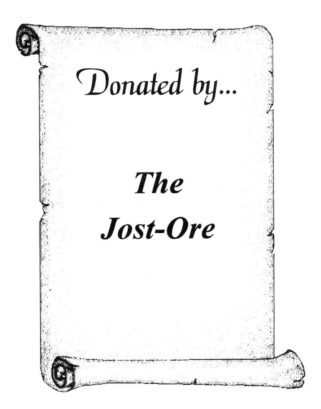

Donated by...

The
Jost-Ore

E.F. Jost
Buffalo
March, 1986

LAWRENCE'S LEADERSHIP
POLITICS AND THE
TURN AGAINST WOMEN

LAWRENCE'S LEADERSHIP POLITICS AND THE TURN AGAINST WOMEN

Cornelia Nixon

University of California Press
Berkeley
Los Angeles
London

University of California Press
Berkeley and Los Angeles, California

University of California Press, Ltd.
London, England

"Manifesto" is quoted by permission of Laurence
Pollinger, Ltd. and the Estate of Mrs. Frieda Lawrence
Ravagli.

Library of Congress Cataloging-in-Publication Data

Nixon, Cornelia.
    Lawrence's leadership politics and the turn against
women.
        Bibliography: p.
        Includes index.
        1. Lawrence, D. H. (David Herbert), 1885–1930—
Political and social views.   2. Politics in literature.
3. Misogyny in literature.   4. Women in literature.
5. Sex in literature.   I. Title.
PR6023.A93Z7559   1986   823'.912   85–14006
ISBN 0–520–05431–8 (alk. paper)

Printed in the United States of America
1   2   3   4   5   6   7   8   9

Frontispiece: *Renascence of Men*, by D. H. Lawrence.
Watercolor, 12 by 9 inches. Location unknown. Repro-
duced from *The Paintings of D. H. Lawrence*, privately
printed for subscribers only (The Mandrake Press,
1929). Courtesy of the Lilly Library, Bloomington, Indiana.

For Alex and Fred, who helped

We have to break away, back to the great unison of manhood. . . . It is a choice between serving *man*, or woman. It is a choice between yielding the soul to a leader, leaders, or yielding only to the woman, wife, mistress, or mother.

D. H. Lawrence, *Fantasia of the Unconscious*

Contents

Acknowledgments   xi

Introduction:
Enemy of Mankind   1

1
From Garden to Swamp   19

2
The Saner Sister   53

3
The Snake's Place   113

4
Surpassing the Love of Women   170

Conclusion:
Private Parts and Public Events   229

Index   235

Acknowledgments

I would like to thank Laurence Pollinger Ltd. and the estate of Mrs. Frieda Lawrence Ravagli, as well as the Humanities Research Center, the University of Texas at Austin, for permission to quote from Lawrence's unpublished manuscripts. The University of California, Berkeley, and Indiana University provided the fellowship and grant support that made this project possible. I am grateful, furthermore, to Thomas Laqueur, Michael Rosenblum, James C. Cowan, William H. Pritchard, Ernest Callenbach, Doris Kretschmer, Barbara Ras, and Victoria Nelson for excellent readings and suggestions. Most of all, I would like to thank Alex Zwerdling, for asking me to consider this question, for challenging me to refine my answers, and for scrupulous editing and judicious encouragement; Frederick Crews, for his advice and support at every stage of this project; and my husband, Dean Young.

Introduction

Enemy of Mankind

How can we say that a writer turns? It must first be agreed that a writer's thoughts, opinions, and feelings can be discerned in the work and abstracted from it in a meaningful way: that attitudes within the work reflect the writer's thoughts or feelings at the time of writing. With a writer less clearly didactic than D. H. Lawrence, we can make no such assumption: Gertrude Stein's feelings about roses, for instance, are not obvious from her famous statement concerning them: "Rose is a rose is a rose is a rose."[1] Lawrence's ideas and feelings are evident in his works, however, because he was often trying to persuade his audience to embrace them. He believed that the novel "can inform and lead into new places the flow of our sympathetic consciousness,"[2] and he considered the same ideas in his fiction that he formulated separately in philosophical polemics. Even before he started issuing social manifestos he declared, "I do write because I want folk—English folk—to alter, and have more sense."[3]

Other plainly didactic writers have undergone changes in thinking. Lawrence's sometime-nemesis Sigmund Freud, for instance, revised his theory in a way that is similar to one of Lawrence's changes. In his early writings Freud maintained that the principal conflict in the personality takes place be-

1. Gertrude Stein, "Sacred Emily," *Geography and Plays* (1922; rpt. New York: Something Else Press, 1968), 187.
2. D. H. Lawrence, *Lady Chatterley's Lover* (Florence, 1928; rpt. New York: Grove Press, 1957), 117.
3. *The Letters of D. H. Lawrence*, vol. 1 (1910–1913), ed. James T. Boulton (Cambridge: Cambridge University Press, 1979), 544. This volume will hereafter be cited in the notes as Cambridge *Letters 1*.

tween "the interests of self-preservation and the demands of the libido," and he regarded cruelty and aggressiveness as simply "a part of sexual life." But during the Great War Freud decided that "as well as Eros there was an instinct of death." He went so far as to conclude, mystically, that "the phenomena of life could be explained from the concurrent or mutually opposing action of these two instincts."

The war also moved Lawrence to find a place in his thinking for what Freud called "the ubiquity of non-erotic aggressivity and destructiveness."[4] In 1914 his perception of human nature was similar to Freud's original view, though differently analyzed. Lawrence saw the instinct for self-preservation (expressed in work and money making) stifling his contemporaries' needs for creative expression and sexual fulfillment. Lawrence thought that people in the Christian era suppressed their true needs because they valued conscious knowledge and spiritual virtue while fearing the body, the senses, and the feelings. He wrote his posthumously published "Study of Thomas Hardy" in 1914, apparently in a millenarian mood, predicting the end of the Christian era and the start of a new age in which work would not overbalance pleasure nor the mind tyrannize the body. Although Lawrence acknowledged that violence might be needed to do away with the old order, he did not recognize it as an expression of a basic need to be destructive. In Lawrence's view the only real needs were enough money to buy necessities and no more, free time and freedom from oppression, and one's proper mate, through whom one might come in contact with eternity.[5]

Less than a year later, however, in the original version of "The Crown," Lawrence had come to see the desire for destruction of self and others as his contemporaries' ruling pas-

---

4. Sigmund Freud, *Civilization and Its Discontents*, trans. James Strachey (New York: W. W. Norton, 1961), 64–67.

5. D. H. Lawrence, "Study of Thomas Hardy," in *Phoenix: The Posthumous Papers of D. H. Lawrence* (New York: Viking, 1936), 398–516. Hereafter this collection will be cited in the text and identified as *Phoenix*.

sion. But in the destructiveness Lawrence still saw a divine spirit. In his view, "sensationalism"—an extreme lust for sex or violence—was "one road to the infinite." Furthermore, he believed a person could experience a "consummation" in destruction or reduction just as in sex. For Lawrence, the process of reduction, the separation of what was joined in growth, took on a power exactly complementary to its opposite, creation or "the life force."[6] Then, in early 1917, while revising *Women in Love*, Lawrence arrived at the conclusion Freud had reached in *Beyond the Pleasure Principle*. In "The Reality of Peace," Lawrence wrote: "There are ultimately only two desires, the desire of life and the desire of death" (*Phoenix* 680). Furthermore, he believed that life itself required the opposition of these two instincts:

> And there is in me the great desire of creation and the great desire of dissolution. Perhaps these two are pure equivalents. Perhaps the decay of autumn purely balances the putting forth of spring. Certainly the two are necessary each to the other; they are the systole-diastole of the physical universe. . . . Shall I deny either? Then neither is fulfilled.
>
> (*Phoenix* 678–79)

Lawrence's vision had always been dualistic, based on a perception of balanced contraries in all creation. But with the discovery that creation and destruction are pure equivalents came moral relativism. Lawrence then necessarily decided to break with the Christian tradition and declared himself a pagan, favoring Heraclitus above all philosophers. In 1915, he developed the idea that there are "opposing infinites," an eternity behind us and one ahead, instead of a single "Eternity" like the Christian heaven.

This change, like Freud's, probably resulted from witnessing a world war. Lawrence made other, more mysterious turns, however, in the year 1915. While writing *The Rainbow*, the politics of which are primarily negative or anarchic, Law-

6. D. H. Lawrence, "The Crown," original manuscript, chapter V. See n. 45.

rence wrote letters arguing for a form of democratic socialism implicitly based on, among other principles, equality of the sexes. Then, a few months later, he announced himself in favor of a "kaiser" and a social system based on "good, better, best." "Liberty, Equality, and Fraternity is the three-fanged serpent" and "the highest understanding must dictate to the lower understandings," he wrote to Bertrand Russell, with whom he had recently been plotting socialist revolution.[7] By 1917, Lawrence believed that personal salvation was to be found in submission to a male leader, a natural hero possessed of wisdom and power. Women in particular would have to learn that submission was for their own good; in Lawrence's new utopia, even the most inferior man would have one follower, namely, his wife. That man would in turn be pledged to a greater, and so on up the hierarchy of dominance. This great army of manhood would march away from their women to build a new world.

In the same short period when his politics reversed, Lawrence apparently became deeply irascible and insulted most of his friends, while a new strain of ranting exhortation appeared in his work. Certain groups in particular came in for his wrath, notably homosexuals and anyone he felt to be "wrong" in "the sex." In fact, he seemed convinced that no one he knew was or could be sexually healthy, and for a few years that phrase became for him almost a contradiction in terms. Lawrence in this period lost faith in sex itself; and, in the eternal war between body and mind, his allegiance tilted noticeably, if not toward the mind, then away from the body, toward transcendence of the very physical being he had glorified in his early works.

These changes are evident in the differing moral universes of Lawrence's two greatest novels, *The Rainbow*, written before, and *Women in Love*, written after the change in his thinking. The only path to self-realization in *The Rainbow* is sexual

---

7. *The Letters of D. H. Lawrence*, vol. 2 (1913–1916), ed. George J. Zytaruk and James T. Boulton (Cambridge: Cambridge University Press, 1981), 364–366. This volume will hereafter be cited in the notes as Cambridge *Letters 2*.

and creative; in *Women in Love*, however, destruction of self and others is a nearly equivalent alternative. Whereas *The Rainbow* rejects all inhibiting political organizations, the later novel argues for the leadership politics that Lawrence was developing in contemporaneous works. And whereas *The Rainbow* centers on strong women, procreative sexuality, and female fecundity in a way that finally, beyond its reservations, is extremely positive, *Women in Love* favors female submission, sexual abstinence, anal sensuality, and union between male friends comparable to marriage. The opposed views found in the novels are supported by Lawrence's contemporaneous nonfiction works.

Lawrence developed his leadership politics at a time when authoritarian political thought was on the rise, and it may be that his path to such thinking was in some way typical. It should be noted that Lawrence denounced fascism itself; nevertheless, his views were similar in many respects to those held by some contemporary European intellectuals sympathetic to fascism. Oddly enough, though in most cases Lawrence neither read nor endorsed such writers, even apparently anomalous elements in his new thought sometimes echo their thinking. The French writer Henry de Montherlant, for instance, suggested that "one of the horrors of war, to which insufficient attention has been paid," was "that women survive it."[8] Although Montherlant was surely jesting, his sense of humor is revealing. He made his views explicit in *Les lépreuses* (1939), where women are carriers of a spiritual "leprosy" dangerous to the health and virility of men. Montherlant blamed women for the "decadence" of France and recommended violence, brutality, bullfighting, and war, Mithraism instead of Christianity, and detached sensuality instead of marriage, as means to revive the virility of the culture. Not surprisingly, therefore, in his *Le solstice de*

8. "Il est vrai qu'une des horreurs de la guerre, sur laquelle on n'attire pas assez l'attention, c'est que les femmes y soient épargnées." Henry de Montherlant, *Les jeunes filles, Romans et oeuvres de fiction non théatrales* (Paris: Gallimard, 1959), 927.

juin (1941), he welcomed the victory of the "virile" Nazis over his own country.

Though Montherlant endeavored to make his position extreme, he did not occupy it alone. The English writer Wyndham Lewis concurred with him in nearly every particular, identifying decadence as "the feminization of culture" and hailing Hitler as a force for racial, economic, and social regeneration.[9] The novels of Pierre Drieu La Rochelle, who collaborated openly with the Nazis, center on young men who are defiled by and reject women's spiritual weakness, shallowness, and materialism. Like the fascist regime he supported, however, Drieu approved of motherhood and childbearing. Genuine (as opposed to proto-) fascist antifeminism was expressed paradoxically, both as an association of femininity with weakness and decadence and as a cult of traditional femininity, glorifying "sacred motherhood."

Although many other writers in this period expressed themselves more diplomatically than Montherlant, Lewis, and Drieu, they held similar political attitudes. W. B. Yeats worked for a time to establish a fascist movement in Ireland, probably because he desired a return to an older, hierarchical order of life, "where all's accustomed, ceremonious." He prayed that his daughter might "become a flourishing hidden tree / That all her thoughts may like the linnet be," rather than, like Maud Gonne, "because of her opinionated mind / Barter . . . every good / By quiet natures understood / For an old bellows full of angry wind."[10] Yeats, like Lewis, Drieu, Montherlant, and the fascists, viewed democracy as feminine and authoritarianism as masculine, while making clear that he preferred authority and masculinity to their opposites.[11]

9. Wyndham Lewis, *The Art of Being Ruled* (New York, London: Harper's, 1926), passim; and *Hitler* (London: Chatto and Windus, 1931).

10. W. B. Yeats, "Prayer for My Daughter," *The Collected Poems of W. B. Yeats* (New York: Macmillan, 1956), 186–87.

11. W. B. Yeats, *A Vision* (New York: Macmillan, 1937), 263; *On the Boiler* (Dublin: The Cuala Press, 1938), 28; and "A General Introduction to my Work," in *Essays and Introductions* (New York: Macmillan, 1961), 519.

As James E. Miller, Jr., and others have argued, T. S. Eliot's poetry reveals queasiness on the subjects of women and sexuality and may contain buried homoerotic content.[12] He admired Julien Benda, whose *Belphégor* (1918) listed women, along with Jews, the masses, and democracy, as the enemies of civilization and argued that the age had been poisoned by the "effeminacy" of thought characteristic of mass democracy.[13] And Ezra Pound, who worked openly for Mussolini, seems to have been uneasy about the other gender: "the female / Is an element, the female / Is a chaos / An octopus / A biological process," he asserted in Canto XXIX.[14]

Many authoritarian writers also favored male separatism, yet the most politically outspoken devoted more of their writing to denunciations of women than to plans for a new political organization of virile men. Lawrence, for instance, seemed to have no idea what men would do after turning their backs on women and marching away together, but he returned again and again to the dangerous errors committed by modern women (sexual assertion, presumption to mentality, demands for love from sons) and the antidotes to them ("Back she must go, to the old mindlessness, the old unconsciousness" [*Phoenix* 623]). Montherlant devoted a series of four novels to women's errors (*Les jeunes filles* [1936], *Pitié pour les femmes* [1936], *Le démon du bien* [1937], and *Les lépreuses* [1939]), and criticized women in a volume of essays, *Sur les femmes* (1942).

Aldous Huxley saw a link between Drieu's sexual insecurity and his politics, asserting that Drieu "was a most inadequate lover. The humiliating consciousness of this fact drove

12. James E. Miller, Jr., *T. S. Eliot's Personal Waste Land* (University Park: Pennsylvania State University Press, 1977).

13. William Chace, *The Political Identities of Ezra Pound and T. S. Eliot* (Stanford: Stanford University Press, 1973), 127–28.

14. *The Cantos of Ezra Pound* (New York: New Directions, 1969), 144. I am grateful to Michael André Bernstein, who called my attention to this passage in his "Image, Word, and Sign: The Visual Arts as Evidence in Ezra Pound's *Cantos*," forthcoming in *Critical Inquiry*.

him into misogyny and the politics of violence and authoritarianism."[15] Eric Bentley made similar observations about Carlyle and Nietzsche, connecting sexual failure and the idealization of virility in their heroic political thought.[16] One of the early psychological studies of fascism argued that its appeal was based in part on fear of women. Peter Nathan, in *The Psychology of Fascism*, suggests that women's sexual emancipation in the early twentieth century led many men to "feel woman as a tarantula spider" and to take refuge in essentially homoerotic military and political organizations, including the fascist movements.[17]

It has been said that misogyny was a feature of the "moral climate . . . around the turn of the century."[18] Even some writers whose sympathies were antifascist and leftwing favored purely male political action; as Daphne Patai has shown of Orwell, misogyny and concern for virility may be essential ingredients in liberal thought as well.[19] Yet such writers as Orwell, Hemingway, Malraux, and Gide did not attack women with the fervor that is evident in the works of most of the authoritarian writers; they do not blame women for the decline of civilization, nor do they need to reject all things feminine. Gide even evinced profound sympathy for women's aspirations in his *L'école des femmes* (1929), *Robert* (1929), and *Geneviève* (1936). The particularly antifeminine form of the cult of virility was embraced, I think, only by those writers whose political thought was authoritarian. In some cases, the glorification of masculinity may have provided fascism's

15. Aldous Huxley, letter to Frédéric Grover, quoted in Robert Soucy, *Fascist Intellectual: Drieu La Rochelle* (Berkeley and Los Angeles: University of California Press, 1979), 6.

16. Eric Bentley, *A Century of Hero-Worship: A Study of the Idea of Heroism in Carlyle and Nietzsche, with Notes on Wagner, Spengler, Stefan George and D. H. Lawrence*, 2nd ed. (Boston: Beacon Press, 1957), 26, 161.

17. Peter Nathan, *The Psychology of Fascism* (London: Faber and Faber, 1943), 56–61.

18. John Cruickshank, *Montherlant* (Edinburgh, London: Oliver and Boyd, 1964), 29.

19. Daphne Patai, *The Orwell Mystique: A Study in Male Ideology* (Amherst: University of Massachusetts Press, 1984).

primary attraction for a writer of otherwise dim political understanding (as Robert Soucy suggests of Drieu).[20]

Yet little attention has been paid to these features of authoritarian thought. Sociological analyses of such thinking view it as a reaction to advanced industrialization, scientific rationalism, and democratization. As such, this thinking is usually characterized as antiparliamentarian, antiliberal, anti-Marxist, and antimodern. Even some of those who recognize the importance of fascist and authoritarian gender connotations offer explanations for them that are not period-specific, suggesting, for instance, that this glorification of virility and denigration of "femininity" resulted simply from the patriarchal family structure, which fosters a son's desire to please a dominant father and his fear of being identified with a weak mother.

The mass desire to submit to authority is sometimes attributed to anomie, the insecurity resulting from the breakdown of traditional social relations, and the enthusiasm for authoritarianism among intellectuals in the early twentieth century may be attributed to what Egon Schwarz names "that calling forth of the archaic so characteristic of the intellectual forced into isolation by the fragmentation of modernity."[21] But the specific forms of archaism called forth reveal the nature of this anomie more clearly than "fragmentation" can suggest. Nathan argues that the misogynist and homoerotic elements in fascism can be viewed as responses to the successful agitation for women's political and personal freedom taking place in the same period, and it may be that, when it shares those elements, nonfascist authoritarian thinking is responsive to the same developments. Lawrence's turn toward leadership politics supports this idea; the evidence suggests that such thinking appealed to him primarily as a refuge from powerful women and allowed him to express the homoeroticism he found unacceptable in himself.

---

20. Soucy, *Fascist Intellectual*, 279, 327.
21. Egon Schwarz, *Poetry and Politics in the Works of Rainer Maria Rilke*, trans. David E. Wellbery (New York: Frederick Ungar, 1981), 28.

Much of Lawrence's new, post-1915 thinking can be attributed to his loss of faith in the mass of humanity, for reasons
that have long been recognized; he was horrified by the war,
particularly the war hysteria at home, and in the midst of it
his ambitious new novel, *The Rainbow*, was banned as sala-
cious. His despair at these events was intensified by quarrels
with friends, his own alarming poverty, and his advancing
tuberculosis. But although these publicly admissible disasters
may account for much of the change in Lawrence's thinking,
they do not explain certain elements in it, particularly his new
sexual repugnance and advocation of the cult of manhood.
And while the war was to Lawrence "the spear through the
side of all sorrows and hopes," even his own account of his
life in this period makes clear that he was affected by other
matters as well.[22]

One of the things that obviously concerned him at this
time was his own sexual nature. What happened to Lawrence
during the war years is the subject of Paul Delany's *D. H. Lawrence's Nightmare: The Writer and His Circle in the Years of the
Great War*. Delany agrees that Lawrence underwent a drastic
personal change in the year he finished *The Rainbow*: he began
the year 1915 as an optimistic socialist revolutionary and
ended it as a paranoid antidemocratic misanthrope. Delany's
study is based in part on evidence in letters only now being
published, and this evidence helps to make the causes fit the
effects.

All indications suggest that Lawrence suffered a private disaster in 1915, possibly a crisis of sexual identity. March 1915
was a relatively palmy period for the Lawrences: he had just
finished *The Rainbow*, which already had a publisher, and
they were secure in one home while Lady Ottoline Morrell
was building them another. Then Lawrence visited Bertrand
Russell at Cambridge. While there, he met John Maynard
Keynes and Duncan Grant, reacted violently to their homo-

22. Cambridge *Letters 2*, 268. For Lawrence's account of his life in this
period, see "The Nightmare" chapter of his novel *Kangaroo* (1923), discussed
in chapter 3 and the Conclusion.

sexuality, and went home in a severe depression that was to last for months. Keynes himself believed that Lawrence's reaction was to Cambridge's intellectual quality ("this thin rationalism skipping on the crust of the lava, ignoring both the reality and the value of the vulgar passions, joined to libertinism and comprehensive irreverence").[23]

The brittle rationalism of Cambridge would have repelled Lawrence in any case, but his own description, in a letter to David Garnett (son of Lawrence's editor, Edward), whose friend Frankie Birrell was also homosexual, better accounts for the revolution in Lawrence's emotional state:

> It is foolish of you to say that it doesn't matter either way—the men loving men. . . . I never knew what it meant until I saw K[eynes], till I saw him at Cambridge. We went into his rooms at midday, and it was very sunny. He was not there, so Russell was writing a note. Then suddenly a door opened and K. was there, blinking from sleep, standing in his pyjamas. And as he stood there gradually a knowledge passed into me, which has been like a little madness to me ever since. And it was carried along with the most dreadful sense of repulsiveness—something like carrion—a vulture gives me the same feeling. I begin to feel mad as I think of it—insane.
>
> Never bring B[irrell] to see me any more. There is something nasty about him, like black-beetles. He is horrible and unclean. I feel as if I should go mad, if I think of your set, D[uncan] G[rant] and K[eynes] and B[irrell]. It makes me dream of beetles. In Cambridge I had a similar dream. Somehow, I can't bear it. It is wrong beyond all bounds of wrongness. I had felt it slightly before, in the Stracheys. But it came full upon me in K., and in D. G. . . .
>
> I could sit and howl in a corner like a child, I feel so bad about it all.[24]

In the depression that followed his visit to Cambridge, the association of homosexuality, black beetles, and corruption dominated Lawrence's letters and became linked in his mind with the war:

23. John Maynard Keynes, "My Early Beliefs," in *The Bloomsbury Group: A Collection of Memoirs, Commentary and Criticism*, ed. S. P. Rosenbaum (London: Croom Helm, 1975), 64.
24. Cambridge *Letters* 2, 320–21.

I like men to be beasts—but insects—one insect mounted on another—oh God! The soldiers at Worthing are like that—they remind me of lice or bugs:—'to insects—sensual lust'. They will murder their officers one day. They are teeming insects. What massive creeping hell is not let loose nowadays. . . . hell is slow and creeping and viscous, and insect-teeming: as is this Europe now—this England.[25]

At the same time, all through April and May 1915, Lawrence felt that he was going insane, that he was in "one of those horrible sleeps from which I can't wake. . . . Everything has a touch of delirium."[26] He raged against life in general ("What a vile, thieving, swindling life!"), against his contemporaries ("What a horrible generation!"), against the men doing the estimates for repairs to his cottage at Garsington ("These vile greedy contractors, they set my blood boiling to such a degree, I can scarcely bear to write"),[27] against the Germans ("I too hate the Germans so much, I could kill every one of them. . . . I would like to kill a million Germans—two million"),[28] against all humanity ("I wish I was a blackbird. . . . I hate men").[29] In a calmer moment, he proclaimed the correctness of Shelley's belief in "the principle of Evil, coeval with the Principle of Good."[30]

By the time he was writing the first draft of *Women in Love*, Lawrence's depression was acute. For most of 1916, he sounds unbalanced, judging from both his friends' descriptions of his behavior and his own letters.[31] Many of his letters from 1916 are homicidal: "There are very many people, like insects, who await extermination"; "When I see people in the distance . . . I want to crouch in the bushes and shoot them silently with invisible arrows of death." The homicidal feeling is directed especially at men: just before the passage last quoted, he says, "I have got a perfect androphobia," and he singles out the *paterfamilias* for his particular loathing: "I see them—fat men in white flannel trousers—pères de famille—

---

25. Ibid., 331.   26. Ibid., 339.   27. Ibid., 324.
28. Ibid., 340.   29. Ibid., 339.   30. Ibid., 315.
31. Paul Delany, *D. H. Lawrence's Nightmare: The Writer and His Circle in the Years of the Great War* (New York: Basic Books, 1978), 229–34.

and the familles—passing along the field-path and looking at the scenery. Oh, if one could but have a great box of insect powder, and shake it over them, in the heavens, and exterminate them."[32] He begins to speak of death as a wonderful thing, both as a means of removing people he hates and as a refuge of peace, cleanliness, and honor for himself. To E. M. Forster he wrote, "I think it would be good to die, because death would be a clean land with no people in it: not even the people of myself. . . . one looks through the window into the land of death, and it *does* seem a clean good unknown, all that is left to one."[33] And to Lady Cynthia Asquith, daughter-in-law to the prime minister, he said, "I am no longer an Englishman, I am the enemy of mankind."[34]

Near the start of this depression, in April 1915, Lawrence received the typescript of *The Rainbow* and made a number of significant revisions, one of which—the completely new ending of chapter 7, in which Will and Anna are released into productivity through deathly sensuality—is the first instance in Lawrence's work, and the only one in *The Rainbow*, in which someone is liberated or made more vital through contact with something deathly. Why did Lawrence make this revision? Delany agrees with a number of Lawrence critics in emphasizing the sodomitic aspect of the sensuality between Anna and Will, and he suggests that Lawrence appropriated sodomy to the heterosexual camp as "a challenge to the homosexuality that had so disturbed him in Grant, Keynes, and Frankie Birrell."[35] But the nature of Lawrence's reaction, following his visit to Cambridge, is more complex and less rational than this analysis allows.

One theme emerging in Lawrence's letters at this time is

32. Cambridge *Letters 2*, 650.

33. *The Letters of D. H. Lawrence*, vol. 3 (1916–1921), ed. James T. Boulton and Andrew Robertson (Cambridge: Cambridge University Press, 1984), 21–22. This volume will hereafter be cited in the notes as Cambridge *Letters 3*.

34. Cambridge *Letters 2*, 648.

35. Delany, 125, 85–90. See also Charles Ross, "The Revisions of the Second Generation in *The Rainbow*," *Review of English Studies*, n.s. 27 (1976): 277–95.

that we are all violent and corrupt and that we must acknowledge the corruption within us. It is clear from his own work—especially the original "Prologue" to *Women in Love*,[36] in which Birkin's attraction to Gerald is openly erotic—that on the subject of homosexuality Lawrence protested too much. Perhaps he recognized, consciously or unconsciously, his own blood-brotherly love for Russell and John Middleton Murry in the "putrescence" of the Cambridge homosexuals. Quentin Bell believed that Lawrence's reaction could have been the result of "discovering, or rather suspecting, homosexual passion, not only in others but within himself"; Bell thought the passion was for young David Garnett (nicknamed "Bunny") because Lawrence also condemned Garnett's circle of attractive friends.[37] Even Keynes understood that Lawrence was "jealous, irritable, hostile" primarily because "he was evidently very fond of Bunny; and when he saw *him* being seduced by Cambridge, he was yet more jealous, just as he was jealous of Ottoline's new leanings that way."[38]

Lawrence's works from the succeeding year show that he was aware of homoerotic desires in himself: the second half of the original (1915) "Crown," as well as the "Prologue" to *Women in Love* and the first post-*Rainbow* draft of that novel (both written in 1916), is largely concerned with the problem of young men who are attracted only to other men. Even the travelogue *Twilight in Italy* (revised during the summer of 1915) is narrated by a young man with homosexual leanings. Lawrence's discovery of a desire in himself that he could neither accept nor kill explains why, from April 1915 onward, he is convinced that everyone harbors a well of decay and destruction within—"we refuse to acknowledge the passionate evil that is in us. This makes us secret and rotten"—and that

36. D. H. Lawrence, "Prologue to *Women in Love*," ed. George Ford, *Texas Quarterly* (1963): 98–111. Reprinted in *Phoenix 2: Uncollected, Unpublished and Other Prose Works by D. H. Lawrence* (New York: Viking, 1973), 92–108. This collection will hereafter be cited in the text and identified as *Phoenix 2*.

37. Quentin Bell, *Bloomsbury* (London: Weidenfeld and Nicolson, 1968), 70–76.

38. Keynes, "My Early Beliefs," 51.

to acknowledge it, even to act on it, would be liberating.[39] Perhaps it would have been for Lawrence. Instead, he continued to equate homosexuality with the foul maw of death, raged against his age for its deathliness, and at the same time tried to rehabilitate death, to find a positive value in corruption.

He also began to formulate a political scheme that would channel his apparent desire for bonding with other men and render it acceptable to himself as a force for rebuilding the world once the war had destroyed the old political order. And he began to denounce women, blaming them, and their self-conscious sexuality in particular, for the state of the world. Heterosexuality itself, therefore, was identified by Lawrence in this period with self-destructiveness. This position reversed his views at the time of writing *The Rainbow,* when he believed that men should go to women to get their "souls fertilised by the female . . . (not necessarily woman but most obviously woman)," in order to get a vision, one that "contains awe and dread and submission" on the part of the man, "not pride or sensuous egotism and assertion."[40] His later conjunction of homoeroticism and negative feelings about women was of course not a logical necessity, but Lawrence definitely felt that sexual love between men was "complemented by the hatred for women,"[41] and occasionally he even blamed assertive women for the genesis of such desires in men.[42]

To trace the development of Lawrence's thought and the possible reasons for changes in it, we must look closely at the earliest gestation of his new ideas, which first became appar-

39. Cambridge *Letters* 2, 315.
40. Ibid., 218.
41. The quotation is from the 1916 draft of *Women in Love;* I took it from the typed portion of the definitive typescript in the Humanities Research Center, the University of Texas at Austin, 324. See chapter 1, n. 15, and chapter 3, n. 20.
42. D. H. Lawrence, *Fantasia of the Unconscious* (1922), rpt. in *Psychoanalysis and the Unconscious/Fantasia of the Unconscious* (New York: Viking, 1960), 143.

ent in the final revisions to *The Rainbow* and are gradually defined through drafts of *Women in Love* and the works contemporaneous with it. This study should make apparent, incidentally, that the fact of single authorship is not a principle of coherence unifying works as disparate as *The Rainbow* and *Women in Love*. Lawrence was not a self-conscious writer, but even he recognized the difference between the two novels when he said that *Women in Love* contained the "results in one's soul of the war: it is purely destructive, not like *The Rainbow*, destructive-consummating."[43] Elsewhere he did assert that *The Rainbow* and *Women in Love* were "really an organic artistic whole"—but perhaps disingenuously, since he was trying to convince his American publisher to issue the two as *Women in Love*, volumes 1 and 2, thereby disguising the earlier novel and possibly making it salable in England.[44] Nevertheless, critics have traditionally used the two novels to explain each other, as if they were one coherent whole—a practice that in some cases has meant straining to yoke heterogeneous ideas together.

Lawrence's artistic personality is such that most cross reading among his works is risky. He valued nothing more in a creature, particularly himself, than spontaneity, impulse, the unrestricted motion of life. "We should ask for no absolutes, or absolute," he says in "Why the Novel Matters"; "My yea! of today is oddly different from my yea! of tomorrow. My tears of tomorrow will have nothing to do with my tears of a year ago" (*Phoenix* 536). His poetics were Romantic, organic, Coleridgean, the idea being to get the piece out whole, in its own form and following its own logic—even when he was patchily revising a completed novel with a new conception in mind, layering a new structure on the old one. He was always passionate about his own ideas and unconscious of or unconcerned about changes in them. He sometimes drastically revised a piece published in a magazine for later publication in a book, even telling the reader that he altered it "only a very

43. Cambridge *Letters* 3, 143.
44. Ibid., 459, 439.

little"—as in the note to the 1925 publication of "The Crown" (the only version of that work readily available today), which is profoundly different from the original, partially published version of 1915.[45] He probably believed it himself or believed that he saw more truly into the matter at the later date or that he knew better what it was he originally wanted to say. Like Ezra Pound, who periodically issued variant lists of the world's greatest literature, Lawrence would urge idea x one year and the perhaps contradictory idea y the next, without saying, "Last year I thought x, but now I think y." Instead, with a Whitmanesque indifference to consistency, he would simply say "x, x, x!" one year, and "y, y, y!" the next.

In his letters and essays Lawrence left a remarkably complete record of his thoughts, but it is the record of a running stream. Even roughly contemporaneous works need to be compared with an eye to possible discrepancies, and his late works seldom illuminate his early ones. *The Plumed Serpent* (1926) clearly has little in common with *Sons and Lovers* (1912). Yet critics routinely use an even later work, *Lady Chatterley's Lover* (1928), as if it were the key to all of Lawrence, revealing ideas he had held all along but could not openly express, and *Fantasia of the Unconscious* (1922) as if it were Lawrence's definitive statement, when in fact it is just the longest, and not even the last, of his many philosophical formulations.

Naturally, just as a running stream is always water, most elements of Lawrence's vision are constant, and certain convictions deepened through his life. But even apparently identical images in separate works do not necessarily share meaning or even connotation. Lawrence used certain metaphors

45. The revised version of "The Crown" appears in *Reflections on the Death of a Porcupine* (1925; rpt. Bloomington: Indiana University Press, 1969) and in *Phoenix 2*. Only the first three chapters of the original were ever published: in *The Signature*, nos. 1–3 (4 October, 18 October, and 4 November, 1915). The first three chapters were only slightly revised for the 1925 publication, but Lawrence thoroughly changed the last three. The original version of chapters IV–VI exists only as a holograph manuscript in the Humanities Research Center, the University of Texas at Austin. Hereafter this manuscript will be cited in the text and identified as CMS.

and images all his life, even though he meant different things by them at different times.

Besides the novels of the Brangwensaga and the essays mentioned thus far ("Study of Thomas Hardy," "The Crown," "The Reality of Peace," and *Twilight in Italy*), works from the period of Lawrence's development that will concern us include "The Education of the People," *Aaron's Rod*, *Movements in European History*, and the original versions of Lawrence's essays on American literature. In some cases, the versions of these works actually written during the war years differ from those that are readily available in print. After the war, Lawrence camouflaged some of his most controversial new ideas while revising some of the pieces in which they first appeared (such as "The Crown" and the essays on American literature), and the exclusive use of final versions partially conceals the ideas that emerged in his work while he was writing *Women in Love*. In the early 1920s, Lawrence discussed some of these ideas in camouflaging terminology, and he recanted most of them by the time he wrote *Lady Chatterley's Lover*. In this study, therefore, I shall cross-read only works that were actually written in the same period and shall rely on evidence that, in some cases, has never been published.

1

From Garden to Swamp

Lawrence's Brangwensaga began as a single novel ("The Sisters," 1913) and remained so through two more drafts; it was as a single novel ("The Wedding Ring," 1914) that early versions of both *The Rainbow* and *Women in Love* were first rejected by a publisher. Lawrence apparently burned these early manuscripts, but surviving fragments indicate that it was the material of *Women in Love* rather than *The Rainbow* that dominated the earliest version. The story of *The Rainbow* was probably written in reverse chronological order, with Ursula's story first, her parents' in the second "Sisters," and her grandparents' in the revision that followed the rejection of "The Wedding Ring." It was not until this fourth drafting, in January 1915, that Lawrence realized that he had too much material for one novel. He decided to publish the first half of the story as *The Rainbow*, which he sent to his typist on March 2, 1915.[1]

More than a year passed before he began to rewrite what he was still calling "the second half of *The Rainbow*," a year—as we have seen—of considerable change both in Lawrence's life and in his thinking.[2] He finished a longhand draft in June 1916, then typed the greater portion of it himself, making such considerable revisions and additions that the typescript

---

1. Mark Kinkead-Weekes, "The Marble and the Statue: The Exploratory Imagination of D. H. Lawrence," in *Imagined Worlds: Essays on Some English Novels and Novelists in Honour of John Butt*, ed. Maynard Mack and Ian Gregor (London: Methuen, 1968), 375–76, 384; and Charles Ross, *The Composition of* The Rainbow *and* Women in Love: *A History* (Charlottesville: University Press of Virginia, 1979), 25–29.
2. Cambridge *Letters* 2, 629.

was in effect another draft. He continued to make holograph revisions to the typescript until the novel found a publisher in 1920, the most massive revision having probably occurred in 1917, with another series in 1919.[3] This novel, which we now know as *Women in Love*, is strikingly different from the surviving fragments of its earliest draft, "The Sisters." The system of thought behind it is also distinguishable from that of the novel to which it is supposed to be a sequel. The proximity in time of their respective compositions would make this difference remarkable in itself even if it did not represent a change in Lawrence's vision that would affect the rest of his work.

In its sixty-five-year span, *The Rainbow* shows a continuous progression in the kinds of experience described, but there is unity in that progression, in the ontological optimism that gave the book its title. The characters in *The Rainbow* want to become creative, productive, fulfilled people, and with varying degrees of difficulty most of them never stop striving toward that end. The opposite course, resignation to a destructive, mechanical way of living, is chosen only by peripheral characters, and once they have made that choice, they are dropped; the novel's focus remains on the unresigned characters and their struggles toward personal fulfillment. At the book's end, the heroine of the third generation has survived the climactic throes of her struggle, and she is granted a vision that promises a better future life.

Readers might reasonably expect the sequel to fulfill the promise of the rainbow that appears on the book's last page; if *Women in Love* does that, it does so less with optimism than with apocalyptic despair. *Women in Love* resumes the story of the Brangwens after a gap of only five years in the characters' lives but in an ontologically opposite world. The majority of the characters in *Women in Love* are mechanical and uncreative beings; they are not only alienated and pessimistic but capable of producing destructive energy with an intensity not

3. Ross, *Composition*, 118–23.

found in characters in *The Rainbow*. How this transformation grows out of the progression in *The Rainbow*, and how it represents a change in Lawrence's view of the world, we may begin to discover by examining the lives of the characters in both books.

The shift is accomplished largely through a change in setting, prepared for at the end of *The Rainbow* by the move from rural Cossethay to the colliery town of Beldover. The Marsh Farm, the Brangwens' link to "blood intimacy" with the land, disappears without a trace in *Women in Love*, and the characters seem to have taken a step forward into the twentieth century, where they are surrounded by cars, machinery, and "the latest improvements."[4] This move introduces several new circles of characters whose analogues are at most marginally present in *The Rainbow*: the machinelike miners, the Crich family, the bohemian artists, and "the slack aristocracy that keeps touch with the arts" (10). In fact, the cast of characters is almost entirely changed. Of the characters who appear in both books, Gudrun is only slightly developed in *The Rainbow*, and Will and Anna appear only in two small scenes in *Women in Love*, where they seem like relics from another age.

Only Ursula is a central character in both books and forms the bridge between them. On the surface, she is the same character: on the third page of the second novel, she is described as being essentially the same "kernel" waiting to sprout that she was at the end of *The Rainbow*. Indeed, much of her behavior in *Women in Love* is understandable only in relation to her early childhood responses to her father and her shattering attempt to find fulfillment in self-centered love with Anton. Yet her position relative to the other characters is strikingly different in the second book and underscores the change in her world. *The Rainbow* moves through its sixty-five years focusing on one family to the virtual exclusion of the rest of humanity, showing the historical development of a free-thinking, self-responsible person who defines herself as

---

4. D. H. Lawrence, *Women in Love* (1920; rpt. New York: Viking Press, 1960), 41. Hereafter this edition will be cited in the text.

an individual rather than as a member of any group and who rejects the traditional values of the earliest generation, namely its beliefs in established religion and the concept of the domestic family. The second book places this same person in a culture in which everyone is self-defined and the traditional values have been virtually abolished. In *The Rainbow*, Ursula is the avant-garde; in *Women in Love*, she is the most traditional major character, and the others are much further along the track she started down in *The Rainbow*.

The first of the "new" characters we meet is Gudrun, who, in the opening dialogue of the book, denounces marriage and motherhood while admitting that she wants the "experience" of marriage. She complains that *"Nothing materialises!* Everything withers in the bud . . . everything—oneself—things in general"* (2). This assertion of the stillborn state of the world is not sincerely endorsed by Ursula, who has a prescient feeling of something about to bloom in her own future. Gudrun is, in all, rather domineering with Ursula, aggressively unconventional, convinced of her own superiority, and at the same time dissatisfied with her life and even herself. The world does not respond to her desires by offering her the life she has imagined; she has a sense of frustrated potentiality in herself, that she will never become the person she was meant to be. Perhaps at some point Gudrun has desired to be a wife and mother; but now that she is withering in the bud, the possibility is abhorrent to her. Still, she wants the "experience": not for fulfillment, but to know with her mind what marriage is like.

We learn later that Gudrun is also deeply ambivalent: for although she is "hurt" by the ugliness of the colliery town and its residents, she is strongly attracted to it and must spend her evenings in town with the miners. The miners are always associated both with a dark, underworld power and with machinery (since they are part of the mine's machinery). Attracted to them, she feels herself to be "like a new Daphne, turning not into a tree but a machine." She becomes the lover of a mining engineer, since she craves "to get her satisfaction of" the dark spirit of the town (108). There is an affinity between her and the miners: "The same secret seemed to be working in the souls of all alike, Gudrun, Palmer, the rakish young bloods, the gaunt, middle-aged men. All had a secret sense of power, and of inexpressible destructiveness, and of fatal half-heartedness, a sort of rottenness in the will" (110).

It seems that Gudrun, who is powerless to fulfill herself, since she is withering in the bud and fatally half-hearted, has great power of another sort: that power is dark, secret, inexpressibly destructive, associated with fatality and rottenness, and seems to create or to come from a mechanized self. That is what Lawrence would call Gudrun's allotropic state, and it is not directly translatable into visible behavior.[5] In relation to other people, Gudrun is consistently willful, arrogant, and aggressive; her will is only rotten and half-hearted in the sense that her urge toward fulfillment has turned back on itself and become instead an attraction to mechanization and destruction. Most of the things that fall into these last categories are not immediately recognizable as either mechanical or destructive; one of the primary objectives of *Women in Love* is to identify both inward and outward manifestations of the urges to destruction and fulfillment. What these things are and why Lawrence considers them to be mechanical and destructive should become more clear as we proceed: in Gudrun's behavior, the principal evidence that she is "turning not into a tree but a machine" includes her attraction to the destructive power in the miners and her desire to know or experience rather than to be.

The elements of assertive will, unconventionality, intense ambivalence, and attraction to the destructive forces in one another are evident in nearly all of the new characters, who also seem to lack a secure integrity of the self. Gerald's assertive will has made him "the God of the machine" (220). Though he tries to impose a measure of conventionality on his increasingly anarchic family, it is not from any inherent belief in custom, but, one suspects, rather because a certain

5. Cambridge *Letters* 2, 183.

order in human relationships is necessary for the smooth running of "the social mechanism," beyond which he finds nothing to believe in ("I suppose I live to work" 48; life "doesn't centre at all. It is artificially held *together* by the social mechanism" 51). Gerald's will not only runs the mines but holds together his own being, which is in danger of collapsing in on its own hollowness: "He was afraid that one day he would break down and be a purely meaningless babble lapping around a darkness. . . . It was as if his centres of feeling were drying up. . . . But his will yet held good" (224–25).

Hermione's will is exercised not on the running of machines but on the related activity of being relentlessly conscious and acquiring as much purely mental knowledge as possible. Every countermanding of her will collapses her, and Birkin's mere description of something she cannot understand is enough to destroy her: "She swallowed, and tried to regain her mind. But she could not, she was witless, decentralised. Use all her will as she might, she could not recover. She suffered the ghastliness of dissolution, broken and gone in a horrible corruption" (82). Halliday, the London bohemian, is a character of two wills, one for a "pure" girl and one for the "filth" or "dissolution" of Minette/Pussum,[6] and he manipulates both women. Minette, on the other hand, is completely without will, a complementary vacuum to the overextension of other people's. All four of these characters are in constant danger of dissolving and are attracted to that which causes them to dissolve.

Even though they are not exempt from the general malady, Birkin and Ursula do have healthier instincts: they are repelled by the self-destructiveness of the other characters and are attracted to the vitality in each other and in the natural world. Ursula has a strong affinity with the creatures around her: at various times she is compared to a berry (136), a but-

---

6. Lawrence originally named this character Pussum and made her dark; he changed her name to Minette and made her a blonde in response to a libel suit. See Robert Chamberlain, "Pussum, Minette, and the Africo-Nordic Symbol in *Women in Love*," *PMLA* 78 (September 1963): 407–16.

terfly (111), and a cobra (144). She wonders "if the trees and the flowers could feel the vibration" of church bells "and what they thought of it" (16). She identifies with "the horses and cows in the field. Each was so single and to itself . . . single and unsocial as she herself was" (236). She condemns Gerald for his need to dominate his mare, who "has as much right to her own being, as you have to yours" (130). Birkin despairs of mankind, which he believes to be destroying itself, but he manages to feel apocalyptic optimism in the thought that humanity is only one "particular expression" of what Lawrence, like Shaw, sometimes called "the life force" (both writers modifying Nietzsche's *Wille zur Macht* and Bergson's *élan vital* for their own purposes). Birkin believes that, after mankind is destroyed, this force will produce "a new embodiment, in a new way" (52). When he is nearly killed by Hermione, Birkin instinctively seeks the touch of green growing things, the "coolness and subtlety of vegetation travelling into one's blood . . . this lovely, subtle, responsive vegetation, waiting for him, as he waited for it" (100).

This sympathetic relationship with nature is a function of the vitality of each, which Ursula sees as "a curious hidden richness . . . the powerful beauty of life itself" in Birkin (38), and Birkin calls "a golden light . . . like spring, suffused with wonderful promise" in her (241). Their liveliness, as well as their sympathy with other creatures, places these two characters in contrast with Gerald, Gudrun, and Hermione, who are rotten or empty inside and need to bully and even to ridicule animals. Hermione, for instance, laughs at a swan (80), Gerald takes pleasure in terrifying his mare (102–4), and Gudrun both denounces a rabbit (234) and mesmerizes some wild cattle (159).

Aside from this difference, however, Birkin and Ursula have much in common with the self-destructive characters: both are extremely individualized, self-assertive, self-conscious, and often deeply ambivalent. They are not immune to self-destructive desires but have what amounts to a religious belief in a creative force beyond human consciousness. In *The Rainbow*, Ursula complains of the modern delusion that humanity's "illuminating consciousness . . . comprised sun and stars, and the Creator,"[7] and in *Women in Love* she declares, "No, it is so *irreverent* to think that everything must be realised in the head. Really, something must be left to the Lord, there always is and always will be" (133). And though the terms in which he expresses it are startlingly aggressive, Birkin's idea is similarly antagonistic to the mind and implies a corollary belief in vitality when he tells Hermione, "If one cracked your skull, one might get a spontaneous, passionate woman out of you. . . . You've got to learn not-to-be, before you can come into being" (36–37). Furthermore, both have a sort of reverence for their lives, a belief in the spiritual nature of life, which sometimes expresses itself in the use of biblical images and phrases to describe their perceptions of everyday reality: Birkin sees Beldover "like Jerusalem to his fancy" (247), as Ursula sees Ilkeston in *The Rainbow*, and she perceives Birkin to be "one of the sons of God," for whom she has been waiting all her life (305–6).

Birkin and Ursula eventually find the way toward a new relationship, perhaps the beginning of a new form of life, through a process that cracks the individualized, self-centered, self-conscious, ambivalent, and purely mental consciousness, which Lawrence elsewhere calls the ego or "the envelope of the achieved self."[8] Their new relationship is the synthesis of a dialectic begun in *The Rainbow*, which is a version both of the Fortunate Fall and of a Joachite view of history: in the beginning humans lived in unconscious unity with a divine universe. The fall was into consciousness, separation, and sorrow; but, painful as the second stage is, it is necessary to allow for a rise to a higher, conscious unity with the divine, a simultaneous realization that one is single and separate, ruled by the law of one's individual being and yet participating in the divinity of all life.

7. D. H. Lawrence, *The Rainbow* (1915; rpt. New York: Viking Press, 1961), 437. Hereafter this edition will be cited in the text.

8. "The Crown," original manuscript, chapter IV, 12; and the 1925 version in *Reflections on the Death of a Porcupine*, passim for "ego."

This dialectic is set up in *The Rainbow*. That novel records a gradual process of individuation, each generation producing characters with a stronger sense of self and a greater inclination to view their relationships to others as competitive. Tom and Lydia have a brief period of struggle before settling into a deeply peaceful harmony; neither feels that self-assertion is as important as their marriage. Anna and Will are violently competitive, each trying to master the other, with Anna proving generally the stronger; it is only through their participation in violent sensuality, something deeper than the will of either, that they come to, if not harmony, at least peaceful, productive coexistence.

When they first choose each other as lovers, Ursula and Anton approach love primarily as self-gratification, each augmenting the self-image of the other, providing both with a sense of power: "For the first time she was in love with a vision of herself" (291); "His will was set and straining with all its tension to encompass her and compel her. . . . If he could only set a bond round her and compel her!" (318).[9] Ursula's desire is not for Anton, but for ever more powerful singleness: "Oh, for the coolness and entire liberty and brightness of the moon. Oh, for the cold liberty to be herself, to do entirely as she liked" (317). Later, again aspiring for the moon, she nearly destroys Anton in her attempt to wring her confirmation from him (478–79). In this action Ursula becomes a destructive force, just as Gerald and Gudrun become later: "a sudden lust seized her, to lay hold of him and tear him and make him into nothing" (319); "as if suddenly she had the strength of destruction . . . She held him pinned down at the chest, awful. The fight, the struggle for consummation was terrible" (479).

Concomitant with the increasing individuation and willed competition, *The Rainbow* traces a steady decline in the traditional values that provide the earliest characters with mean-

9. The published versions say "encompass him" but the manuscript, in the Humanities Research Center, University of Texas at Austin, says "encompass her," which clearly makes more sense in the context.

ing and identity. Each generation is better educated, more verbal, more given to purely mental activity than the last. The book reflects this progression in its increasing presentation of dialogue, largely composed of arguments that become steadily more intellectual. Tom is enraged by Lydia's occasional verbal reminiscences, both because they emphasize her separateness from him in the past and because, unworldly as he is, he is shocked and confused by the decadence of scenes that Lydia takes for granted, scenes from her aristocratic childhood in nineteenth-century Poland—such as her father's importing whores by the trainload: "And there she sat, telling the tales to the open space . . . laughing when he was shocked or astounded, condemning nothing, confounding his mind and making the whole world a chaos, without order or stability of any kind." Tom is not especially verbal, and he separates himself from Lydia rather than engaging in verbal conflict; but soon "out of nowhere, there was connection between them again," a connection that always existed in something other than words (57).

They cannot engage each other consciously, and therefore their union is never complete; yet neither is dissatisfied with it. Both have other sources of emotional satisfaction: Lydia in her past and her children, Tom in his work, his step-daughter, and the fellowship of pubs, and both in their fundamental religious beliefs, which are not expressed so much in organized religious practice as in a religious view of ordinary life. In an unusually articulate moment, Tom says, "when a man's soul and a woman's soul unites together—that makes an Angel. . . . Bodies and souls, it's the same" (135).

The next generation of Brangwens has the same resources but is more willful and better educated. Anna and Will argue about religion, opposing their individual beliefs with the force of their competitive wills. For both there is now a separation between the ordinary world and religion, which is contained in the physical building of the church. Will's work provides him with money but no satisfaction, and Anna deprives him not only of his art but also of some of his satisfaction in religion. She argues him out of his unquestioning belief in the gospels, forcing him to a separation of soul and mind: "The miracle was not a real fact. She seemed to be destroying him. . . . And yet he did not care about the Bible, the written letter. . . . He took that which was of value to him from the Written Word, he added to his spirit. His mind he let sleep" (168–69).

Disappointed by the failure of their union, each creates a private source of satisfaction that seems designed to exclude the other and reject the other's point of view. Anna is contemptuous of the physical rituals and symbols of the church, so Will commits himself passionately to them. Will wants to give himself completely to Anna and depend on her, so she turns her attention instead to her children and is absorbed in a long "sleep of motherhood" (418). This condition of maximum separation seems to limit the development of Anna and Will as people: Anna lives only through her children, and Will longs for but feels incapable of participation in public life.

Unlike Tom and Lydia, Anna and Will have consciously constructed barriers between themselves to protect each self from the negating, competitive other, and they cannot feel their unconscious connection. The only way they could come to a tender, loving union would be to break consciously through the barriers they have constructed, and they seem unwilling or unable to do that. Instead, they resolve their struggle by discovering a virtue in separation. Suddenly recognizing each other as autonomous—free, independent, inscrutable, and therefore "cruel" and "dangerous"—they are overcome with lust: "They had no conscious intimacy, no tenderness of love. It was all the lust and the infinite, maddening intoxication of the sense, a passion of death" (234). As with Milton's Adam and Eve, heightened consciousness separates Anna and Will from God, from satisfaction in their work, and from each other, and the recognition of otherness leads to lust, to sex that is not communion but the rifling of an object by a subject. As is also arguably the case in *Paradise Lost*, however, acting on the lust is both "deathly" and the best they can do in their fallen condition. Anna and Will, though they never form a sympathetic union, begin to live more fully, and Will is "set free" to take part in public life (235).

Their children are even further from the Garden. Ursula's normal consciousness is empirical rather than spiritual, yet she adheres more strictly than her parents do to the outward form of religion, keeping the Sabbath holy and utterly separate from the rest of the week. The religious dimension has been driven from six days of the week and corraled into the seventh, where its effect is intense: "On Sundays, this visionary world came to pass. . . . She lived a dual life, one where the facts of daily life encompassed everything, being legion, and the other wherein the facts of daily life were superseded by the eternal truth" (274–75).

This dichotomous arrangement leaves the greater part of her week destitute of meaning, and Ursula searches with her characteristic intensity for alternative sources. She embraces serially the beliefs and the occupations that gave meaning to the lives of her progenitors; with each, however, she is disillusioned. She realizes that her religious passion is actually a displacement of sexual longing; she refuses to become the mechanical being she feels she must be to succeed in worldly work; she leaves the university when it fails to fulfill her expectation that it can replace religion; and she rejects the alternative of domesticity as too narrow for a conscious, educated being. With no other sources of meaning and internal satisfaction, she places an intolerable burden on her relationship with Anton.

When this relationship fails, she passes through a kind of self-death. The development of her consciousness has taken her beyond all help from the world as it is; she feels a desire to which life is not responsive. At this point, she presumably has choices. A more pragmatic character might admit defeat and either compromise with the given conditions, commit suicide, or wall herself off from further disappointment by ceasing to believe in a correspondence between human desire and what life is capable of delivering. Ursula chooses the spiritual rather than the empirical perspective, and the book ends on a note of triumph. Her optimistic rebirth implies the unpragmatic assumption that if life is no longer responsive to human desire, then life is about to change. Her self-death is only death to the old form of her life: she emerges from it believing herself to be the kernel of a new vital form that will take root when she casts off "this old, decaying, fibrous husk" of parents, lover, Beldover, Nottingham, England, "the world of things" (492).

This separation of the self from the traditional sources of meaning and identity—religion, work, the land, and the domestic family—is a kind of fall, and it happens in *The Rainbow*; in relation to this fall, *Women in Love* is the postlapsarian world and follows predictably from the earlier novel. Even Gerald, outwardly the champion of custom, agrees with Birkin that "there's no God" (51). The church appears only as an "old institution," useful for weddings and funerals (92). For most of the characters, work has become dead and mechanical—Birkin will "drop it as soon as I am clear enough" (124), Ursula finds it something to be endured while she waits for her life to begin (45), Gudrun makes plans to flit away from it (203) and does not even take her art very seriously (87). Only Gerald is emotionally involved in his work, but it is not a simple, natural exercising of his talents in meaningful activity. It is more like a terrible emotional need: "Gerald was as if left on board of a ship that was going asunder beneath his feet, he was in charge of a vessel whose timbers were all coming apart" (213); "And it was his will to subjugate Matter to his own ends. The subjugation itself was the point" (216). Feeling his old world falling apart, he destroys his father's system in the mines and creates a new order of such mechanical purity that when it is finished "Gerald was hardly necessary any more" and he begins to wonder "what he was" (224).

The satisfactions of the domestic family are hardly considered by the new characters: Minette/Pussum finds her pregnancy "beastly" (61), Gudrun declares herself to "get no feeling whatever from the thought of bearing children" (3), and even Ursula, who does seem to want children (3), finds her parents' lives to be "so *nothing* . . . there's no meaning in it" (365–66) and wonders why every woman wants "a hubby and a little grey home in the west" (367). Conventional marriage comes in for general disapproval: Gerald toys with the idea as a way of structuring himself, but none of the others can tolerate the thought of a stable, social marriage, *"égoïsme à deux"* (344). Birkin and Ursula enter into an "absolute, mystic" marriage of the spirit, adding "legal marriage" as "a mere question of convenience" (343); and in their life they will have no home, no fixed location, but rather "freedom *together*" (143).

The burden of satisfaction, then, is placed by the new characters, just as it was by Ursula in *The Rainbow*, on romantic love. Ursula herself wants to give romantic love another try, until Birkin makes it clear to her that that is not what he wants and forces her to realize that ordinary romantic love will never fulfill them. At the stage of ego development that they and the other characters have reached, romantic love can only be a repetition of the fight for self-gratification that Ursula experienced with Anton or of the power struggle between Birkin and Hermione. The "star balance" Birkin desires and convinces Ursula to try for is both less personal and more permanent than romantic love. It is recognizably a new form of relationship, intended to allow for the reintegration of mental consciousness with what Lawrence calls "blood consciousness" in cerebral individuals; it incorporates both conscious and unconscious connections and allows for permanent separateness in permanent union. As such, it is a synthesis of the thesis and antithesis embodied in the first two generations of *The Rainbow* and a reasonable fulfillment of the promise at that book's end.

Birkin's "star balance" is, however, also a betrayal of the expectations developed in *The Rainbow*. As we shall see, the promise of *The Rainbow* is for sexual fulfillment, procreative oneness with the divine, and an end to mechanical servitude. It is, furthermore, a promise for all people. But the fulfillment, when it arrives in *Women in Love*, is asexual, antifertile, undemocratic, and deeply misanthropic: only Birkin and Ursula are saved, and they turn away from the rest of humanity, which is "gone . . . down the slope of mechanical death," like the Gadarene swine (361).

There is, furthermore, another woman in love, whose story is given at least equal prominence in the second novel; and her way of loving, even her very being, has no true antecedent in *The Rainbow*. The relationship of Gerald and Gudrun is like an earlier one except for a crucial difference in intention: Ursula and Anton naively try to encompass each other for their own gratification and fail, while Gudrun and Gerald know in advance not only that they will fail but that theirs will be a mortal struggle, and they are attracted to each other for that reason. They want nothing from each other but the ultimate sensations, ultimately murder and death, and along the way the exhilaration of terrible battle with a rival who is equal in destructive power. They do not seek happiness or the satisfactions of positive desire. They feel pleasure only in "the activity of departure," in destruction, corruption, reduction, dissolution, the coming apart of themselves, their souls, minds, and bodies.

Nearly everyone in *The Rainbow* is in process, passing through destructive states as part of a dialectic that returns them to creation. The few characters who take the pragmatic alternative that Ursula does not take, to wall off the self from disappointment, seem to separate themselves thereby from the living cosmos and therefore from vitality. Winifred Inger and the younger Tom Brangwen are in some ways prototypes of Gerald and Gudrun: both pairs embody the errors that are possible for overly mental modern humanity. Winifred and Tom take "a ghoulish satisfaction" from the "slavery" imposed on human beings by "that symmetric monster of the colliery" (348–49); they are attracted to each other in spite of mutual fear and revulsion (346); and they live in "marshy, bitter-sweet corruption . . . where life and decaying are one" (350). But Tom and Winifred do not take vitality from this corruption. Instead, both of them seem to be dying: "He had the instinct of a growing inertia, of a thing that chooses its place of rest in which to lapse into apathy, complete, profound indifference. He would let the machinery carry him" (351). Winifred becomes to Ursula a "heavy cleaving of moist clay, that cleaves because it has no life of its own" (343). Ursula and Anton, too, are "killed" in some way by their struggle to use each other for selfish gratification; in the end, they are "like two dead people" (480).

But *Women in Love* introduces the idea that one may go on living and flourishing after losing "organic hold" on the source of life. Gerald and Gudrun, for instance, seem to gain vitality from destruction, particularly from the unconscious pact they have with each other, by which Gudrun appears to be at Gerald's mercy but will be the ultimate victor (234). In this novel, frozen water is the supreme symbolic form both of corruption (which is antiorganic, antivital) and of mechanization (which is abstract, inhuman), and Gerald is always associated at his strongest and most beautiful with frost, ice, and snow. Near the end of his fatal struggle with Gudrun, he seems to be growing both more mechanized and more powerful: "He felt strong as winter, his hands were living metal, invincible and not to be turned aside. . . . He was super-humanly strong and unflawed, as if invested with supernatural force" (391–92).

Gudrun fears Gerald, but she is stimulated by the danger and the challenge to outwit him: "She knew her life trembled on the edge of an abyss. But she was curiously sure of her footing. She knew her cunning could outwit him. She trembled, as she stood in her room, with excitement and awful exhilaration" (454). Gudrun feels rapture near, and desire for, the perfect frozen center of the Alps, to climb into which would be her "consummation" (391, 400); she declares "the complete moment of my life" to be one in which she is knocked into "oblivion" by a toboggan ride. Both Gerald and Gudrun find ecstasy in mountain sports, which are described as "moving in an intensity of speed and white light that surpassed life itself, and carried the souls of the human beings beyond into an inhuman abstraction of velocity and weight and eternal, frozen snow" (411).

The desire to surpass life itself and achieve eternal perfection is one of the things Gerald and Gudrun have in common, and in this they are more Promethean than satanic. Gerald and Gudrun are usually seen as manifestations of the apocalypse, evidence of the desperate condition of humankind and the need for its death and renewal. Indeed they are that, and the satanic associations of the imagery surrounding them are undeniable.[10] But they are not simply satanic, any more than Milton's Satan is; they are not the objectification of all error, a simple foil for Birkin and Ursula. Lawrence's attitude toward them is complex, as becomes obvious when we compare his treatment of Gerald and Gudrun to that given their prototypes in *The Rainbow*. By the end of their brief history, Winifred and Tom do seem to be simply coagulations of error; they are presented almost entirely externally and become almost one-dimensional villains; they are even physically nauseating (350). The emphasis on the revulsion they inspire in Ursula suggests that the lesbian Winifred and the cynical mine manager Tom revolted the man who wrote *The Rainbow*; the mine owner in *Women in Love*, however, is a tragic hero, and his decadent lover remains beautiful and often sympathetic, even occasionally heroic, as in "Gudrun in the Pompadour." That Lawrence made his satanic figures into fully realized, complex, often sympathetic characters in the second novel suggests at least a change in his treatment of the opposition. In *The Rainbow* characters who oppose themselves to Lawrence's idea of creative fulfillment become of marginal importance to the novel, but in *Women in Love* the opposition is so important that they are sometimes hard to distinguish from the home team.

Gerald and Gudrun are identified (by Birkin, but in a way that the book bears out) with a form of life that Birkin calls "the destructive creation." It proceeds from "the dark river of dissolution" and is therefore ontologically opposite to vital creation, which is produced by "the silver river of life." Some-

10. See Kathleen M. Miles, *The Hellish Meaning: The Demonic Motif in the Works of D. H. Lawrence* (Carbondale: Southern Illinois University Monographs, Humanities Series, 2, 1969).

how the process of dissolution or decay is capable of creating life. It spawns not only Gerald and Gudrun but recognizable natural creatures: swans, lotuses, lilies, mud flowers, water plants, seals, and rabbits, as well as bats, beetles, rats, and snakes (164). Some critics explain the "destructive" nature of these creatures by saying that they are on their way to death, like Tom and Winifred, or that they are signs of the apocalypse.

Such readings, however, miss the full force of Lawrence's oxymoron. Dissolution and destruction are the mirror opposites of growth or "synthetic creation." Dissolution is the separation of elements joined or "composed" in growth; after death, that which was joined separates, *de*composes, dissolves, corrupts, returns to dust. Following the characteristic duality of his thinking, Lawrence went a step further with the mirror opposition between growth and decay: if life is created by the synthesis of elements, it should also be created by their coming apart again.

Later, Lawrence would make an even greater peace with the forces of destruction. His postwar cosmogony in *Fantasia of the Unconscious* (1922) has the earth, sun, and moon being created from the decay of the first creature's body.[11] But in *Women in Love* the principle of decay generates only an inverted version of the physical universe. Birkin sees the process of synthetic creation as having "lapsed" in nature, leaving only the process of separation, which "ends in universal nothing." For the moment, the natural world looks the same, but creation is running down.

The special creations of the inverse process are associated with water and therefore with dissolution and, in Lawrence's symbolic logic, with mechanization. Lawrence's identity of dissolution with mechanization or abstraction is difficult to grasp, but it is central to *Women in Love*. A person who aspires to the condition of a machine—who wants to fix the imperfect

11. D. H. Lawrence, *Psychoanalysis and the Unconscious/Fantasia of the Unconscious* (New York: Viking, 1960), 63.

flux of organic life, who seeks to control himself and his environment by force of will—is for Lawrence more like an inorganic abstraction than a living creature. Hence Lawrence associates mechanization with all the words signifying organic decay, and he slides easily back and forth between the two concepts: the miners are mechanized, and their wills are rotten (110); so is Gudrun's, and she is turning into a machine (108)—specifically, toward the end, into a clock (457). Gerald wills himself to become an abstraction while he fears that his self is dissolving to nothing (224–25). Rot naturally inspires nausea and horror, as does the idea of mechanizing a human into a robot or a clock, and to associate anything with such images is clearly to judge it negatively. Yet in *Women in Love* the desire to transcend the imperfect organic flux into abstraction, if taken far enough, becomes the Promethean desire for eternal perfection, "surpassing life itself." Hence the miners' hearts die within them when Gerald creates the "new order" in the mines, which is "strict, terrible, inhuman," but they are also "exalted by belonging to this great and superhuman system . . . beyond feeling or reason, something really godlike" (223).

In the world of this book, mechanization is the human form of the destructive creation, and neither mechanization nor the destructive creation is a purely negative development. Whereas in the natural world corruption has taken over the process of creation, human beings have lost the desire for creative fulfillment and have increasingly mechanized their environment and themselves. What Lawrence thought of as mechanization of the self begins with the pessimistic choice to wall oneself off within a willbound ego. This choice may stem from a disjunction between desire and the world's capacity to fulfill it (as in Gudrun's case), but it is experienced, defensively, as a lapse of desire for productive happiness. What is walled out is both the flux of change and the possibility of fulfillment, which in Lawrence's philosophy at the time he wrote "Study of Thomas Hardy" could only come through a leap beyond the self, into the "unknown" or the "beyond." The unknown is both an unpredictable, unstructured way of living, outside safe convention, and an ontological state of oneness with Lawrence's idea of God or the infinite or the eternal world. To make this leap, a person must open the shell of the ego—shed all self-control—and become vulnerable to the flux of elemental forces sweeping over one from within and without. The leap is actually made in sex, as Lawrence stated in "Hardy": "In love, a man, a woman, flows on to the very furthest edge of known feeling, being, and out beyond the furthest edge. . . . the act, called the sexual act . . . is for leaping off into the unknown, as from a cliff's edge, like Sappho into the sea" (*Phoenix* 441).

Obviously, mechanization is the refuge of the cautious. Unfortunately, the mechanized self continues to yearn for fulfillment; these yearnings are translated into a desire for violent sensation, which may be experienced without discarding the protective shell of the ego. Extremes of lust and violence are therefore parodic substitutes for the exhilaration of fulfillment, and they stand in relation to it exactly as the destructive creation stands to the synthetic one. Just as the natural world is running down since the lapse in synthetic creation, the wave of humanity that includes all of the major characters in *Women in Love* is flattening out and losing its momentum. But, once again, the process of destruction is startlingly creative. Gudrun, Palmer, and the miners are not only inexpressively destructive, they are powerful (110); Gerald is growing strong as winter; Hermione only gains access to intense vitality in her attempt to kill Birkin (98). In fact, that murderous moment is Hermione's "consummation"—just as it would be Gudrun's to die in the snow, just as it nearly is Gerald's to kill her in the snow. Gerald's soul opens "wide, wide . . . in wonder" as he strangles her (463); Hermione feels she must kill Birkin to break down the walls around herself (98). The suggestion is that each of these destructive acts is, or would be if it were completed, a kind of rebirth in destruction—a breaking of the ego, a leap into the unknown. When the image of Sappho leaping from a cliff appears in *Women in Love* (183), it characterizes a desire for self-realization not in sex but in death.

Self-regeneration through murder or suicide is an idea central to the original unpublished chapters of "The Crown." As noted briefly in the Introduction, this version of Lawrence's philosophy was written in the spring and summer of 1915, when he was making final revisions to *The Rainbow* and before he began the major draftings of *Women in Love*. Only the first three chapters of the original "Crown" have ever been published; they appeared in *The Signature* in the fall of 1915. The last three chapters exist only as a holograph manuscript at the Humanities Research Center of the University of Texas at Austin. When Lawrence published "The Crown" in *Reflections on the Death of a Porcupine* in 1925, he revised the previously published chapters only slightly, but he completely rewrote the three unpublished ones (see Introduction, n. 45). These unpublished chapters give us an excellent view of Lawrence's state of mind between *The Rainbow* and *Women in Love*, and I will refer to them often throughout this study (identified in the citations as CMS, with chapter and page numbers).

In "The Crown," for the first time, Lawrence's philosophy includes a second path to redemption. While writing this essay, he observed around him what he took to be "a perverted, mental blood lust" in his contemporaries' reactions to the war. He wrote to the pacifist Bertrand Russell that "your basic desire is the maximum of desire of war, you are really the super-war-spirit. What you want is to jab and strike, like the soldier with the bayonet, only you are sublimated into words."[12] "The Crown" helps to explain this strange charge. There Lawrence argues that "the whole nation" is "engaged, vividly, vitally, fundamentally engaged in the process of reduction and dissolution," reaping the reward of "sensational gratification in the flesh or . . . within the mind." (This self-destructive gratification is what Lawrence describes, here and elsewhere, by the term "sensationalism.") The advanced, intelligent, sensitive people (like Russell) all seek now a "con-

---

12. Cambridge *Letters* 2, 392.

summation in reduction"; that is why Europe is at war (CMS IV, 5–8). They are in some sense, furthermore, right to want such a perverted consummation. Surprisingly, extremes of lust and violence are not a dead end: "Sensationalism . . . is one road to the infinite." Though "the climax of this progression is in horror, torture, and extreme death . . . only the finely developed soul can go through all the degrees of Sadisme" (Lawrence's spelling; CMS V, 2–3).

The idea still is to go "beyond the furthest edge of known feeling," but into sadism or into masochism—plunging the bayonet joyfully into the enemy or getting one's own leg shot off. The result may be release and rebirth:

> A man may be sufficiently released by a fall on the rope and a dangling for a few seconds of agony in mid-space. That may finally reduce his soul to its elements, set it free and child-like, undo all the perhaps false development of ages in his soul, make him elemental and unformed again. Then he can begin anew to develop, to build up, to unify, to create. So that the near touch of death may be a conversion to life, a liberation to the principle of the creative absolute.
>
> (CMS V, 4)

The fall on the rope *may* be sufficient, but Lawrence seems to have first observed this release in a maimed soldier at the seaside. The soldier's leg had been blown off in the war, and Lawrence imagined that he was "glowing still from the consummation of destruction and pain and horror, like a bridegroom just come from the bride." He had a soul that was "so clean and new born and fine" and "he was so strong in his new birth" that other people crowded around him, "almost beside themselves. They wanted his consummation, his perfect completeness in horror and death" (CMS V, 8–9).

In "Hardy" the consummated "bridegroom just come from the bride" has achieved self-realization through sex. But in the original "Crown" that kind of creative fulfillment is no longer possible, and Lawrence implies that sex was never a means to it:

> For a hundred years we have been given over to the slowly advancing progress of reduction, analysis, breaking-down, dissolution. Now we have reached the point when the sex is

exhausted, and there can be no more reduction through passion: when criticism and analysis are exhausted in the mind, all the units broken down that can be reached. There remains only the last experience, the same to all men, and to all women, the experience of the final reduction under the touch of death.

(CMS V, 5)

Sex is here a means to "reduce" rather than create the self, whereas in "Hardy," "the *via media* to being, for man or woman, is love, and love alone" (*Phoenix* 410). Leaping off a cliff is certainly self-destructive, but Lawrence means it only as a metaphor for complete self-abandon; the other images for sexual fulfillment are all of the synthetic creation. To be sexually fulfilled is to flower like the poppy, to "sprout into the unknown," to "fly the flag of myself, at the extreme tip of life," and to become thereby more, "the complete Me," as the fiery flower is "the thing itself at its maximum of being"—and possibly to leave seeds behind (*Phoenix* 402–9). But the original "Crown" implies not only that "sex is exhausted" now but also that it never was anything *but* destructive: "In sex, we have plunged the quick of creation deep into the cold flux of reduction, corruption, till the quick is extinguished" (CMS V, 7).

Women in Love seems to share this view of sex as something rather horrifying that is going out of style. As we shall see in chapter 3, the way Birkin and Ursula attain the unknown is subtly but clearly distinguished from sexual passion. Birkin, Hermione, Gerald, and Gudrun are among those described in the original "Crown" who have gone to the end of experience in the sexual line without being released and reborn. Hermione needs to have her skull cracked, and Gerald needs to crack someone's, to achieve a consummation in "reduction" or "Sadisme." Though Birkin at last discovers another way and tries to convert Gerald to it, the only release dramatized as accessible to Gerald and Hermione in the novel is the consummation through homicide.

Neither of the attempted murders is successfully completed and therefore we cannot know what would have resulted if they had been. If Gerald had killed Gudrun, would he have broken permanently out of his mechanical ego and become free and whole? Would Gerald have remained part of the destructive creation, or would he have been "converted to life," like the maimed soldier, after a "consummation of destruction," and have joined Birkin and Ursula as travelers on the new path, jobless, homeless, open to the flux of change? This we cannot know, though the tragic ending of the book suggests the latter.

The possibility of renewal through homicide does appear in Lawrence's work before "The Crown" and *Women in Love*. In one of Lawrence's earliest stories, "A Fragment of Stained Glass" (1911), a serf kills a horse with an axe and sets fire to the manor, committing crimes so violent as to register almost like murder, yet remains the story's hero; and "The Prussian Officer" (1914) is a study in necessary homicide. The orderly who kills his officer, in a burst of repressed instinct, is swept out of ordinary life into the unknown: "The village and the white-towered church was small in the sunshine. And he no longer belonged to it—he sat there, beyond, like a man outside in the dark. He had gone out from everyday life into the unknown, and he could not, he even did not want to go back." The orderly and the peasant react as healthy animals to extreme provocation; both are held in subjection by social structures that take no account of the individual, and both are physically abused by those in command of them. Killing the officer is presented as a healthy reaction of the orderly's instinctual being: when he strangles the officer it is because "the instinct which had been jerking at the young man's wrists suddenly jerked free. He jumped, feeling as if he were rent in two by a strong flame." And his unconscious decision finally to fight back seems to be identical with his having at last found self-definition; as he approaches the officer for the last time he has "a core into which all the energy of that young life was compact and concentrated . . . hard there in the centre of his chest was himself, himself, firm, and not to be plucked to pieces."[13]

13. D. H. Lawrence, *The Prussian Officer* (1914; rpt. Cambridge: Cambridge University Press, 1983), 16, 13–14.

The orderly and the peasant are heroically healthy when they break out to become renegades, to live briefly in the beyond before they die. But murder is not the only way for the serf or the orderly to be released into the beyond. Each has chosen a woman and is clearly capable of finding fulfillment with her, sexual fulfillment of the sort described in "Hardy" (which was written the same year as "The Prussian Officer"); that they are prevented from doing so intensifies the tragedy in these stories. Nothing intrinsic in the nature of either character necessitates violence as the only path to release from the ego; Gerald and Hermione, and probably Gudrun as well, are the first characters in Lawrence's work for whom that is true.

And even the normative relationship in *Women in Love* represents a change from Lawrence's earlier dynamic of self-realization: the way Birkin and Ursula break through to new health seems to involve a similar violation of vitalist morality. The climactic breakthrough occurs in the tearoom scene in "Excurse," when Ursula discovers an "unthinkable" power in Birkin, "floods of ineffable darkness and ineffable riches." She finds this power in his buttocks and proclaims them a "source deeper than the phallic source . . . further in mystery than the phallic source." This discovery reveals him to her as "one of the sons of God . . . not a man, something other, something more"—as in some way surpassing humanity (305–6). And Birkin himself feels like "an Egyptian Pharaoh . . . subtle, full of unthinkable knowledge and unthinkable force . . . like the immobile, supremely potent Egyptians" (310).

This scene might appear to be merely a primitivist ritual by which Birkin and Ursula establish an unconscious connection between themselves if these terms were newly introduced. We have heard them all before, however, and in contexts that link them with the most extreme forms of destruction, with the rush of humankind down the Gadarene slope and the imminent annihilation of the white races. In "Moony," Birkin experiences a kind of prophetic trance in which he realizes that he has two choices: he can continue with the rest of his race on the course toward "snow-abstract annihilation," perfect mechanization, and, therefore, dissolution of the self. Or he can break free into "pure, single being, the individual soul taking precedence over love and desire for union," accepting the "obligation of the permanent connection with others" but never forfeiting "its own proud individual singleness" (247).

Birkin understandably chooses the second course and goes off to propose to Ursula, but not before he has dwelt on the horrors of the alternative. He identifies the process of slow death now occurring in his own culture with the decline of a West African civilization, which he sees revealed in one of its artifacts, the statue of a woman. The cause of this decline as Birkin sees it is to be found in the souls of the people who constitute that culture: "The desire for creation and productive happiness must have lapsed, leaving the single impulse for . . . knowledge arrested and ending in the senses." The process is essentially the same as the mechanization of the self just described. And here we learn more about the "violent sensation" desired by the mechanized or dissolving self: it is "mystic knowledge . . . such as the beetles have, which live purely within the world of corruption and cold dissolution." "Knowledge such as the beetles have" becomes more clear when we hear that "this was why the Egyptians worshipped the ball-rolling scarab," and when we remember Birkin's emphasis on the statue's "protuberant buttocks." The scarab is a dung beetle; the ball it rolls is excrement. Later, in "The Ladybird," written when Lawrence had decided that "the principle of decomposition . . . set the globe rolling," the hero explains that the Egyptians identified the scarab with "the creative principle";[14] for Birkin, however, it is an emblem of ghoulish decadence. Whatever acquiring its knowledge might mean for a human, such knowledge is "very, very far . . . beyond the phallic cult . . . far beyond the scope of phallic investigation" (245–46).

"Phallic knowledge" is presumably reproductive, part of synthetic creation. The sensual knowledge of thoroughly decayed humans is beyond phallic investigation and, therefore, beyond even sodomy; it seems to have little to do with sex at

---

14. D. H. Lawrence, "The Ladybird" (1923); rpt. in *Four Short Novels* (New York: Penguin, 1976), 97.

all. Whereas sex and reproduction belong to the "silver river of life," the large intestine is clearly the body's "dark river of dissolution," in which what was joined is separated. Therefore, whatever knowledge it may have to impart belongs with the destructive creation, with the "abhorrent mysteries" in which Gerald and Gudrun are "implicated" (234), with "sewer rats" like Loerke (419), with all the violent and putrescent decadence that Birkin and Ursula want to escape.

Imagine our surprise, then, when this escape begins with Ursula's discovery of a power deeper than the phallic in Birkin's buttocks, a source that is dark, fluid, and Egyptian. This would seem to be "knowledge such as the beetles have"; and what it reveals is the tremendous, even superhuman power of the forces of dissolution. Because Birkin has them in his body, he is "full of unthinkable knowledge and unthinkable force"; he is also "more than a man." Un-Promethean as the context is, what Birkin has sounds suspiciously like what Gerald and Gudrun want.

For some reason, Lawrence wanted us to connect the normative relationship of Ursula and Birkin with the worst decadence. The manuscript provides evidence that Lawrence created this paradox intentionally, since Birkin's meditation in "Moony" and the relevant sections in "Excurse" were written in the same ink (blue-gray) between the lines of the definitive typescript; both were apparently added in the major period of revision (1917).[15] And the published novel makes clear that deathliness is now an integral part of Lawrence's idea of regeneration. In "Excurse," Birkin wants Ursula to "take" him as he has "taken her . . . at the roots of her darkness and shame—like a demon, laughing over the fountain of mystic corruption which was one of the sources of her being" (296).

15. This manuscript is in the Humanities Research Center, University of Texas at Austin, which calls it "the definitive typescript"; Charles Ross, *Composition*, calls it "the final draft," since the first editions were set up from it. In any case, it was made in 1917 and Lawrence made holograph revisions to it in two periods of revision, one in 1917 (blue-gray ink), one in 1919 (reddish brown ink). I will refer to it as the definitive typescript (WLTS). See Ross, *Composition*, 100–101, 115–18, 120–23.

In the dark of Sherwood Forest she does so, releasing both of them to the "star balance" and making Birkin "night-free, like an Egyptian, steadfast in perfectly suspended equilibrium" (311). For some reason, touching the anus of the beloved creates a new relationship between them; for some reason too, the anus is a "source of being."

This novel asks us to accept a complex relationship between vitality and decay, and critics have seldom been able to do it. As Jeffrey Meyers points out, "The equation of the anus with the life source is such an obscene and outrageous idea that some of the most perceptive critics have either ignored it entirely or else refused to face [its] full implications," which for Meyers means facing "Lawrence's homosexuality."[16] One way to avoid facing this outrageous idea is to conflate *Women in Love* with its sister novel and interpret Birkin and Ursula's release as if it were identical to the clearly sexual fulfillments in *The Rainbow*—for this life in or through corruption is a new development in *Women in Love*. Lawrence himself implied as much when he said that *Women in Love* "is purely destructive, not like *The Rainbow*, destructive-consummating."[17] Even critics who recognize, however, with F. R. Leavis, that "*Women in Love* is wholly self-contained, and, for all the carryover of names of characters, has no organic connexion with *The Rainbow*," resist Lawrence's evaluation of the later book.[18] In fact, such critics as Leavis, Julian Moynahan, H. T. Moore, and Graham Hough have so succeeded in establishing a wholesome, socially acceptable version of Lawrence, Lawrence as the priest of love, that others, notably Colin Clarke and Frank Kermode, have recently felt a need to reassert the other side.

In 1921 John Middleton Murry was outraged by *Women in Love* (even before he realized that he was one of the models

16. Jeffrey Meyers, "D. H. Lawrence and Homosexuality," in *D. H. Lawrence: Novelist, Poet, Prophet*, ed. Stephen Spender (London: Weidenfeld and Nicolson, 1973), 145.
17. Cambridge *Letters* 3, 143.
18. F. R. Leavis, *D. H. Lawrence: Novelist* (New York: Knopf, 1968), 109.

for Gerald), and he led the attack that was to keep Lawrence in dubious repute until his rescue by Leavis. In his review of *Women in Love*, Murry denounces the ambiguous relationship between the social decline of "the African process" and the consummation in "Excurse." He declares Lawrence a public menace, his "consummation . . . a degradation," and his book "an attempt to take us through" the African process.[19]

In *Son of Woman* (1931), Murry elaborates this attack, drawing primarily biographical conclusions from it. He postulates that "Lawrence changed while *Women in Love* was actually being written: that he really did mean to reject the way of sensuality and dissolution, and that he succumbed to it in spite of himself." Murry's violent ambivalence toward Lawrence got in his way, and his assertion that Lawrence's work was an attempt to compensate for his sexual failure should probably not be taken as the unbiased truth. Still Murry was astute on certain themes that have only recently reappeared in Lawrence criticism. He focused relentlessly on the asexual nature of the relationship desired by Birkin: "A sexual marriage in which he does not have to satisfy the woman, where the sexuality, being transformed into sensuality, may give him the opportunity of reasserting the manhood he had lost—this is precisely Lawrence's dream."

Very few critics have taken seriously Murry's charge that in Birkin's brave new world "the phallic relation is to be superseded, by a new sexuality of separateness and touch."[20] Marguerite Beede Howe makes a strong case for Murry's reading in *The Art of the Self in D. H. Lawrence*, her useful study of Lawrence's ego psychology. She finds *Women in Love* to be "puritanical tragedy, where to assert one's male sexuality is the hubris that attracts divine retribution. . . . Whereas

19. John Middleton Murry, "The Nostalgia of Mr. D. H. Lawrence," *Nation and Athenaeum* (August 13, 1921); rpt. in his *Reminiscences of D. H. Lawrence* (London: Jonathan Cape, 1933), 218–27.

20. John Middleton Murry, *Son of Woman* (London: Jonathan Cape, 1931), 113–15.

Gerald is an adult, sexual male, his counterpart Birkin is not."[21] Most critics, however, have assumed that Birkin and Ursula have genital sex as well, and the novel does suggest, paradoxically, that they eventually do. When it occurs, however (as will be discussed in chapter 3), it seems to be an early version of the sexuality in *The Plumed Serpent* and *Lady Chatterley's Lover*. As the famous exchange between Kate Millett and Norman Mailer made clear, Lawrence denounced conscious sexual pleasure for women in these late works and had his heroes use sex as a means of teaching submission to assertive modern women.[22] Lawrence's campaign against self-centered women was lifelong, and in many of his early works young male characters are painfully reticent about sex (Paul Morel in *Sons and Lovers*, Tom Brangwen in *The Rainbow*, Alfred Durant in "Daughters of the Vicar," and Severn in "The Old Adam"). But Birkin's reluctance is an escalation of both themes, and he is the first of Lawrence's heroes (to be followed by Cipriano and Mellors) consciously to withhold his sexual favors.

Lawrence clearly felt that Birkin was going beyond sex rather than shrinking from it, and more sympathetic critics have considered the matter from that point of view. These critics classify the scenes of supraphallic sensuality with what they see as instances of sodomy in Lawrence's work, the first of which some of them believe occurs between Anna and Will in *The Rainbow*. G. Wilson Knight pioneered this reading in "Lawrence, Joyce, and Powys." Though he notes that "in *Women in Love* the implements are fingers" and the act is what some critics have called an "anal caress," Knight regards it as an early version of the sodomy in *Lady Chatterley's Lover*, which is often read simply as a gesture of forgiveness for what Lawrence calls "the oldest shames of the body." Knight says that Lawrence "is trying to blast through this degradation to a new health" and that "the deathly is found to be

21. Marguerite Beede Howe, *The Art of the Self in D. H. Lawrence* (Athens, Ohio: Ohio University Press, 1977), 69, 76.

22. Norman Mailer, *Prisoner of Sex* (Boston: Little, Brown, 1971), 98–115; and Kate Millett, *Sexual Politics* (New York: Doubleday, 1970), 237–93.

the source of some higher order of being; contact with a basic materiality liberates the person."[23] After 1915 Lawrence's work often asserts the need to accept shame and corruption in oneself, and the need to accept it in the beloved seems to be part of Birkin's motivation in *Women in Love*. He wonders, "When would she so much go beyond herself as to accept him at the quick of death?" When he touches her "fountain of mystic corruption," he is "laughing, shrugging, accepting, accepting finally" (296).

One wonders, however, if this theme sufficiently explains the separate appearances in the novel of supraphallic sensuality as both the most decadent and the most regenerative forms of human interaction. Mary Freeman confronts this contradiction by placing Birkin and Ursula among the damned: they willingly participate in "the sense of decay permeating the whole social order" and thereby "in some measure convert a death agony to a death ecstasy."[24] Frank Kermode more fully registers the paradox in "Lawrence and the Apocalyptic Types," in which he describes the act performed by Birkin and Ursula as a "harrowing of hell" that "amalgamates heaven and hell, life-flow and death-flow, in one act." Kermode is analyzing Lawrence's use of the Book of Revelation: "He has in mind what he takes to be the basic figure of the mystery behind revelation—that is the point . . . where life and death meet."

Kermode's subject is the conflict between apocalyptic mysticism and novelistic realism in Lawrence's work. He thinks that *Women in Love* succeeds because the mystical typology is subdued by the realism, as it will not often be in Lawrence's later fiction. His explanation of the supraphallic contradiction is entirely typological, however, and leaves no explanation for

23. G. Wilson Knight, "Lawrence, Joyce and Powys," *Essays in Criticism* 11 (1961): 403–41. For further discussion, see Mark Spilka, "Lawrence Up-Tight or the Anal Phase Once Over," *Novel* 4 (1971): 252–67; and George Ford, Frank Kermode, Colin Clarke, and Mark Spilka, "Critical Exchange," *Novel* 5 (1971): 54–70.
24. Mary Freeman, *D. H. Lawrence: A Basic Study of His Ideas* (Gainesville: University of Florida Press, 1955), 65.

the act as a realistic, historical choice (which, as we shall see in chapter 3, Lawrence clearly thought it was). He relies on the similarity between Lawrence's novel and earlier apocalyptic literature, such as the Book of Revelation: "Decadence and renovation, death and rebirth, in the last days, are hard to tell apart, being caught up in the terrors."[25]

Colin Clarke examines further sources for Lawrence's paradoxical treatment of decay in *River of Dissolution: D. H. Lawrence and English Romanticism*. Lawrence was steeped in Romantic poetry. Wordsworth, Shelley, and Keats influenced his poetry as much as the Bible did his novels,[26] and Clarke finds a powerful Romantic influence in the novels as well. Clarke argues that ambiguous treatment of dissolution is inherent in the Romantic tradition, and that *Women in Love* brings the ambiguity to the surface and makes it fully conscious for the first time. He shows Lawrence both using and playing with certain themes in the poetry of his Romantic predecessors, including: images of dissolution becoming images of sublimation; confusion between the dissolving of consciousness and a dissolving of the substantial world of sense; the possibility of a confusion between surrendering to the sleep of vision and surrendering to the sleep of death; and the slide from fading into reverie or trance to fading into passion or death. Clarke believes that Lawrence is both doing what Keats did—flirting with glamorous death—and revealing something about that desire. Seen clearly, the desire for dissolution is part of an antinomial paradox that goes something like this: "Only through submission to disintegration can the disintegrated condition be superseded"; or, "holiness is quite other than degradation, and also is nourished by degradation."

25. Frank Kermode, "Lawrence and the Apocalyptic Types," *Critical Quarterly* 10 (1969): 14–38.
26. For an analysis of the Romantic influence on Lawrence's poetry, see Sandra M. Gilbert, *Acts of Attention: The Poems of D. H. Lawrence* (Ithaca and London: Cornell University Press, 1972). For the influence of the Bible on Lawrence's novels, especially *The Rainbow*, see George Ford, *Double Measure: A Study of the Novels and Stories of D. H. Lawrence* (New York: Holt, Rinehart and Winston, 1965).

Clarke argues persuasively that *Women in Love* "in effect 'affirms'" both of the latter propositions "more or less continuously." He is not saying that dissolution is part of a phoenix-like dialectic, a necessary burning of the old before the new can arise—that is Knight's argument, the "blast through degradation to new health." Clarke argues that "the effect of Lawrence's art is to discourage in the reader any tendency to reach a single and ready-defined judgment" on the "human value" of various experiences; that in fact the reader must "admit the disintegrative impulse to be an 'equal alternative' to the integrative."

Clarke is right: Lawrence's vision is antinomial and morally relativistic in *Women in Love*. I think Clarke is wrong, however, when he calls *The Rainbow* an unsuccessful attempt to create the same paradoxes. He says that *The Rainbow* is groping toward "the audacious double-talk of *Women in Love* but achieving, instead, an effect of uneasy equivocation"; that it "only 'half-says' . . . that corruption, violence, bestiality, 'all the shameful things of the body' are both degrading and life-enhancing." Clarke thinks that Lawrence had decided this already but did not know how to embody it in art: that the strategy of the earlier book is not "sufficiently flexible" to allow his paradoxes to appear as other than contradictory.[27] He makes leaps, however, to get to this conclusion. For instance he associates Skrebensky's "African night" with corruption,

27. The conclusion that *The Rainbow* is an early, imperfect version of *Women in Love* is one to which several studies on Lawrence's development have come. Stephen J. Miko's *Towards* Women in Love (New Haven: Yale University Press, 1971) traces Lawrence's development as a religious writer, his struggle for a means to show the workings of transcendent forces in realistic characters and events. Miko registers little change in Lawrence's thinking and focuses instead on the refining of his technique. Miko's use of the 1925 version of "The Crown" may have caused him to miss some of the changes in Lawrence's thinking; he even seems unaware of the existence of the original, which would have been the appropriate version to use in a developmental study covering Lawrence in 1915 (Miko 212–14). Mark Kinkead-Weekes, in "The Marble and the Statue," also focuses primarily on Lawrence's technique. He explains the content of the novels as both the effect and the cause of all change: using the surviving drafts, he argues that the technical discoveries Lawrence made in the act of writing account for the changes in his work.

even while admitting that "the concept of corruption is not invoked explicitly" in connection with it, and conflates the fluid darkness of the love scenes between Ursula and Anton with Birkin's river of dissolution—reading all images of water, darkness, and Africa retroactively from their associations in *Women in Love*, in which, as we shall see, their meanings are quite different. He objects to the ending of *The Rainbow* because "we are left with the impression that corruption is merely *antithetical* to this new life" promised by the rainbow[28]—but that impression, I think, corresponds quite accurately to the theme of *The Rainbow* as a whole.

Clarke is not without evidence for his reading of *The Rainbow*. There is one passage that supports his interpretation: the sequence at the end of "The Child" in which Will and Anna are released and made whole through a sensuality that Lawrence insists is "deathly." That scene is a late addition, however, added by Lawrence after his thinking had already begun to change. The novel as a whole is not ambivalent toward corruption, though that scene is, and it seems more reasonable to read a single sequence through the dynamic of the whole novel. Such a reading is provided in the next chapter.

28. Colin Clarke, *River of Dissolution: D. H. Lawrence and English Romanticism* (London: Routledge and Kegan Paul, 1969), 35, 50, 84, 52, 42, 67.

2

The Saner Sister

At the end of *The Rainbow*, Ursula has an optimistic vision of the coming regeneration of the human race, embodied in the symbol that gives the book its title: "she knew that the sordid people who crept hard-scaled and separate on the face of the world's corruption were living still, that the rainbow was arched in their blood and would quiver to life in their spirit." The rainbow is an unequivocally hopeful sign here, riding as it does on the book's biblical typology. It is a covenant, though apparently not with God, who is not mentioned in the concluding passage. "Heaven" appears four times, though each time it is a place roughly coterminous with "sky": the rainbow is in "the space of heaven," "its arch the top of heaven," and the new human race will rise "to the light and the wind and the clean rain of heaven . . . the world built up in a living fabric of Truth, fitting to the over-arching heaven" (494–95).

When the new covenant is fulfilled, heaven will be brought down to earth and the natural world will be the terrain of religious significance. Similarly, if we have to decide who the parties to the covenant are, the part assigned to God in the Bible seems to be taken by humanity, or humanity in conjunction with the natural world, or by the blood, rather than by an extraterrestrial being. The promise of the rainbow, which arches in the blood of corrupt modern people, is physiological, at least metaphorically so: the promise is that the people will "cast off their horny covering of disintegration, that new, clean, naked bodies would issue to a new germination, to a new growth." The earth itself will shed its manmade shell: "The old, brittle corruption of houses and factories" will be "swept away." One wonders how literally the book's last paragraph is meant to be taken. Since even jaded modern people do not in any realistic sense have a "horny covering," it is one thing to say this will be "cast off," and quite another to imagine "houses and factories swept away" (495). As stated, this vision is blithely apocalyptic and oblivious of practical difficulties.

However Lawrence envisioned "the earth's new architecture," the old is still in place, and even more corrupt, in *Women in Love*. The mining town Ursula views with such horror at the end of the earlier novel is the principal setting of the later one, and the people we meet are more "sordid," "hard-scaled," "separate," and "corrupt" than anyone in *The Rainbow*. Perhaps Lawrence always intended to make the second book not a vision of the solution but a more compelling statement of the problem. George Ford has pointed out that the biblical imagery of *The Rainbow* establishes Ursula as a prophet who will help to lead the way into the promised land.[1] Perhaps Lawrence intended, having established her as a prophet, to send her through a trial in the underworld, analogous to Jonah's sojourn in the whale's belly or Christ's three days in the tomb.

Perhaps, in other words, Lawrence knew when he wrote the end of *The Rainbow* that in the next book the covenant would not be fulfilled, or not fulfilled exactly as promised. Still, the Book of Genesis is strongly evoked throughout *The Rainbow*; and since the biblical rainbow promises that the waters will cover the earth no more (and that promise is kept), we have no reason to expect that the catastrophe will continue in the sequel. Lawrence himself may have recognized that, in relation to the promise of *The Rainbow*, *Women in Love* is a betrayal: for a time he considered calling the second book *Noah's Ark*.[2] Though this title suggests survival (as well as how to achieve it), the biblical ark was built before, not after, the rainbow. Such a sequence might be poetic

1. George Ford, *Double Measure: A Study of the Novels and Stories of D. H. Lawrence* (New York: Holt, Rinehart and Winston, 1965), 137.
2. Cambridge *Letters* 3, 183.

license, or it might reflect a change in Lawrence's original scheme.

If Lawrence's vision of the coming regeneration of humanity underwent a change between the two books, there ought to be ample evidence of it in the books themselves and in other works contemporaneous with them. The ambiguity we have already noticed in *Women in Love* is the most persuasive evidence—since Murry, some readers have said, in effect, of Birkin and Ursula: this is no ark, this is more flood. But of course this ambiguity represents a change in vision only if *The Rainbow* is not morally ambiguous in the way that *Women in Love* is. One way to judge whether *The Rainbow* partakes of such ambiguities, or is even groping toward them, is to liberate it from its sister novel and to read it as if the second book had never been written. Accordingly, this chapter will first explicate some of the most controversial images and events in *The Rainbow* by referring only to that work and to works contemporaneous with it. Then both this chapter and the next will follow those images that also appear in the second novel to see if they survive the transference intact or undergo change.

One assumption of this reading is that *The Rainbow* makes sense, that it is a coherent, consciously crafted whole (something not all critics have been willing to grant it). Looked at separately, the April 1915 revisions do give a vitality to destruction that was not in the original and that conflicts with the main themes of the novel. But that ambiguity was increased by proof revisions, probably demanded by the publisher, that both obscured the nature of the destruction and made it more clearly negative; and the paradoxes introduced by the revisions have saner connotations in relation to the novel in which they appear than they will in the later work.

In the April revisions (made by hand on the definitive typescript),[3] Lawrence changed the second generation more

3. The corrected typescript of *The Rainbow* is in the Humanities Research Center, University of Texas at Austin. Hereafter this manuscript will be referred to as the definitive typescript and will be cited in text as RTS.

than any other part of the novel, increasing the violence not only of Anna and Will's release but also of their conflict. For instance, he made Will more in love with his art after his marriage, so that Anna's taking it away from him is a betrayal, whereas in the earlier version his interest in art spontaneously declines when he has Anna. The fighting itself is made more violent and the combatants more conscious of what they are doing: whereas Will "seemed to hurt her womb callously" in the March typescript, he does so "to take pleasure in torturing her" in the revision and the published text (149); and he is merely "ugly" and "vicious" in the typescript in spots where, after the April revisions, he is "evil" and "malignant" (RTS 227–42).

Even in the typescript version of *The Rainbow*, however, Will and Anna fight violently. In fact, the passage that Clarke finds the most "prophetic" of *Women in Love* remains unrevised from the typescript:

> At first she went on blithely enough with him shut down beside her. But then his spell began to take hold of her. The dark, seething potency of him, the power of a creature that lies hidden and exerts its will to the destruction of the free-running creature, as the tiger lying in the darkness of the leaves steadily enforces the fall and death of the light creatures that drink by the waterside in the morning, gradually began to take effect on her. Though he lay there in his darkness and did not move, yet she knew he lay waiting for her. She felt his will fastening on her and pulling her down, even whilst he was silent and obscure.
>
> She found that, in all her outgoings and her incomings, he prevented her. Gradually she realized that she was being borne down by him, borne down by the clinging, heavy weight of him, that he was pulling her down as a leopard clings to a wild cow and exhausts her and pulls her down. . . . Why did he want to drag her down, and kill her spirit? . . . Why did he deny her spirituality, hold her for a body only? And was he to claim her carcase? . . . "What do you do to me?" she cried. . . . "There is something horrible in you, something dark and beastly in your will."
>
> (181–82)

Clarke sees here an "antinomy—a vision of horror and perversity imposed, immediately, upon a no less cogent vision of potency and life"; he calls Will's dependency "weakness-in-strength" and argues that "what is being deviously suggested is that the potency can't be had *without* the degradation." It is true that Anna is horrified and that Will is full of potent life. Whether or not there is anything perverse or unnatural about the situation is another matter, as is the question of whether or not Will's power comes from his degradation, which would make this image a perverse-vital antinomy of the sort that informs *Women in Love*. Clarke thinks it is, because of "its ambiguous stress on enforced *downward* movement."[4]

The trouble is that Clarke applies to *The Rainbow* a vocabulary that develops a special significance in *Women in Love*. He calls Will as a tiger "reductive," a word that in his analysis is used to designate all forms of disintegration that incorporate a downward movement, including the metaphor of Western man as the Gadarene swine rushing down the slope to extinction and Ursula's downward stroking of Birkin's buttocks in "Excurse." This use of the term is inspired by some of the least appetizing passages in *Women in Love*, including: "There was only the inner, individual darkness, sensation within the ego, the obscene religious mystery of ultimate reduction, the mystic frictional activities of diabolic reducing down, disintegrating the vital organic body of life" (443).

As we can see from this passage, when Lawrence thinks something is "reductive," he calls it that; he does so even in *The Rainbow*, in which he uses each of the terms for organic decay at least once ("reducing" appears in one of the revised scenes, *Rainbow* 228). And even though there is an undeniable downward movement in the tiger's pulling down of its prey, as well as destruction for the prey, it is difficult to see the analogy between this image and that of the Gadarene swine. That tigers hunt cows is a fearsome fact of nature, a matter of instinct and survival; used as a metaphor for a man's desire, it highlights the fact that humans are animals and that their desires are natural. The Gadarene swine story, however, evokes an unnatural situation: when domestic pigs

---

4. Colin Clarke, *River of Dissolution: D. H. Lawrence and English Romanticism* (London: Routledge and Kegan Paul, 1969), 46–49.

commit suicide, the world has gone mad. This biblical parable also appealed to Dostoyevsky as an appropriate image for the decline of Western civilization (see his epigraph to *The Possessed*), and part of its point for both writers has to do with the perversion of nature it implies (Birkin sees his contemporaries rushing "down the slope of mechanical death" 361).

When compared to the hunting tiger in *The Rainbow*, this image is emblematic of one of the changes in Lawrence's thinking: *The Rainbow* asserts the need for conscious humans to recognize the divinity in their own animal life, whereas *Women in Love* implies that it is too late for that now. In the later novel, the downward movement is life-coming-apart: decaying flesh, disintegrating selves, the end of the world. But in *The Rainbow*, that motion seems to be just bringing-humanity-down-to-earth, countering its mistaken desire for transcendence. The rainbow symbol presides over this novel because it rounds back to stand on the ground.

One of the progressions *The Rainbow* records is a growth of consciousness and consequent conflict with animal life. Anna is the most conscious member of the Brangwen family up to her time, and it is she who is horrified by the "something horrible," "something dark and beastly" in her husband. The generations of farming Brangwens live in intimate harmony with animal (that is, beastly) life and the cycles of nature. The beginning of *The Rainbow* describes their life, emphasizing that they live by "instinct" and by touch: "They felt the rush of the sap in spring . . . the pulse and body of the soil . . . the pulse of the blood of the teats of the cows beat into the pulse of the hands of the men" (pulses we can hear beating in this line). In the wintertime, when their bodies are forced to be inactive, the men practically freeze over: "the men sat by the fire and their brains were inert, as their blood flowed heavy with the accumulation from the living day." The men do not think, because they are "impregnated with the day."

The women are somewhat more mental: "on them too was the drowse of blood-intimacy. . . . But the women looked out from the heated, blind intercourse of farm-life, to the spoken world beyond." The men live by the blood, which is here as in all of Lawrence's work the center of animal being, as the mind is the center of conscious thought in words. Even the women are closer to animal life than to verbal consciousness in the early generations. The "spoken world" is "beyond": "they heard the sound in the distance, and they strained to listen"(2).

Lydia, though she becomes a Brangwen farmwife, comes from the outer world, where she was formerly married to a Polish intellectual. She speaks several languages, knows several countries, and therefore embodies all the glamor of culture outside the farm for Tom, the first of the Brangwen farmers who is educated enough to appreciate it. It is no surprise, then, that her child, Anna, who is both the most advanced Brangwen woman and the child of a foreign intellectual, leaves the farm altogether and, at least as a young woman, identifies more with her mind than her body.

She is enough of a Brangwen, however, to be attracted to her stepcousin Will, who is repeatedly designated as living from his animal being: he is like "some animal, some mysterious animal that lived in the darkness under the leaves and never came out, but which lived vividly, swift and intense" (102). This polarity naturally creates a conflict between them. Will is not a farmer, though we repeatedly see him working in the garden and he lives more by touch than by thought. He is a religious artist, dedicated to ritual and the physical embodiments of religious passion, and his faith is uncritical in a way that infuriates Anna. His faith is in fact somatic. He has to "extinguish" his mind when Anna forces him to see "with the clear eyes of the mind" that water cannot turn to wine: "Brangwen loved it, with his bones and blood he loved it, he could not let it go" (168).

Will is an evolutionary step beyond the inert brains of the farming Brangwens, but his development is within their line: he lives for a vital mystery, a force beyond himself to which he has access through his blood and which Lawrence even describes with animal and vegetable metaphors. The cathedral at Lincoln is "a great involved seed," "the perfect

womb," and "a gloom of fecundity." It unifies in itself all the
contraries of which organic life is made, and therefore transcends them: "Containing birth and death, potential with all
the noise and transition of life," it is "away from time, always
outside of time" (198). Will responds to it not with his mind
but with his soul and in a way that imitates sexual response:
his soul rushes forward to "touch" the mystery and to come
to its "consummation" in "ecstasy."

Anna resists the pull of this mysterious ecstasy with her
mind and thereby ruins it for Will. Anna is always, literally
and figuratively, laughing in church, and she gradually secu-
larizes him.[5] She rejects the cathedral as a counterfeit absolute, standing illegitimately in place of the sky, the stars, and
the earth; if it is outside time and change, it is not part of
organic life at all. Will yearns for perfect timeless stasis in the
cathedral, something like the inert, impregnated condition of
the Brangwen farmers, whereas Anna feels claustrophobic.
"She had always a sense of being roofed in" by the cathedral,
and she wants to be free of its pull, to decide for herself (200).

She rejects the similar timeless perfection of their honey-
moon, which is what Will is trying to reinstate when Anna
feels that he is "pulling her down" like a leopard: "Here was
a poised, unflawed stillness that was beyond time, because it
remained the same, inexhaustible, unchanging, unexhausted
. . . the heart of eternity, whilst time roared far off" (141).
Anna decides to leave this eternal state, to give a tea party.
She wants to be part of the outside, social world, and she
wants to be a separate person from Will, just as in the cathedral "she claimed the right to freedom above her, higher than
the roof" (200).

In the ensuing struggle Anna sees herself as a creature of
light and mind who wants "to be happy, to be natural, like

5. One excellent analysis of Lawrence's religious thought begins with
consideration of this image, which recurs in his work. See James B. Sipple,
"Laughter in the Cathedral: Religious Affirmation and Ridicule in the Writings of D. H. Lawrence," in *The Philosophical Reflection of Man in Literature*, ed.
Anne-Teresa Tymienieck (Dordrecht: Reidel, 1982), 213–44.

the sunlight and the busy daytime," while she thinks Will
unnatural, "like the darkness covering and smothering her"
(166), motivated only by "his own dark-souled desires" (170).
For Will, the terms are different. What he wants is simply
unity: "Why could she not be with him, close, close, as one
with him?" (175); "She was his ark, and the rest of the world
was flood" (183). At the same time, she is destroying him
spiritually, forcing him to realize that "the miracle was not a
real fact"—removing both his ark and his cathedral at once.
When he fights back like a leopard, he is fighting for his life:
"She seemed to be destroying him. He went out, dark and
destroyed, his soul running its blood. And he tasted of death.
Because his life was formed in these unquestioned concepts"
(168).

Anna and Will each have something to learn: Anna, that
the night is as natural as the day; Will, that static unity is
unnatural for two separate, live creatures. What each of them
learns is to be more natural, and if the struggle by which they
learn this is destructive, it is not perverse or ambiguously nat-
ural-unnatural, as "reduction" is in *Women in Love*. For it to be
so, Anna would have to be exhilarated and attracted by his
dragging her down, as Gudrun is by Gerald's, and Will would
have to be made potent because he is being destroyed—
would have to run on the energy created by his own dissolution, as Gerald, Hermione, and Gudrun do.

But the concurrence of dissolution and power in Will is not
a cause-effect relationship. Will's power is innate: it is that of
the animal that lives in darkness. His tendency to dissolve,
on the other hand, is a late development in his character, following his marriage to Anna and her refusal to live in perfect
unison with him. In the course of their conflict, he loses the
degradation, but not the potency; he stops being weakly dependent, whereas he and his darkness continue to be at least
as powerful as they were before.[6]

6. The description of the marital struggles between Anna and Will is prophetic of *Women in Love* in a small way. It contains the only instance in *The
Rainbow* in which darkness clearly is associated with something like decay:

Later on, Ursula will have to learn both of her parents' respective lessons—to live singly, and to trust the unconscious darkness. Her ruminations, which are more conscious and articulate than theirs, help to explain their conflict and its resolution. Toward the end of *The Rainbow*, Ursula meditates on the darkness and finds, like Birkin in the next novel, that a "dark stream" is the reality beneath the facade of modern humanity, the truth behind its belief in its own progress and in the virtue of its social organization. There, however, the similarity between the two streams ends.

> She could see, beneath their pale, wooden pretense of composure and civic purposefulness, the dark stream that contained them all. They were like little paper ships in their motion. But in reality each one was a dark, blind, eager wave urging blindly forward, dark with the same homogeneous desire.
>
> (448)

Whereas Birkin's dark stream is horrible, cold, disintegrating, a river of dissolution that somehow produces life from the dismantling of organic matter, Ursula's is a wave of desire, eager, urgent, blind, and dark. This homogeneous desire is not to experience "a myriad subtle thrills of reduction, the last subtle activities of analysis and breaking down," as it is in *Women in Love* (443). It is, in fact, more or less the opposite: not to dissolve one's organic being but to be "a wild animal," a "dark, fertile being," and a "dark vital self" (448–49). It is, as Ursula discovers, to be a leopard, and to live from one's blood:

> She was free as a leopard that sends up its raucous cry in the night. She had the potent, dark stream of her own blood, she had the glimmering core of fecundity, she had her mate, her

---

"She wanted to desert him, to leave him a prey to the open, with the unclean dogs of the darkness setting on to devour him" (166). The uncleanliness of the dogs may have something to do with decay. Will, however, is consistently seen as a clean, lovely creature of darkness. Therefore creatures of darkness, and darkness itself, do not necessarily have anything to do with degradation. It is Will's fear of being alone that is imaged in the unclean dogs, as it is Anna's desire to be free, separate and rational ("a creature of light") that creates her horror of the darkness in Will.

complement, her sharer in fruition. So, she had all, everything.

(449)

Ursula's potent dark stream is actually the blood, just as Birkin's is at least implicitly the intestines. The blood is here both
potent and dangerous, frightening and fecund, associated
with leopards and with fruitful mating—warm, life-giving,
and rich, whereas Birkin's river is cold, deathly, and repellent.

Ursula sees the bloodstream as the reality cloaked by social
conventions after she is reunited with Anton Skrebensky in a
passage that echoes "Anna Victrix." Like Will, Anton is potent, animal, and vulnerable: when Ursula first sees him
again, she thinks he has "some of the horseman's animal
darkness," and can "only feel the dark, heavy fixity of his
animal desire." She fears him, because "he wanted something that should be nameless," yet she is attracted to him
because he is vulnerable: "in his dark, subterranean male
soul, he was kneeling before her, darkly exposing himself"
(443). Here her point of view is very like Anna's: she is in a
highly conscious state, toward the close of her college years,
and she sees Anton's darkness as both a bit degrading to him
and dangerous to herself.

But soon she is absorbed into his darkness and transformed by the experience. In the love scenes following their
reunion, the references to darkness are almost too frequent to
count. The description of the river Trent reinvokes the terms
used for the bloodstream ("dark water flowing in silence
through the big, restless night made her feel wild"), and the
lovers beside it experience "subtle, stealthy, powerful passion, as if they had a secret agreement which held good in the
profound darkness," until "their blood ran together as one
stream." They become "darkness cleaving to darkness . . .
one stream, one dark fecundity" (445–47).

Like Clara and Paul beside the same river in *Sons and Lovers*, they leap beyond social convention into sexual fulfillment. But whereas Clara and Paul visit the river in the daylight, Lawrence makes Ursula and Anton's consummation
profoundly dark, to oppose it imagistically to the light of consciousness: "Once the vessel had vibrated till it was shat-

tered, the light of consciousness gone, then the darkness reigned, and the unutterable satisfaction" (447). Darkness is also opposed to the lights of the city and to the human social facade, beneath which the proper burgher is "a lurking, blood-sniffing creature," a "primeval darkness falsified to a social mechanism" (448). This darkness gives Ursula and Anton something they could not find in the light: Ursula has "all, everything," Anton suddenly has "the clue to himself" (449), and together they enter "the dark fields of immortality" (451).

Even before Anton's return, Ursula realizes that her life has been lived too much in the light, that to deny the leopard lurking within is to freeze oneself in a state of permanent potentiality, like a seed unable to sprout:

> That which she was, positively, was dark and unrevealed, it could not come forth. It was like a seed buried in dry ash. This world in which she lived was like a circle lighted by a lamp. This lighted area, lit up by man's completest consciousness, she thought was all the world: that here all was disclosed forever. Yet all the time, within the darkness she had been aware of points of light, like the eyes of wild beasts, gleaming, penetrating, vanishing. And her soul had acknowledged in a great heave of terror only the outer darkness. This inner circle of light in which she lived and moved, wherein the trains rushed and the factories ground out their machine-produce and the plants and the animals worked by the light of science and knowledge, suddenly it seemed to her like the area under an arc-lamp, wherein the moths and children played in the security of the blinding light, not even knowing there was any darkness . . . turning their faces always inward towards the sinking fire of illuminating consciousness, which comprised sun and stars, and the Creator, and the System of Righteousness, ignoring always the vast darkness that wheeled round about . . . wheeled round about, with gray shadow-shapes of wild beasts, and also with dark shadow-shapes of the angels, whom the light fenced out, as it fenced out the more familiar beasts of darkness. . . . and some having given up their vanity of the light, having died in their own conceit, saw the gleam in the eyes of the wolf and the hyena, that it was the flash of the sword of angels, flashing at the door to come in . . . like the flash of fangs.

(437–38)

The fangs are a part of life that scientific rationalism denies in its "vanity of the light"; contemporary humanity is so deluded by the power science and knowledge have given it that it thinks its "illuminating consciousness" is the Creator. But there are things one cannot see if one looks only at the light. Just as the sun and the stars exist independently of human consciousness, so does the Creator. There are angels out in the darkness, and they are revealed in the flash of fangs—in animal aggression, which social, productive humanity has denied and repressed.

Ursula's discovery here seems to be approved by her author, who pursues the same line of thought, using similar imagery, in "Study of Thomas Hardy." He argues that the beauty and greatness of Hardy's novels reside in a quality he "shares with the great writers, Shakespeare or Sophocles or Tolstoi." All these writers surround "the little human morality play" with "the terrific action of unfathomed nature; setting a smaller system of morality, the one grasped and formulated by the human consciousness within the vast, uncomprehended and incomprehensible morality of nature or of life itself, surpassing human consciousness." Although the insignificant human morality seems to be a "charmed circle," it is all the time surpassed by "the wilderness raging round" (*Phoenix* 419).

Elsewhere in "Hardy" Lawrence declares that "the final aim of every living thing, creature, or being is the full achievement of itself" (*Phoenix* 403), and in *The Rainbow* Ursula is also allowed to share this insight with her author. In the botany laboratory she gets "a glimpse of something working entirely apart from the purpose of the human world. . . . there the mystery still glimmered" (436). A professor (named Dr. Frankstone, to associate her with the errors of Dr. Frankenstein) suggests to Ursula that there is no reason to "attribute some special mystery to life" just because "we don't understand it as we understand electricity": "May it not be that life consists in a complexity of physical and chemical activities, of the same order as the activities we already know in science?" Ursula then looks through the arc lamp of a microscope at a unicellular "plant-animal lying shadowy in a boundless light" and wonders if the professor is right: "Was she herself [a] . . . conjunction of forces, like one of these?" But turning the light of scientific knowledge on live creatures does not illuminate certain mysteries: "What then was its will? . . . What was its intention? . . . what was the purpose?"

The answer comes in a second epiphany: "It intended to be itself. . . . Self was a oneness with the infinite. To be oneself was a supreme, gleaming triumph of infinity" (440–41). Life in any form is a triumph for a force not visible under the arc lamp of rationality and not subject to or owned by humanity. But if the source of life is infinite, then simply to be oneself, to be alive, is to be part of infinity. The idea of self enters Lawrence's conception because of how life appears, in discrete creatures, each of which must consider its own well-being first in order to prosper and yet is never more a part of the whole urge of life than when so prospering, and because human beings can be alive without being truly themselves, denying all that is natural to them and forcing their lives into conformity with abstractions. In "Hardy," Lawrence distinguishes the self-fulfilling individual from the merely "selfish or greedy person": "a man of distinct being, who must act in his own particular way to fulfil his own individual nature . . . chooses to rule his own life to its own completion, and as such is an aristocrat" (*Phoenix* 439).

Ursula's two epiphanies are further explained in several letters Lawrence wrote during the final drafting of *The Rainbow*. Most of his letters of January and February 1915 concern the ideal community he hoped to found, which he often called "Rananim" and which would be the embodiment of a godly way of life, based on a rejection of the anthropocentric perspective. Writing to E. M. Forster (whose novel *Room with a View* was published in 1908), Lawrence announced:

> It is time for us now to look all round, round the whole ring of the horizon—not just out of a room with a view; it is time to gather again a conception of the Whole: . . . a conception of the beginning and the end, of heaven and hell, of good and

evil flowing from God through humanity as through a filter, and returning back to God as angels and demons.

We are tired of contemplating this one phase of the history of creation, which we call humanity. We are tired of measuring everything by the human standard: whether man is the standard or criterion, or whether he is but a factor in the Whole whose issue and whose return we have called God.

Humanity is only an expression of something that issues from and returns to God, not itself important; and the larger whole "wheels round" it, just as the darkness does around Ursula. This same letter explains that Lawrence's Rananim would reject class, money, and "personal salvation," yet it would be composed of "many fulfilled individualities seeking greater fulfilment."[7] The opposition between "personal salvation" and "fulfilled individuality" seems to underlie Ursula's second vision. The self that the cell possesses is not personal but infinite, an individual embodiment of infinity rather than an ego. An ego is a closed, fixed entity that needs to be consistent, rational, and conventional, whereas an individual embodying infinity is open to impulses, unfixed, in flux.

The artificiality of the self conceived as ego, the idea that we are not fixed entities but mercurial conductors of impersonal forces, is always at the center of Lawrence's thought, especially at the time he wrote *The Rainbow*. He began to articulate the idea in *Sons and Lovers*, in which Paul felt himself and Clara to be "only grains in the tremendous heave that lifted every grass blade its little height, and every tree, and every living thing . . . To know their own nothingness, to know the tremendous living flood which carried them always, gave them rest within themselves."[8] Lawrence's aim in *The Rainbow* is to show that the characters are expressions of these impersonal forces and that "the old stable ego of the character," or of the person, is a hurtful fiction perpetuated by the rationalist tradition.[9]

7. Cambridge *Letters 2*, 265–66.
8. D. H. Lawrence, *Sons and Lovers* (1913; rpt. New York: Penguin, 1976), 354.
9. Cambridge *Letters 2*, 183.

Ursula herself is educated in that tradition, and the book's final chapters record her disillusionment with it and her progress toward Lawrence's way of thinking. Her first major step is to see something dwelling in the darkness outside the arc light of scientific knowledge, something that nevertheless is "an intensely-gleaming light of knowledge"; the difference is in the adjective. The eyes of the jungle beasts are "points of light . . . gleaming"; there is a "gleam in the eyes of the wolf and the hyena." Like "the flash of fangs" and angels' swords and the "glimmer" of the mystery of life, a gleam is a transient light from a natural source, different from the electric glare of the arc light. It reveals things not observable under the arc light of the microscope, such as infinity and that in us which partakes of it: "Electricity had no soul, light and heat had no soul," but "to be oneself" "was not limited mechanical energy, nor mere purpose of self-preservation and self-assertion" (441). Presumably, the creature asserts itself in order to live, but in doing so it participates in eternity. If even the life of a single-celled animal is a "triumph of infinity," and if the gleaming eyes of predators are "the flash of the sword of angels," then so is the pulling down of a wild cow by a leopard.

Ursula had to go into the darkness to gain this understanding. Gleams are not visible in the daylight, and the soul acknowledges "only the outer darkness" (437). When she goes to Anton, then, directly after this epiphany, she is seeking not regression to bestiality but progression to self-realization: to "come forth" as "that which she was, positively." Nevertheless, Lawrence clearly does not mean that she will "find herself" consciously, since this form of self-realization is accomplished without effort by protozoa.

The apparent atavism of the proposal is an intentional insult to human vanity, not a genuine recommendation that we return to the animal state. In "Hardy," Lawrence considers the ills of the modern world to be caused by overemphasis on the mind at the expense of the flesh and the feelings. He explains the tragedy of Jude and Sue in *Jude the Obscure* as

> owing to centuries and centuries of weaning away from the
> body of life, centuries of insisting upon the supremacy and
> bodilessness of Love, centuries of striving to escape the condi-

tions of being and striving to attain the condition of Knowledge, centuries of pure Christianity. . . . And this tragedy is
the result of over-development of one principle of human life
at the expense of the other: an over-balancing; a laying of all
the stress on the Male, the Love, the Spirit, the Mind, the Consciousness; a denying, a blaspheming against the Female, the
Law, the Soul, the Senses, the Feelings.

(Phoenix 503, 509)

Like many others in his time, Lawrence in this period identified the mind as male and the body as female. Unlike many
of his contemporaries (and unlike his own later position),
however, he deplored the rationalist, patriarchal valorization
of mentality and maleness and tried to evoke a new reverence
for the flesh and the female, to right the balance.

Therefore Ursula's progression to self-realization involves
giving herself over to her fleshly impulses, living entirely "in
the sensual sub-consciousness" and "mocking at the ready-
made, artificial daylight of the rest" (448). By the end of the
book she has broken all connection to the matrix of social
structures regulating human interaction, a move Lawrence
clearly approves. In another letter written while he was drafting *The Rainbow*, he complained that

> this present community consists, as far as it is a framed thing,
> in a myriad contrivances for preventing us from being let
> down by the meanness in ourselves or in our neighbours. But
> it is like a motor car that is so encumbered with non-skid, non-
> puncture, non-burst, non-this and non-that contrivances, that
> it simply can't go any more. . . . Every strong soul must put
> off its connection with this society, its vanity and chiefly its
> fear, and go naked with its fellows.

Lawrence's Rananim was to be based on this trusting anarchy
and on "fulfilment in the flesh of all strong desire" rather than
on self-denial, control, and sacrifice.[10]

Putting off the connection with society is, paradoxically,
the best one can do not only for oneself but also for other
people, as several letters from the period explain: "There
comes a point when the shell, the form of life, is a prison to

10. Ibid., 271–73.

the life. Then the life must either concentrate on breaking the shell, or it must turn round, turn in upon itself, and try infinite variations of a known reaction upon itself." Lawrence plans to "smash the frame," which means that "the land, the industries, the means of communication and the public amusements shall all be nationalised," removing economic worries so that everyone might be free to fulfill their "individualities": "There must be an actual revolution, to set free our bodies. For there never was a free soul in a chained body."[11]

Ursula is taking the first steps toward freeing her own soul and body when she rejects social convention, the rationalist perspective, and human solipsism. When she is doing so, her eyes glimmer like those "of a wild animal . . . dilated and shining" (448). Her parents have the same look toward the end of their struggle. Will can "see with his gold-glowing eyes his intention and his desires in the dark"; and Anna has a "curious rolling of the eyes, as if she were lapsing in a trance away from her ordinary consciousness . . . when something threatened and opposed her in life, the conscious life." She develops this trick after "she learned not to dread and to hate him, but to fill herself with him, to give herself to his black, sensual power, that was hidden all the daytime." Will seems purely of the animal zone outside the arc light; Lawrence even says that his face is "not very human." Anna is now under Will's spell "when the darkness set him free": "then she answered . . . with a soft leap of her soul." She seems almost split between the two zones, and impersonally related to Will: "she was the daytime" and "they remained as separate in the light, and in the thick darkness, married"; "he called not to her, but to something in her, which responded subtly, out of her unconscious darkness" (213–14).

Will's dark potency remains; what is gone is his dependence. A few pages after the passage in which Anna feels that he is dragging her down like a leopard, the two qualities begin to split apart, and the situation consequently improves for

11. Ibid., 283–86.

Anna and Will. She locks him out of the bedroom, and he suffers all the terrors of an abandoned child until "something gave way in him." He realizes that "he must be able to be alone." In this discovery he is reborn:

> He was himself now. He had come into his own existence . . . born at last unto himself. . . . Now at last he had a separate identity. . . . Before he had only existed in so far as he had relations with another being. Now he had an absolute self—as well as a relative self.
>
> (187)

Will needs to learn this because he has thought Anna's presence to be necessary to his very life, and the spouse who is asked to breathe for two will naturally feel smothered. But in the context of the whole novel, Will's rebirth has larger implications: by being born into himself, he comes into oneness with the infinite. Anna has either known this innately or learned it by participating directly in the mystery of creation. When she dances, naked and pregnant, she is celebrating both her separate life and her participation in eternity: "she danced there in the bedroom by herself, lifting her hands and her body to the Unseen, to the unseen Creator who had chosen her, to Whom she belonged. . . . she had to dance before her Creator in exemption from the man" (179–80).

Like Ursula's story, Anna and Will's concerns the recognition of divinity in one's own animal life. Anna precedes Will to this realization, perhaps because she is a woman and therefore closer, in Lawrence's view, to the flesh, though she originally identifies with her mind. She also more readily appreciates the beauty of earthly life, is impatient with religious transcendence, and has a sense of self separate from her husband. Despite Will's association with animals, and even after his rebirth as an independent self, he has yet to discover that the infinite he seeks is not in heaven but on earth. When he does, he and Anna are both transformed through sensual experience that seems to, but in context does not, partake of the moral ambiguities of Birkin and Ursula's consummation.

Will experiences transcendent ecstasy in Lincoln Cathedral

until Anna forces him to see the gargoyles, one of which she thinks is a satiric portrait of the artist's wife. Though he resists her, he recognizes then that not everything there partakes of infinity, and he loses "that which had been his absolute, containing all heaven and earth." To see eternity in a building is as much an error as to assume that human consciousness is the creator. Just as the arc light shows only a partial truth, excluding the dark angels, the cathedral has "still the dark, mysterious world of reality inside, but as a world within a world, a sort of side show" (202).

Will and Anna get along better after this, but neither is quite complete. We hear of Will that "in spirit, he was uncreated," and of Anna that "her soul had not found utterance," though "her womb had" (203). It is in this period that they devote themselves to separate works, Will to the physical church and Anna to the children. They seem to be connected only sexually, and they simply go apart when they experience conflict. Anna is satisfied with her motherhood, but Will is "aware of some limit to himself, of something unformed in his very being . . . some folded centres of darkness which would never develop and unfold whilst he was alive in the body." Lawrence reemphasizes in the last sentence of the chapter that this "darkness . . . would never unfold in him" (207). He seems prepared to leave Will there, with no further development, and the title of the next chapter indicates a shift of focus to Ursula. In the April revisions, however, Lawrence greatly expanded and revised the end of "The Child," creating a climactic resolution to the story of Anna and Will.

The deathly but liberating sensuality they discover is clearly parallel to what Birkin and Ursula experience: Lawrence calls it "deathly," "a passion of death," "violent and extreme as death"; it is also "immoral and against mankind" (234). Yet, when they give themselves up to it, their "inward life was revolutionised," they are finally "absorbed in their own living," and Will is at last fulfilled: "His intimate life was so violently active, that it set another man in him free" (235). The rainbow is even invoked to bless this deathly union, since what inflames Will's "infinite sensual violence" is "the rolling, absolute beauty of the round arch" in Anna's body (234).

The association of death with self-realization and the optimism of the rainbow does seem to make this event a creative-destructive, vital-deathly antinomy of the sort Lawrence creates in *Women in Love*. Yet in the novel in which it appears, immorality and antisocial behavior have healthy, unambiguous connotations; and before the proof revisions required by a timid publisher, this sensuality was associated not with cold death but with the magnificent violence of leopards and tigers.

This immoral self-indulgence is clearly part of the process of bringing Will down to earth that began with the loss of his transcendent absolute in the cathedral. Lawrence makes this connection explicit:

> He had always, all his life, had a secret dread of Absolute Beauty. It had always been like a fetish to him, something to fear, really. For it was immoral and against mankind. So he had turned to the Gothic form, which always asserted the broken desire of mankind in its pointed arches, escaping the rolling, absolute beauty of the round arch. But now he had given way, and with infinite sensual violence gave himself to the realisation of this supreme, immoral, Absolute Beauty, in the body of woman.
>
> (234)

Will's ecstasy in the cathedral centers on the Gothic arches there, which "leapt up from the plain of earth, leapt up in a manifold, clustered desire each time, up, away from the horizontal earth" (199). Lawrence makes it clear that he wants Will to respond only to the Gothic arch at this time: Lincoln is primarily Gothic, with round arches only on the west front. Anna and Will enter from the west, and Will says, "It is a false front." It is only when they reach the interior, which is Gothic, that "his soul [rises] from her nest" (198).[12]

Keith Sagar is surely right when he explains that the round arch is a kind of horizontal, since it returns to earth unbroken;

12. Marguerite Beede Howe, in *The Art of the Self in D. H. Lawrence* (Athens, Ohio: Ohio University Press), 44, bases part of her reading of this section of the novel on the assumption that Lincoln has Roman or Norman arches, that is, arches that are round like the "absolute beauty" of a woman's body, but this is not the case.

he connects it to all things terrestrial, including the Brangwen farm and animal being, whereas the Gothic arch is vertical, representing spiritual aspiration, the "broken desire" of humans to transcend their earthly nature.[13] That Will longs to leap to "the climax of eternity, the apex of the arch" makes him seem inconsistent in the early chapters, since he is also described as being darkly animal (199). Lawrence's symbolic reading of architecture in "Hardy" may make Will more coherent: there, cathedrals are the static female principle realized in art (*Phoenix* 457). Will is always yearning for the female, but he cannot be satisfied because he is looking in the wrong place. Not that he lets his religious ecstasy replace sexual desire, as has sometimes been assumed;[14] he is always enthusiastically sexual, much more so than Anna. In the beginning of their marriage, she wants to give him "love, pure love . . . as of flowers, radiant, innocent," but "he did not want flowery innocence. He was unsatisfied. . . . from his body through her hands came the bitter-corrosive shock of his passion upon her, destroying her in blossom" (178). Yet he is only fulfilled when he moves his absolute to earth, to the body of his wife.

The descendent nature of this consummation may explain why it is "immoral and against mankind." In the modern era, Western cultures are committed to transcending the conditions of organic life, and we believe so completely in abstractions as to be willing to sacrifice any individual's actual desires "for the greatest good of the greatest number." Anton Skrebensky identifies with such abstractions as the nation, the army, the white man's burden, "the whole." Ursula detests him for this, and Lawrence makes clear that he agrees with her:

> He could not see, it was not born in him to see, that the highest good of the community as it stands is no longer the highest

13. Keith Sagar, *The Art of D. H. Lawrence* (Cambridge: Cambridge University Press, 1966), 45.

14. Scott Sanders, *D. H. Lawrence: The World of the Five Major Novels* (New York: Viking, 1973), 71.

good of even the average individual. He thought that, because the community represents millions of people, therefore it must be millions of times more important than any individual, forgetting that the community is an abstraction from the many, and is not the many themselves. Now when the statement of the abstract good for the community has become a formula lacking in all inspiration or value to the average intelligence, then the "common good" becomes a general nuisance, representing the vulgar, conservative materialism at a low level.

(327)

Because he lives for the nation rather than himself, Anton has no definite desires of his own and believes that not self-realization but war is "about the most serious business there is." Therefore he appears to Ursula "like nothing": "It seems to me . . . as if you weren't anybody—as if there weren't anybody there, where you are" (308–9).

In "Hardy," Lawrence describes the conflict between distinct individuals, those who attempt to fulfill their own natures, and the "average," "the communal morality," that attempts to inhibit them. The hidden message he finds in *Jude the Obscure* is that "the old, communal morality is like a leprosy, a white sickness: the old, antisocial, individualist morality is alone on the side of life and health" (*Phoenix* 437). Will's desire for transcendence, Anna's flowery love, and Anton's belief in the common good are all part of the white sickness, the bourgeois sublimation of impulse in favor of a bloodless idea of virtue based on self-denial.

It is against this "communal morality" that Will and Anna's sensuality transgresses: they "throw everything overboard, love, intimacy, responsibility. . . . They abandoned in one motion the moral position, each was seeking gratification pure and simple." They are liberated from the idea of themselves as a married pair who must be good and loving to each other, selfless, sacrificing their own desires for the needs of the family. Acting instead on their own selfish impulses, they are even "cruel" and "hostile" to each other (232).

The uninhibited gratification of self entailed in their discovery of "Absolute Beauty" is consonant with the use of "absolute" we noticed first. An "absolute self" is free and independent, presumably thinks primarily of itself, yet is a triumph of infinity when it does so. Will's sense of self is further separated from Anna just before their deathly orgy begins: he goes to another woman but does not feel connected to her, either. Though he cares "nothing" about Jenny—she is "just the sensual object of his attention"—nevertheless he finds "a new creation to him, a reality, an absolute, an existing tangible beauty of the absolute" in the round arch ("one small, firm curve") of her side (226–27).

When he goes home, he and Anna are like strangers to each other. Like Ursula at the end of the novel, he now has "no real relation with his home"; he looks "almost sinister" because "absolved from his 'good' ties." He is aloof, indifferent, unaffected by and unaware of Anna, and her immediate thought is, "So, he was blossoming out into his real self," having usually been "mute, half-effaced, half-subdued"—not real because imperfectly asserted. At first she is angry and regrets the loss of their intimacy and her supremacy. Then she feels a new attraction to him: "something was liberated in her" and "she challenged him back." Both of them become "free lances," seeking their own ends (231–32).

The self that Ursula sees later on as "one with the infinite" is similarly selfish, amoral, and sensual. She asserts her independence from all "good ties" at the end of the book, at a time when her soul has become "itself forever"; and Anton finds "the clue to himself" through a sexual experience that is "dark," associated with jungle animals and contrasted to communal behavior. Like the final experiences of Anna and Will, the lovemaking of Ursula and Anton has a sadistic element and is not based on conscious intimacy but on pure sensual desire: "She knew, vaguely, in the first minute, that they were enemies come together in a truce. Every movement and word of his was alien to her being" (442). Yet both are freed from social convention and made one with the infinite the first time they make love:

> She passed away as on a dark wind, far, far away, into the pristine darkness of paradise, into the original immortality. She entered the dark fields of immortality.

> When she rose, she felt strangely free, strong. She was not
> ashamed,—why should she be? . . . Whither they had gone,
> she did not know. But it was as if she had received another
> nature. She belonged to the eternal, changeless place into
> which they had leapt together.

Before making love, they actually stand "as at the edge of a
cliff" (451), which of course exactly echoes Lawrence's definition in "Hardy" of self-fulfillment through sex.

Like Anna and Will, this pair of lovers is unremittingly
"dark." The difference is that Lawrence has one pair freed by
touching immortality, the other by touching death. The manuscripts help to resolve this discrepancy: the proof revisions
(made in the summer of 1915) substitute the words "deathly"
and "like death itself" for visual imagery that explicitly links
Anna and Will's sensuality to the angelic flash of fangs. In the
April 1915 version, Will

> wished he were a cat, to lick her all over; and then a tiger-cat,
> to eat her, tear her with his mouth: he wished to wallow in
> her, to bury himself in her flesh, cover himself over with her
> flesh. He wished he were a cat, to lick her with a rough, grat-
> ing, lascivious tongue: a tiger-cat, to lick till the blood came,
> so he could lap it up till it ran from the corners of his mouth:
> so he could tear her flesh with his mouth.
>
> (RTS 352)

All this was cut in proof and replaced with this tame sentence: "He wished he had a hundred men's energies, with
which to enjoy her" (234). Similarly, whereas in the April version he is so inflamed that he is "ready to murder her for
sheer inability to be satisfied of her," in the proof revision he
is "ready to perish" for the same reason (RTS 352, *Rainbow*
234). Charles Ross may be right when he suggests that these
and many other of the proof revisions were made at the publisher's insistence in an unsuccessful attempt to head off censorship by the government.[15] The idea of "deathly" sensuality

---

15. Charles Ross, *The Composition of* The Rainbow *and* Women in Love: *A
History* (Charlottesville: University Press of Virginia), 42–57.

is vague and, therefore, less offensive than the explicit violence Will wants to wreak on Anna.

But this revision also obscures the thematic associations that previously made sense of this passage. The vagueness, combined with the ultimate negativity of death, usually forces readers to conclude that what Anna and Will are doing is wrong—and confusingly so, since it results in a renewal of life for all concerned. For instance, Mark Kinkead-Weekes, one of Lawrence's most perceptive critics, says of Anna and Will: "they 'die' and are renewed, but it is 'pure death,' purely dark, and a renewal of the dark side of themselves only." As Ross points out, this is "to ignore the beneficial liveliness it achieves."[16]

When Will was not deathly but a tiger-cat, lapping up her blood, his immoral, antisocial sensual violence was clearly, in the context of the novel, a step in the direction of life and health. Ursula's later epiphanies are similarly "immoral and against mankind" because they deny the anthropocentric perspective and argue for the free expression of impulse instead of brotherly love, civic duty, patriotism. Skrebensky's allegiance to the abstract nation and his desire to go to war are in comparison much more deathly. War, especially modern war, is another thing only humans do—killing not to eat, not to get a mate, not with natural weapons against a personal rival, but coldly, without desire, without touching the enemy, and with nothing to gain that is necessary or meaningful to an individual's life—only to a nation's. As Ursula says, "we aren't the nation," and if you define yourself as an abstraction instead of a live creature, you may seem "as if you weren't anybody" (309). Lawrence's idea of fulfilled individuality implies a potential for violence but not for war; Ursula may be "a lurking, blood-sniffing creature with eyes peering out of

---

16. Mark Kinkead-Weekes, "The Marble and the Statue: The Exploratory Imagination of D. H. Lawrence," in *Imagined Worlds: Essays on Some English Novels and Novelists in Honour of John Butt*, ed. Maynard Mack and Ian Gregor (London: Methuen, 1968), 393; and Charles Ross, "The Revisions of the Second Generation in *The Rainbow*," *Review of English Studies*, n.s. 27 (1976): 295.

the jungle darkness" (448), Will may be ready to murder Anna for inability to be satisfied of her, but neither of them desires to use a machine gun. The manifestations of this atavism seem to be, in fact, sexual rather than lethal.

Even with the proof revisions, Anna and Will's consummation in death can be shown to have primarily healthy associations in the novel. "The pristine darkness of paradise" into which Ursula and Anton leap sounds both like Eden, temporarily restored to them when they relinquish their "illuminating consciousness," and like the other side of death, the usual location of "the dark fields of immortality." It also sounds that way when Tom and Lydia leap into it:

> Blind and destroyed, he pressed forward, nearer, nearer, to receive the consummation of himself, he received within the darkness which should swallow him and yield him up to himself. If he could come really within the blazing kernel of darkness, if really he could be destroyed, burnt away till he lit with her in one consummation, that were supreme, supreme. . . . It was the entry into another circle of existence, it was the baptism to another life, it was the complete confirmation. . . . Everything was lost, and everything was found. The new world was discovered, it remained only to be explored. . . . it was the transfiguration, glorification, the admission.

Lawrence emphasizes that Tom must be destroyed to become himself. The darkness must "swallow" him, he must "really . . . be destroyed," "burnt away" in the "blazing kernel," "losing himself to find her, to find himself in her" (90–91). The darkness that destroys him will "yield him up to himself."

The later, more individualized generations think more of finding themselves individually than of losing themselves to find their partners, or themselves in their partners. But Tom's fulfilling self-immolation is in other respects similar to what happens in the next two generations: the old world, the old self are well lost for the new creation, which is only reached by being destroyed, or by touching death, or by passing away into the dark fields of immortality. All three alternatives sound like the phoenix cycle, the new rising from the ashes of the old, and like the biblical assertion in "Hardy" that the leap into the unknown is death to the old self: for "he who would save his life must lose it" (*Phoenix* 409). They involve individuals coming into being as themselves through contact with something that is beyond human life but not above it: they have access to it only through their lovers, and the "destruction" described is simply sexual, a humorless version of the Renaissance pun on dying. Lydia is "the awful unknown" to Tom; Anton "opens out into the unknown" (for a time) for Ursula; Anna and Will know death, the passage to the ultimate unknown, in each other.

These cycles are also versions of the Christian dialectic, but brought down to earth. Death is not the end, but the beginning, of eternal life; and heaven is here on earth, achievable in marriage ("when a man's soul and a woman's soul unites together—that makes an Angel. . . . Bodies and souls, it's the same" 135). And in the cathedral scene, the only passage besides the end of "The Child" that was completely redrafted in the April revisions, death is simply identifiable with the source of life, the place from which all life comes and to which it returns:

> Spanned round with the rainbow, the jewelled gloom folded music upon silence, light upon darkness, fecundity upon death, as a seed folds leaf upon leaf and silence upon its root and flower, hushing up the secret of all between its parts, the death out of which it fell, the life into which it has dropped, the immortality it involves, and the death it will embrace again.
>
> (198–99)

The seed falls "out of" death into life, and the whole process of birth and death "involves" immortality, since each finite seed and self is an expression of the infinite. As used here, death is another name for the infinite or the source of life.

Touching death should therefore be an appropriate rite of passage to self-realization. The old form of the individual's life is destroyed in the touch, leaving only the soul, which then experiences unification with the infinite to a degree that is usually only possible after death or before birth—between lives, as it were. The result is a new self, one with the infinite.

At least that is how the scene looks viewed in context, but it is also the harbinger of quite a different idea expressed a few months later in the original version of "The Crown." Whereas in "Hardy" sex is a means to "flower" and become one's complete self, in this essay (written only a year later) "passion means the reacting of the sexes against one another in a purely reducing activity. . . . in sex, we have plunged the quick of creation deep into the cold flux of reduction, corruption, till the quick is extinguished." Lawrence implies that sex for earlier generations (such as Anna and Will's) was merely a means to achieve "the final reduction": "for a hundred years we have been given over to the slowly advancing progress of reduction." In his own time, however, "the sex is exhausted, and there can be no more reduction through passion" (CMS V, 3–7).

How, then, can we separate the deathly sensuality of *The Rainbow* from what Birkin and Ursula experience in *Women in Love*? Is not their consummation also a phoenix cycle? The phoenix is a mythical representation of the vegetative year, in which new growth appears magically where the old has fallen, the secret being in the seed that also falls and lies unnoticed. But the African sensuality of *Women in Love* is associated with a culture that is permanently caught in one phase of the vegetative cycle: "the desire for creation" has "lapsed" in them, and they "fall from the connection with life and hope." The African process begins "when the soul in intense suffering breaks, breaks away from its organic hold like a leaf that falls" (245–46). Apparently, "soul" means in *Women in Love* what it does in *The Rainbow*. The soul has an "organic hold"—on the infinite, the source of life?—a hold that can be broken, after which it will never see spring again, only autumn. The individual is not dead but has lost "pure integral being" and cannot produce anything new. Again, a world in which such things happen is not the natural world, but a world gone mad.

Birkin and Ursula do rise, phoenixlike, from their African

sensuality, and they are newly created as single beings. The difference is in what they had to touch—in what, by implication at least, is therefore the new unknown, the new infinite. The unknown in "Hardy" is like the darkness in *The Rainbow*: fecund and frightening, alive and powerful. The darkness can be sinister because it hides predators with flashing fangs, but it also covers seeds as they germinate; it is the twin unknown, out of which life comes and to which it returns. In *Women in Love*, on the other hand, darkness can be "obscene," "disintegrating," "diabolic," "frictional," having to do with decay and "the dark river of dissolution." And in a letter to Forster from 1916, the unknown that Lawrence longs for is not loss of self in sexual fulfillment but actual death: "one looks through the window into the land of death, and it *does* seem a clean good unknown, all that is left to one."[17] In both novels, darkness and the unknown are actually within and reachable only by acknowledging "the dark stream that contains us all"—which in one novel is identifiable with the bloodstream and repressed animal instinct, and in the other with the bowels, sadism, corrupt sexuality, and suicidal desire.

This distinction remains clear despite an extraordinary coincidence of imagery between certain scenes in the two novels. For instance, Ursula and Anton sink into a dark, African river of terror and sensuality. What they fear excites them sensually, and this rather decadent excitement leads to their consummation:

> Then in a low, vibrating voice he told her about Africa, the strange darkness, the strange, blood fear.
> "I am not afraid of the darkness in England," he said. "It is soft, and natural to me, it is my medium, especially when you are here. But in Africa it seems massive and fluid with terror— not fear of anything—just fear. One breathes it, like the smell of blood." . . . Gradually he transferred to her the hot, fecund darkness that possessed his own blood. He was strangely secret. The whole world must be abolished. . . . A turgid, teeming night, heavy with fecundity in which every molecule of

17. Cambridge *Letters* 3, 22.

matter grew big with increase, secretly urgent with fecund desire, seemed to come to pass. . . . they walked the darkness
beside the massive river.

(446)

Yet even though the "massive river" Trent clearly becomes
like the "massive, fluid terror" of Africa, there is no reason to
suppose this river has anything to do with corruption or dissolution—quite the opposite. Things are not rotting, coming
apart, dissolving, disintegrating in this darkness; they are
growing "big with increase." In *Women in Love*, wherever
there is water or fluidity there is dissolution, but the same is
not true in *The Rainbow*.

Neither is there any reason to equate the two appearances
of Africa. Both images associate Africa, conventionally, with
darkness, but just as darkness has different connotations in
the two novels, so does the dark continent. Anton's Africans
live in terror, presumably of the jungle and the leopards and
tigers within it; yet even their fear is warm and fecund, as the
jungle is. Birkin's Africans are cynical, corrupt, cold creatures
like insects, and Birkin attributes no emotions to them. They
have "died, mystically," and they live like the beetles, "purely
within the world of corruption and dissolution." Because they
have gone "far beyond the phallic cult," one wonders how
they reproduce and carry on this "long process—thousands
of years it takes, after the death of the creative spirit" (245–
46).

Similarly, whereas in *Women in Love* Egypt is associated
with both a deathly power and knowledge of corruption
"such as the beetles have" (246), it has no such associations
for Lawrence in his *Rainbow* period. In the later novel Hermione is "powerful" as she and her friends sit like "the dead"
in "the hall of kings in some Egyptian tomb" (91), Birkin is
"like the immobile, supremely potent Egyptians" after Ursula
discovers his dark power (310), and the anal caress promises
to make him "night-free, like an Egyptian" (311). When he
was writing the earlier novel Lawrence was already fascinated by the image of Egypt and associated it with a divine or
suprahuman force that needed to be recognized. But in a let-

ter from 1914, the power he sees expressed in Egyptian sculp-
ture has nothing to do with corruption:

> The vision we're after, I don't know what it is—but it is some-
> thing that contains awe and dread and submission, not pride
> or sensuous egotism or assertion. I went to the British
> museum—and I know, from the Egyptian and Assyrian sculp-
> ture—what we are after. We want to realise the tremendous
> *non-human* quality of life. . . . Behind us all are the tremen-
> dous unknown forces of life, coming unseen and unperceived
> as out of the desert to the Egyptians, and driving us, forcing
> us, destroying us if we do not submit to be swept away.[18]

Soon Lawrence would decide that the "non-human forces"
sweeping through human life included the power of dissolution and corruption, and he would continue to connect them
with Egypt. But the ball-rolling scarab has no place in *The
Rainbow*, nor does the rejection of procreative sexuality associated with it in *Women in Love*. In the letter just quoted, the
"tremendous unknown forces of life" can only be approached
with the help of "the female": "there is no getting of a vision
. . . before we get our sex right: before we get our souls fertilised by the *female*. . . . only some female influence (not necessarily woman, but most obviously woman) can fertilise the
soul of man to vision or being."[19] Not beetles and corruption
but women and fertility are close to the divine in *The Rainbow*.

Lawrence protested too much when he said, in 1926, "And I,
who loathe sexuality so deeply, am considered a lurid sexuality specialist."[20] He earned the reputation by writing *Sons and
Lovers* and *The Rainbow*, books that show no loathing for sex
but treat it more openly than his contemporaries were willing
to accept. Like all his work, *The Rainbow* indicts conscious
modern sensation seeking; but, unlike much of his work, it

18. Cambridge *Letters* 2, 218.
19. Ibid.
20. *The Collected Letters of D. H. Lawrence*, ed. Harry T. Moore (New York:
Viking, 1962), vol. 2, 954. This volume will hereafter be cited in the notes as
Moore *Letters* 2.

celebrates the most ancient and ordinary kind of sex, passionate procreative love between men and women.

Though sex is the path to redemption in his early works, Lawrence approved of it even then only as a *means*—to the unknown, to a sense of one's place in relation to the great impersonal forces, which altogether means "to being." Like most theologians of sex, Lawrence thought sex as an end in itself was self-abuse, even during the period of "Hardy" and *The Rainbow*. Once the discovery of oneself is made, it cannot be repeated, and "the repeating of a known reaction upon myself is sensationalism." But if a person ventures beyond the known in sex, he may not only fulfill himself but help others: a letter from February 1915 asserts that the true aim of sex is to "venture in upon the coasts of the unknown, and open my discovery to all humanity."[21] Clearly, when Lawrence wrote this letter, he had not yet decided, as he says in the original "Crown," that heterosexual union is now sought only by the backward people, those who have not traveled to the confines.

Most of "Hardy" is a hymn to the glories of sex. There, "the supreme desire of every man is for mating with a woman, such that the sexual act be the closest, most concentrated motion in his life . . . of which all the rest of his motion is a continuance in the same kind." When such mating is achieved, "the woman of his body shall be the begetter of his whole life." Such sexuality is a spiritual as well as a physical fulfillment: "Does not a youth now know that he desires the body as the *via media*, that consummation is consummation of body and spirit, both?" (*Phoenix* 444–45, 469).

Viewed in the light of the later work, the sexual breakthrough in *The Rainbow*'s second generation may be a harbinger of a loathing for sex. But insofar as it fulfills that function, that passage thereby separates itself from the rest of the novel, in which sexual fulfillment comes not through the "reduction" of "The Crown," but through the "leap" of "Hardy."

21. Cambridge *Letters* 2, 284–85.

There is reductive sexuality in *The Rainbow* as well, but it does not lead to fulfillment. One source of confusion in the criticism is that Lawrence has Ursula and Anton embody both possibilities at different times in their affair; they are only enriched through one kind of sex, however, whereas the other destroys them.

Anton Skrebensky is Lawrence's portrait of overly mental modern man: he is too civilized, and his life is drying up because of the imperative to be selfless, to love his neighbor, to serve humankind. Through most of the book, Skrebensky, like Gerald, does not know how to fulfill himself and therefore proposes to give his life to the running of "the social mechanism." As long as he is doing that, his affair with Ursula can only strengthen both of their egos. Ursula falls in love not with Skrebensky but "with a vision of herself" (291), and all she wants from·him is to feel beautiful; he is closed and complete in himself, and he can invest only his body in sex, "let his soul do as it would" (315). They are the quintessentially modern lovers that Lawrence describes in "Hardy." Both see themselves as primary, "receiving gratification" from "the administration" of the other; and "it is this attitude of love, more than anything else, which devitalizes a race, and makes it barren" (*Phoenix* 491). Together they can only destroy each other with shallow, ego-gratifying sensuality, presided over by the moon, while Ursula yearns to "leap from the known into the unknown" (316), "yearning for something unknown" (477). She tries vainly to wring it out of Anton, who, since he is trying to be an abstraction instead of a live self, does not open into the unknown: "She knew him all round, not on any side did he lead into the unknown" (473).

For a period in their affair, however, he does. When he first returns from Africa, he announces that "the whole world must be abolished," seduces Ursula, and neglects his work. The difference in him is that his blood is "possessed" by the "hot, fecund darkness" and "the strange blood fear" of Africa (446); and, because of this fear and fecundity, he is able to discover "the clue to himself, he had escaped from the show, like a wild beast escaped straight back into its jungle. . . . He felt rich and abundant in himself" (449). Together Ursula and Anton now enter "the dark fields of immortality" (451). But even fulfillment, the clue to himself, is not enough to keep Skrebensky from reverting to type, and he becomes again the conventional, social man, Lawrence's paradox of a man who has no live self because he is both egocentric, and therefore closed to the source of life, and selfless in his dealings with others.

The first sign of his reversion is his desire to marry Ursula, even though "to make public their connection would be to put it in range with all the things which nullified him, and from which he was for the moment entirely dissociated" (453). Now he is a live, rich being only when he is with her, and immediately a corpse when she has left (456–57). He wants definitely to marry her and to go to India, and he re-aligns himself with imperial England. In argument with Ursula he goes back to defending the government and the greatest material good for the greatest number, and he becomes afraid of Ursula, "of her body," which was previously the route by which "he had discovered the clue to himself" (460–61).

He becomes pale, bleached out, "like a body from which all individual life is gone" (462). Ursula is sexually transported now only outdoors with her eyes open: then "it was as if the stars were lying with her and entering the unfathomable darkness of her womb, fathoming her at last. It was not him" (464). Ursula then notices men who are what Anton no longer is: animal, full-blooded, African—first the taxi driver (467), then the Sicilian hotel porter, who has "an almost African imperturbability" (472).

Ursula now becomes a destructive harpy as she tries to wrest from him what he can no longer give. Once again, he can only give her his body, and she even reverts to wanting to feel beautiful, not recognizing that her longing, in the late moonlit scenes as in the early ones, is for the unknown. Their struggle leaves them both "dead" for months after they separate; and Anton, now a banally superficial inhabitant of the world of light, is afraid of the darkness, even the darkness of

England. He identifies Ursula with "the darkness, the challenge, the horror. . . . He wanted to marry quickly, to screen himself from the darkness, the challenge of his own soul" (482). Anton has failed the challenge to become a single being, and, unlike Conrad's Kurtz, he unambiguously rejects the part of himself identified with African darkness, even though it once was his own and made him "rich and abundant in himself," "free," a "consummate being," "infinitely potent," an inhabitant of the "dark fields of immortality" (449–53).

Ursula, too, is "inert, without interest or strength" (483). When she finds that she is pregnant, her life is at such a low ebb that she decides to submit to marriage with Anton. Lawrence makes this prospect sound like suicide: "she should join him again and her history would be concluded forever" (485). She is jarred out of this state by the horses, which are the most vivid, frightening animal presences in the novel and clearly linked both to the immortal sensuality she once had with Anton and to a special manifestation of the infinite forces within.

Ursula's horses may be Lawrence's most successful symbol, by his own definition of a "great symbol" as opposed to an allegorical image:

> You can't give a great symbol a "meaning," any more than you can give a cat a "meaning." Symbols are organic units of consciousness with a life of their own, and you can never explain them away, because their value is dynamic, emotional, belonging to the sense-consciousness of the body and soul, and not simply mental. An allegorical image has a *meaning*. Mr. Facing-both-ways has a meaning. But I defy you to lay your finger on the full meaning of Janus, who is a symbol.[22]

Nearly everyone who has written on *The Rainbow* has tried to lay a finger on the full meaning of the horses, and the variety of the results testifies to the irreducibility of the symbol. So

---

22. D. H. Lawrence, "Introduction to *The Dragon of the Apocalypse*," in his *Selected Literary Criticism* (1931; rpt. ed. Anthony Beal, New York: Viking, 1966), 157.

does the presence in the scene of another, previously unnoticed meaning:[23] the horses are subtly identified with Ursula's unborn child, and their behavior mimics childbirth.

How one reads Lawrence's opposition between humanity's animal nature and its civilized behavior often determines the interpretation of this scene. Many critics have suggested that those churning hooves and flanks refer to sensuality and animal vitality, and some quote a passage from the later Lawrence in which he identifies horses in dreams with sensuality.[24] But since Ursula both runs for her life from the horses and is reborn into a new life, arguably because she meets them, interpretation of the horses' significance is split. Some critics see her escape into "the smaller, cultivated field, and so out to the high-road and the ordered world of man" (488) as a rejection of sensuality and an affirmation of the impulse to build civilization. Because Ursula hopes to marry Skrebensky before meeting the horses, and is glad to have escaped that fate soon afterwards, these critics identify Skrebensky with the horses and emphasize his sensuality, his "horseman's animal darkness," rather than his characterization as a builder of empire. In this view, the horses represent something to be transcended and kept under control.[25]

The other major interpretation is that the horses represent the vitality of nature, repressed in civilized humanity, which surges up in Ursula to keep her from betraying her quest for fulfillment by marrying Skrebensky. Critics holding this view often emphasize that Skrebensky is a shallow, cynically sensual imperialist who has betrayed his vital self and is there-

23. Most of this section appeared as "To Procreate Oneself: Ursula's Horses in *The Rainbow*" in *English Literary History* 49 (Spring 1982): 123–42.

24. D. H. Lawrence, *Psychoanalysis and the Unconscious/Fantasia of the Unconscious* (New York: Viking, 1960), 199.

25. See, for instance, H. M. Daleski, *The Forked Flame: A Study of D. H. Lawrence* (London: Faber & Faber, 1965), 123–24; F. B. Pinion, *A D. H. Lawrence Companion* (New York: Barnes & Noble, 1978), 158–59; and Scott Sanders, *D. H. Lawrence*, 92. Eugene Goodheart, *The Utopian Vision of D. H. Lawrence* (Chicago: University of Chicago Press, 1963), does not mention the horses but does offer an interesting argument for Lawrence's favoring the daytime world of civilization in *The Rainbow*.

fore unable to provide Ursula with the fulfillment she seeks. The horses, then, represent what Skrebensky lacks, and they come like avenging angels to block her path, to remind her that the goal of her quest is not security but transfiguration, a new life, in which the sensual vitality they represent will not be transcended but incorporated. She escapes the horses because animal vitality in its purest form is dangerous, but she rises renewed, like the phoenix, after being seared by this power. Critics holding this view often see mythic allusions in the horses, especially to the four horsemen of the apocalypse and to Pan, the hooved god of forests and herds, who in later classical mythology became the universal god.[26]

Though I think the second (sometimes called the "vitalist") view is truer to the novel, the evidence for the first interpretation should not be ignored: Lawrence's endorsement of natural vitality is qualified. There is, however, another reading of the horse scene that the present examination will not support. Some critics holding roughly the vitalist view think that the missing element in Ursula's affair with Skrebensky is male potency and that the horses remind her of what she will have to do without if she marries him.[27] In 1921, six years after writing The Rainbow, Lawrence identifies horses in dreams with "the great sensual male activity" and asserts that "the greatest desire of the living spontaneous soul is that this very male sensual nature, represented as a menace, shall be actually accomplished in life."[28] Applying this assertion to Ur-

26. See, for instance, Mary Freeman, D. H. Lawrence: A Basic Study of His Ideas (Gainesville: University Presses of Florida), 46–47; Graham Hough, The Dark Sun (New York: Macmillan, 1957), 71; Kinkead-Weekes, "Marble and the Statue," 407–10; Julian Moynahan, The Deed of Life (Princeton: Princeton University Press, 1963), 66–68; and Ann L. McLaughlin, "The Clenched and Knotted Horses in The Rainbow," D. H. Lawrence Review 13 (Summer 1980): 179–86.

27. See, for instance, Ford, Double Measure, 158–60; Jennifer Michaels, "The Horse as a Life Symbol in the Prose Works of D. H. Lawrence," The International Fiction Review 5 (1978): 116–23; Keith Sagar, "The Third Generation," in Twentieth Century Interpretations of The Rainbow, ed. Mark Kinkead-Weekes (Englewood Cliffs, N.J.: Prentice-Hall, 1971), 67–68. Revised from Keith Sagar, The Art of D. H. Lawrence, 120.

28. Lawrence, Psychoanalysis/Fantasia, 199.

sula and her horses, however, can lead to some alarming conclusions: one critic even feels called upon to assure us that
Ursula does not desire "actual physical union with the animal."[29]

That anyone should feel the need to offer such an assur-
ance tells us less about *The Rainbow* than it does about the
wisdom of relying on Lawrence's encyclopedic prose works
to explain his novels. *Fantasia of the Unconscious*, in which
Lawrence does link horses and male sensuality, was written
in a period when he was obsessed with male dominance and
proclaiming all things powerful to be male. But, as we saw
earlier, in "Hardy" he identifies the mind as male and the
flesh as female, and advocates a new reverence for the flesh
to temper the mental and the male. Chances are, then, that if
Ursula's horses have something to do with the body, the soul,
the senses, or the feelings, they ought to be female instead of
male (*Phoenix* 509).

Similarly, it is true that Ursula is looking for a Son of God,
like those mentioned in Genesis (6:1–4), who marry the
daughters of men, and that Skrebensky has turned out not to
be one; and in *Apocalypse*, written in 1929, Lawrence says:
"The sons of God who came down and knew the daughters
of men and begot the great Titans, they had 'the members of
horses,' says Enoch."[30] Lawrence did not yet know this interesting fact, however, when he wrote *The Rainbow*. It is not in
the Bible,[31] and if he had encountered it in some other source,
he surely would have had Ursula think something about it.
But nowhere is the phenomenon mentioned in *The Rainbow*.

Where it does appear is in *The Book of Enoch*, which Lawrence read in 1929 while preparing to write *Apocalypse*.[32] *The*

29. Ford, *Double Measure*, 160.

30. D. H. Lawrence, *Apocalypse* (New York: Viking, 1931), 98.

31. Robert Young, *Analytical Concordance to the Bible* (New York: Funk and
Wagnalls, 1910).

32. *The Book of Enoch*, trans. R. H. Charles (Oxford, 1906; London: Society
for Promoting Christian Knowledge, 1917), 115–16. Rose Marie Burwell, "A
Catalogue of D. H. Lawrence's Reading from Early Childhood," *D. H. Lawrence Review* 3 (Fall 1970): 292, suggests that Lawrence read a book of Enoch,

Book of Enoch is one of several ancient texts that are biblical in character but not recognized as part of the Bible. It is believed to predate Genesis and may have influenced writers of the New Testament, in which it is mentioned, but it was banned by the Church in the fourth century. The Abyssinian Church, however, preserved *The Book of Enoch* among the books of its Bible, and a translation of this Ethiopic version was first published in Europe in 1821. Since then, ancient scrolls corresponding to and supplementing the Ethiopic version have been discovered.[33]

Enoch's version of the Sons of God would make nonsense of the end of *The Rainbow* if Lawrence had had it in mind. Enoch dwells obsessively on the mating of heavenly beings and women because he believes it constituted the corruption that brought on the Flood. In Genesis, however, the Sons of God are given only brief, cryptic notice and are not clearly implicated in human corruption. Ursula knows only the biblical reference to them, and her Son of God is part of the promise of the rainbow, not the cause of the Flood.

Lawrence's use of the Sons of God in *The Rainbow* is perhaps illuminated by a letter he wrote while working on that novel. He explains the economics of his Rananim as

> communism based, not on poverty, but on riches, not on humility, but on pride, not on sacrifice but upon complete fulfilment in the flesh of all strong desire, not on forfeiture but

given him by Frederick Carter, before writing *Apocalypse* in December 1929. The relevant passage occurs in the Charles translation but not in the other text Burwell names as a possibility (*The Hebrew Book of Enoch*, ed. Hugo Odeberg, London: 1928), which is not a translation of the Ethiopic Enoch. Enoch dreams that stars (symbolic of the Sons of God) fell down, "protruded their parts of shame like horses" and mated with white cows (symbolic of the daughters of men) only in the Aramaic and Ethiopic versions, and not in the Hebrew, which does not concern the Sons of God story at all. Another possible source for Lawrence is the original publication in English of the Ethiopic version: *The Book of Enoch, the Prophet: An Apocryphal Production*, trans. Richard Laurence, Archbishop of Cashel (Oxford: Oxford University Press, 1821), 114–15.

33. J. T. Milik, *The Books of Enoch* (Oxford: Clarendon Press, 1976).

upon inheritance, not on heaven but on earth. We will be Sons of God who walk here on earth, not bent on getting and having, because we know we inherit all things.[34]

These "Sons of God" are the same as the "aristocrats" or self-fulfilling individuals of "Hardy." Moreover, the fact that this letter was written to a woman (Lady Ottoline Morrell) and that he uses the first person plural in reference to the Sons of God should indicate that the term does not even have gender connotations for Lawrence in this period.

Finally, even if the Sons of God in Genesis are superior male beings, they have nothing to do with horses. Neither do the horses in *The Rainbow* have much to do with male potency. If Lawrence is right in *Fantasia* and readers do tend to associate horses with male sensuality, then it is easy to see why Ursula's horses have been experienced as uninterpretable. The language in which they appear suggests instead their association with the exclusively female mysteries of pregnancy, labor, and birth.

Ursula meets the horses soon after realizing that she is pregnant and shortly before losing the child through miscarriage. At first the child is "the heaviness of her heart," then the horses:

> Then gradually the heaviness of her heart pressed and pressed into consciousness. What was she doing? Was she bearing a child? Bearing a child?
>
> (483)

> She knew the heaviness on her heart. It was the weight of the horses. But she would circumvent them. She would bear the weight steadily, and so escape. . . . Suddenly the weight deepened and her heart grew tense to bear it. Her breathing was laboured. But this weight also she could bear. . . . What was it that was drawing near her, what weight oppressing her heart? . . . She was aware . . . of their haunches, so rounded, so massive, pressing, pressing, pressing to burst the grip upon their breasts.
>
> (486–87)

<hr>

34. Cambridge *Letters* 2, 273.

The pressing of the heaviness on her heart is nearly identical in the two contexts. Lawrence also says repeatedly that the weight of the horses is something she can *bear*, though when the weight deepens her breathing is *"laboured."* And his odd usage of "couched" in "her heart was couched with fear, couched with fear all along" (488) seems to be a deliberate clue to the scene's significance.

The whole scene subtly mimics labor and birth. The horses are "gripped, clenched narrow in a hold that never relaxed" (487) like a child in the birth canal, and they thunder upon her in intermittent waves like contractions. When the last and worst of these waves is upon her, she is "as if seized by lightning. . . . the weight came down upon her, down, to the moment of extinction" (488). "Lightning" here is a metaphor for electrifying fear; it may also be a pun on "lightening," an obstetrical term that was in use in 1915 and that Lawrence may have known.[35] "Lightening" is the baby's descent into position to be born; its weight drops lower in the mother's body. Though the term technically refers to an event that happens before labor begins, the fetus does continue its downward progress shortly before delivery. It is probably not a coincidence that Lawrence has Ursula almost simultaneously being "seized by lightning" and feeling the weight come "down upon her, down."

Then he says, "Her heart was gone, she had no more heart," as if the weight pressing upon it had obliterated it. This is like the moment of greatest internal pressure, shortly before birth. Lawrence calls this moment "the crisis," which, though not an obstetrical term, has been used since the sixteenth century to designate the critical moment in an illness when a decisive change occurs, for better or worse. The critical moment in a birth is the delivery, and Ursula now delivers herself from the horses (488–89).

It is not the child who is born from this labor, but Ursula

35. Joseph B. De Lee, *The Principles and Practice of Obstetrics* (London: W. B. Saunders, 1918), 85–86. Frieda Lawrence, mother of three when she met Lawrence, undoubtedly knew the term.

herself. At her last glimpse of the horses, from the safety of the other side of the hedge, she thinks, "she could not bear it. She rose and walked swiftly . . . across the field." It is another assault from the horses she cannot bear here, yet a few pages later we learn that she will not bear the child, either; because the horses are linked to the child and to childbirth, escaping them may be a symbolic miscarriage. Somehow, this experience has forged Ursula's soul: she is very ill afterwards, but "her soul lay still and permanent, full of pain, but itself forever" (490). The birth imagery now refers to Ursula's birth as an independent self, and the child is the constriction against which she must fight in order to be born, because the child is "the bondage, to Skrebensky and Skrebensky's world," to a conventional social life in colonial India and an unfulfilling marriage (491). Now Ursula herself can be identified with the horses: both are fighting to burst a constriction that separates them from eternity. The horses are "running against the walls of time, and never bursting free" (487); Ursula fights to be free of "Anton's world: it became in her feverish brain a compression which enclosed her. If she could not get out of the compression she would go mad" (491). She has burst free after her illness and miscarriage, like a "kernel" from its "shell": then she is "striving to take new root, to create a new knowledge of Eternity in the flux of Time" (492).

At least two events, then, are reflected in the birth imagery in and around the scene with the horses; one is psychological and one is physical. The realistic explanation for the horses' menacing behavior may be that Ursula is beginning to have her miscarriage and disorientedly interprets what she sees through waves of pain and fear. She goes out for the walk in which she meets the horses because of "a gathering restiveness, a tumult impending within her . . . seething rising to madness within her" (485), and after she escapes them she can scarcely walk, though they have not harmed her in any obvious way. She does lose the child in her subsequent illness, and her contractions may have begun when she meets them. As a hallucination, the horses could be an objectification of her sensations.

At the same time, the seething within is a psychological revulsion from her self-betrayal and leads to a new self-realization. Lawrence saw emotions as physical states; his characters become sick or well, weak or powerful according to their psychological condition, and it is characteristic of his work that Ursula's psychological rebirth is associated with an experience similar to physical parturition. That she rejects actual childbearing is also psychologically appropriate because she has conflated the child's existence with imprisonment in a loveless marriage.

The concurrence of spiritual rebirth and physical miscarriage, however, implies a rejection of fertility at a climactic moment in the novel. Ursula is Lawrence's advance guard for the future; she suffers from what he sees as the spiritual diseases of the twentieth century, and the dynamics of her rebirth ought to indicate how he thinks modern humanity will be regenerated. Does she need to reject procreation in order to realize her potential?

Opposing motherhood to fulfillment would seem to make an odd conclusion to a novel that glorifies the fertility of nature and women. As Marguerite Beede Howe puts it, "Almost everything in the book, including the landscape, is feminine; and almost everything feminine is pregnant."[36] Ewes lamb, the earth sprouts, the women bear fourteen children. Even heaven "teems" in *The Rainbow* and has "intercourse" with earth, just as the soil clings to the feet of the Brangwen farmers "with a weight that pulled like desire." No wonder even the men can be "impregnated with the day": "they knew the wave which cannot halt, but every year throws forward the seed to begetting, and, falling back, leaves the youngborn on the earth" (2). Even the darkness is "fecund" in this novel (41, 198), and the night gets pregnant, becomes "a turgid, teeming night, heavy with fecundity in which every molecule of matter grew big with increase" (446).

Those who see the horses as something to be transcended

36. Howe, *Art of the Self in D. H. Lawrence*, 34.

might say that Ursula rejects the mindless physical servitude of motherhood and looks forward to a future of self-responsibility—going beyond her mother, who stopped traveling forward when she fell into "the sleep of motherhood" (418). One of Lawrence's announced themes for *The Rainbow* is "woman becoming individual, self-responsible, taking her own initiative"—perhaps liberating herself from her traditional incarceration in a childbearing body and subordination to maternal duty.[37] But this reading forces a separation between the end and the rest of the novel, in which divinity is indistinguishable from the life in a creature, and the goal of self-realization is reached through experience in the body and is closely associated with procreation. It would seem to be much more in keeping with the rest of the novel, in fact, if Ursula were to be awakened to the spiritual nature of her existence through the experience of childbirth rather than miscarriage, which in its issue is more clearly a manifestation of death than of life.

It is not the physical result of miscarriage, however, that seems to concern Lawrence. In fact, as we shall see, miscarriage is actually perfect for his purposes—though it needed to be associated with the powerful symbol of the horses and accompanied by serious misunderstanding on Ursula's part. By making the progress of Ursula's understanding lag well behind events, Lawrence manages to imply that procreation is not only no hindrance but also a positive means to self-realization if rightly approached. By linking the event with the highly charged imagery of the horse scene, he makes the miscarriage seem consonant with the central theme of the novel, the recurrent discovery by humans of their place in relation to the fecund, frightening divinity revealed in organic life.

The horses are connected both to the irrational violence of wolves and leopards and to the infinite life revealed in the cell's nucleus. As Sagar argues, "the gleam in the eye of the

37. Cambridge *Letters* 2, 165.

wild beast, the flash of fangs, is also the flash of the sword of angels, for the gleam is the very quick of life," and "the urgent, massive fire locked within the flanks of the horses" differs "only in scale from the gleam of the nucleus under the microscope."[38] The horse scene, like Ursula's two epiphanies, is filled with gleams, glimmers, glistenings, and flashes, as well as incandescence and iridescence; and the horses, like the beasts and angels outside the arc light, are dark, powerful, dangerous, gleaming, flashing, haloed, and circling.

The horses seem, then, to embody the savage, irrational divinity that Ursula must recognize in her own being before she can "come forth" as "that which she was, positively" (437); as such, it is appropriate that they should also imitate labor pains. Lawrence's pantheistic God is primarily characterized as the source of life, and the representation of this divinity appropriately incorporates powerful animals and the idea of birth, since these are among the most spectacular manifestations of the life force. Metaphoric leopards and tigers abound in *The Rainbow* as representatives of a deity denied by rational humanity, though charging horses are the best Lawrence could muster, realistically, in the English countryside; and birth, both as metaphor and event, is closely associated in this novel with ontological revelation. Thinking of God primarily as the source of life leads logically to a near-conflation of spiritual regeneration and physical birth, to an almost literal reading of the metaphor of rebirth: God creates, and then recreates, the individual. In "Hardy" Lawrence sees the necessity of a second birth "at the age of twenty or thirty": "the incomplete germ which is a young soul must be fertilized, the parent womb which encloses the incomplete individuality must conceive, and we must be brought forth to ourselves, distinct" (*Phoenix* 433). Both in "Hardy" and in *The Rainbow*, being recreated entails ego loss, a recognition that one does not control one's own life, and a brave naked leap into "the unknown," which constitutes an ontological state of oneness with Lawrence's idea of God. And though in both

38. Sagar, *Art of D. H. Lawrence*, 61, 64.

works sexual passion is the principal means to transfiguration, parturition seems actually better suited to providing the necessary realizations.

And, in fact, pregnancy and birth give Lawrence's characters glimpses of their place in the eternal ordering. Tom Brangwen realizes while attending his ewes in labor that he does "not belong to himself," that he is "submissive to the greater ordering" (35); and again, during the birth of his first child, he sees "the infinite world, eternal, unchanging," in the way his wife looks at him, "as a woman in childbirth looks at the man who begot the child in her: an impersonal look, in the extreme hour, female to male" (76). Anna Brangwen, pregnant, dances before the Lord, "lifting her hands and her body to the Unseen, to the unseen Creator who had chosen her, to Whom she belonged" (179). Ursula, too, realizes only after the birthlike experience of miscarriage that she belongs to the infinite. Her life is not her own creation and she must not attempt to be God by trying to remake a man: "She was glad she could not create her man. . . . She was glad that this lay within the scope of that vaster power in which she rested at last. The man would come out of Eternity to which she herself belonged" (493). These experiences both reveal the divine and are embodied metaphors of Lawrentian rebirth: what is to be brought forth in the woman is within her but not hers and not in her control. Lydia's look at Tom during childbirth is a window into eternity because of her pain and her inability to control what is happening to her; her mere personal ego is powerless and she is revealed as the embodiment of an impersonal force.

To convince the reader that selves are not fixed entities, that the "old stable ego of the character" is a fiction, Lawrence had to dramatize conflicts between his characters' conscious wills and the impersonal natural forces within. The clearest manifestations of these forces are, therefore, violent and frightening to the characters. Childbirth is not only symbolically but also realistically appropriate as an event leading to ontological revelation, since it occurs even in opposition to the woman's will and may threaten her life to bring forth new life. Echoing the Bible in "Hardy," Lawrence argues that "he

who would save his life must lose it," and his use of the masculine pronoun may indicate why he wanted, not childbirth,
but "love, and love alone" to be "the *via media* to being, for
man or woman" (*Phoenix*, 409–10). But choosing a means
equally available to both sexes meant that Lawrence often had
to incorporate imagery of violence and destruction into his
characters' sexual relationships. Tom must be destroyed in order to be consummated: what will destroy him is "the awful
unknown" in Lydia. He seems to fear for his life when he
approaches her too nearly: "He was afraid, he wanted to save
himself" (90). And, as we have seen, the lovemaking in the
next two generations, when it is most fulfilling, is associated
with violence.

Perhaps to mediate the violence, and to associate sex with
a more obvious manifestation of vitality, Lawrence borrowed
the imagery of procreation and attached it to the sexual consummations. Tom's necessary destruction, for instance, is described as entering "really within the blazing kernel of darkness" (91). For similar reasons, Lawrence again used seed
imagery to characterize an event merely violent on the surface
but that he meant for us to see as spiritually if not physically
procreative: Ursula fears for her life from the horses, and her
fear is fecund even on the surface level of the imagery because
it is "a small, living seed of fear" in her heart (486). And after
her miscarriage, Ursula's child is dead but Ursula herself is
"the naked, clear kernel thrusting forth the clear, powerful
shoot . . . striving to take new root, to create a new knowledge of Eternity in the flux of Time" (492). The imagery of
germination here characterizes Ursula's spiritual rebirth and
mediates both the destructive violence of the horses and the
antiprocreative nature of the realistic event.

In *The Rainbow*, metaphoric birth is clearly more important
to Lawrence than actual childbirth, and he articulates this distinction in "Hardy":

> That she bear children is not a woman's significance. But that
> she bear herself, that is her supreme and risky fate: that she
> drive on to the edge of the unknown and beyond. She may
> leave children behind, for security. . . . It is so arranged that
> the very act which carries us out into the unknown shall prob-

ably deposit seed for security to be left behind. But the act, called the sexual act, is not for the depositing of the seed. It is for leaping off into the unknown, as from a cliff's edge.

(*Phoenix* 441)

Bearing children ensures the preservation of the race, but Lawrence laments in "Hardy" that "man" works too hard at self-preservation instead of expressing himself in "begetting children, colouring himself and dancing and howling and sticking feathers in his hair, in scratching pictures on the walls of his cave, and making graven images of his unutterable feelings" (*Phoenix* 398). "Begetting children" may look out of place in this list, until we recognize that Lawrence does not mean bearing or raising children, but simply begetting them, which may be an incidental consequence of something more important. In "Hardy," the highest achievement of life is not the fruit but the flower; the flower does produce seeds, but seeds are not its goal. The red of the poppy is not "the excess that accompanies reproduction," as practical, self-preserving people have called it:

The excess is the thing itself at its maximum of being. . . . Seed and fruit and produce, these are only a minor aim: children and good works are a minor aim. . . . The final aim is the flower. . . . Not the work I shall produce, but the real Me I shall achieve, that is the consideration; of the complete Me will come the complete fruit of me, the work, the children.

(*Phoenix* 402–3)

The point is "to fly the flag of myself, at the extreme tip of life . . . till, like the poppy, we lean on the sill of all the unknown . . . having surpassed that which has been before" (*Phoenix* 406–9). If a child is begotten at the same time, it is, at best, a sort of fringe benefit.[39]

Neither is "Hardy" the only instance in Lawrence's work where begetting and bearing receive unequal treatment. What matters always in the novels is self-realization. If a child is conceived in the process, the pregnancy may be treated as

---

39. "There is the baby, but that is a side issue," Mellors writes to Connie at the end of *Lady Chatterley's Lover* (Florence, 1928; rpt. New York: Grove Press, 1957), 364.

confirmation that what has happened between the man and woman is good; Lawrence bestows remarkably few pregnancies on couples who have not risked themselves together. But children are never actually born to his happy couples, except in *The Rainbow*, and there only after the novel's focus has shifted to the next generation. Elsewhere—for instance, in *Lady Chatterley's Lover*, *The Lost Girl*, and *The Man Who Died*—when the woman becomes pregnant, the man leaves her, promising to return, but the book ends with their prospects uncertain. We do not know if Connie and Mellors will be reunited after their baby comes; Ciccio leaves the pregnant Alvina to fight in the Great War; and Christ's parting promise to the pregnant priestess of Isis is not reassuring.

Couples with children, especially the fathers, are usually extremely unhappy in Lawrence's novels: the father absconds long before the beginning of *The White Peacock*, commits adultery and kills himself in *The Trespasser*, and leaves his wife and children to become an itinerant musician in *Aaron's Rod*. In *Women in Love* the mother of the Crich family is half mad, and Ursula and Gudrun view their parents' life as "so nothing" (365) and doubt that they will have children at all (3). In the stories, a remarkable number of families have only one parent, the other having died or left. If both stay after children come, someone will pay, usually the child ("The Rocking-Horse Winner") or the father ("The Old Adam"), unless both parents are ninnies ("Daughters of the Vicar").

The reasons for this ambivalence are perhaps obvious in the facts of Lawrence's life. That Lawrence's own family was extremely unhappy is recorded in *Sons and Lovers*, and Frieda's forced separation from her children later threatened his marriage; Lawrence apparently came to look on her children as rivals. Yet he was eager to conceive children with Frieda, even before they were living together and despite their poverty and inability to marry quickly. He wrote to her that he objected to birth control: "I do not believe, when people love each other, in interfering there. It is wicked, according to my feeling." He said he would "be glad" if she were already pregnant. His willingness to conceive children when Frieda was still married to someone else was romantic and unconventional and might have been consonant with the discrepancy between fertility and parenthood in his work. When a man and woman leap off the cliff together, they must trust completely in the vaster power and not "interfere" with it in any way. They should be glad to participate in the mystery of life by conceiving a child, though the "responsibility" of children is a separate matter, and more worrisome. In the same letter, he added, "But you see, we must have a more or less stable foundation if we are going to run the risk of the responsibility of children—not the risk of children but the risk of the responsibility."[40]

Lawrence seemed able, in his personal life and in his work, to make a radical distinction between procreation, which to him was a physical event leading to the beyond, and parenthood, which was a position of worldly responsibility perhaps detrimental to the parents, especially the father.[41] When he wrote the letter just quoted, Lawrence was revising *Sons and Lovers*, in which the children "have heaps of vitality" because they are conceived through a passion that Paul thinks gave his mother "everything that was necessary for her living and developing."[42] Yet, as a responsibility, the children bind together a marriage that ruins their parents' lives; the sons are injured, too, because they replace the father in the mother's affections. In the only surviving fragment of Lawrence's next novel, the draft of "The Sisters" that was apparently an early version of *Women in Love*, Gudrun is the first of Lawrence's heroines to be pregnant at the end of a novel. The pregnancy makes Gerald realize that he loves Gudrun, but the fragment, which must be nearly the end of the novel, concludes with Gerald worrying that she will love the child more than she does him.[43]

40. Cambridge *Letters 1*, 402–3.

41. Kohya Shimizu has discussed the same issue in "D. H. Lawrence ni Okeru Seishoku to Sôzô no Kairi o Megulte" [The Distinction Between Creation and Procreation in D. H. Lawrence], *Studies in English Literature* (English Literary Society of Japan, Tokyo), 50 (November 1973), 63–77.

42. Cambridge *Letters 1*, 476–77; D. H. Lawrence, *Sons and Lovers*, 317.

43. "The Sisters" fragments are in the Humanities Research Center, the University of Texas at Austin. As Kinkead-Weekes notes ("Marble and the

Lawrence then wrote all the drafts of *The Rainbow*. That novel, though it celebrates fertility, procreation, and even childbirth as conducive to bearing oneself, also presents children as a hindrance to parents' self-realization. Early in the marriages of the first two generations, the wives are preoccupied apart from their husbands, shutting the husbands out of the unknown and therefore out of "existence." Tom feels excluded by Lydia's history, "the pain of the old life, the dead husband, the dead children" (61); when she is pregnant with his child, she grieves for her lost children and refuses to let Tom comfort her. She becomes "more and more unaware of him, his existence was annulled" (59). Similarly, Anna dances Will's "nullification," naked and pregnant before the Lord, "dancing his non-existence, dancing herself to the Lord, to exultation" (180–81). Absorbed in her children, she becomes satisfied to be "a door and threshold" for other souls, rather than "the wayfarer to the unknown," leaving Will dissatisfied and angry (193). Both Tom and Will turn to their daughters, and, by default, they too become absorbed in the children. Tom seems almost to fall in love with his stepdaughter Anna while feeling insecure because she is not actually his child, and Will makes such emotional demands on the baby Ursula that she is "wakened too soon" (218).

But children are only the fruit and cannot give their parents what they need to flower. After his transfiguration with Lydia, Tom realizes that children are the work of a force that moves through the parents, the same that has remade his life and that comes to him and Lydia through each other:

> What did it matter, that Anna Lensky was born of Lydia and Paul? God was her father and her mother. He had passed

---

Statue," 375) one fragment is numbered 291–96 in a novel that Lawrence intended to be about 300 pages. This scene, furthermore, reads like the final episode of the Gerald-Gudrun story: it is a confrontation, in the presence of Gudrun, between Gerald and Loerke, both of whom want to marry her. Gerald wins, Loerke retires, and Gerald and Gudrun begin to dress their mutual wounds. This version was probably written in 1913. See Ross, *Composition*, 15–22.

through the married pair without fully making Himself known to them.

    Now He was declared to Brangwen and to Lydia Brangwen, as they stood together. When at last they had joined hands, the house was finished, and the Lord took up His abode.

                                       (91–92)

God "passed through" Paul and Lydia Lensky without "declaring" Himself to them, creating children but not complete selves for the parents. Tom and Lydia, too, produce a child before they are transformed; and Anna and Will have four children before they become complete people, at which point "the children became less important, the parents were absorbed in their own living" (235).

    Similarly, only Ursula's flesh was "thrilled" by her pregnancy, while "her soul was sick. It seemed, this child, like the seal set on her own nullity." She must then deny her desire for the beyond: "Only the living from day to day mattered, the beloved existence in the body . . . with no beyond, no further trouble" (483). The child's existence creates a worldly responsibility and makes Ursula think she must marry Skrebensky, despite the fact that he no longer opens into the unknown for her: "Poignant, almost passionate appreciation she felt for him, but none of the dreadful wonder, none of the rich fear, the connection with the unknown, or the reverence of love" (473).

    Yet Ursula is saved from her denial of the spirit by a divine revelation associated with the contractions of her own womb. A child is God's work, but God is only declared to its parents in each other—or, at least, that is the only access to eternity for the father. In the first two generations, the man is dissatisfied after the children come and is transformed when he and his wife find the new world; he looks for it all along in his wife, while she is drawn away from him to a different source. When she is pregnant, the man is annulled and shut out of existence, but God is passing more directly through the woman. When Anna dances Will's nonexistence, she is communing with "the unseen Creator who had chosen her, to whom she belonged" (179). In pregnancy the women seem to have access to the infinite apart from the man, and in giving birth they seem to do, alone, what the man only does in sex: surrender conscious control and give themselves up to the power of the divine forces within.

That is why Lawrence burdens Ursula with a miscarriage. Through it, she can touch the infinite, alone, without a man, and without falling into the sleep of motherhood; she can participate in the mystery of begetting without incurring the responsibility of bearing; she can be reborn into the unknown and remain unencumbered with lover or child afterwards, so that she is free to enter "freedom together" with Birkin. Miscarriage is a daring solution because it risks seeming like a rejection of fertility, which in the rest of the novel is divinity expressing itself; and a woman miscarrying is unlikely to have the same emotional experience as a woman giving birth. That, I suspect, is why Lawrence needed the horse scene: there the miscarriage symbolically joins the unhaltable wave of begetting, the flash of fangs and angels' swords, the gleam of the cell's nucleus, and the impersonal look of a woman in childbirth. The continuity of imagery works below the surface, and the horses appear to be the culmination of a theme that has built throughout the novel, even when we do not understand what they mean. Through the horses, Ursula's miscarriage is so strongly linked to earlier, fruitful labors that the metaphoric fertility resulting from it seems natural: Ursula is a seed shed out of its shell, naked and glistening.

She does not recognize the divinity in the horses, and, realistically, she cannot; the symbolic and realistic levels of the scene would collapse into each other if she were to do anything but try to escape the horses. To keep the realism intact, she needs to be unable to bear the horses; to give her miscarriage the proper symbolic meaning, she also needs to feel unable to bear her actual child. At first she identifies the child with Skrebensky and the conventional world: "the child bound her to him. . . . she fought and fought and fought all through her illness to be free of him and his world" (491). She fights the child because she never thinks of it as a child but conflates it instead with a series of abstractions: the life of the body, a traditional domestic life, Skrebensky's world, and finally the whole "world of things." She fights that world in the form of the child, apparently vanquishing it when she miscarries.

But afterwards, when she sees the child free of abstractions, she realizes she was wrong: "If there had been a child, it would have made little difference, however. She would have kept the child and herself, she would not have gone to Skrebensky" (493). She is clearly in error when she fights the pregnancy, and the slow progress of her understanding allows Lawrence to avoid condemning procreation itself by leaving open the possibility that she could have had the child and still "kept herself," kept the new self that has been born in her, without actually having her do it. If she were to have the child and be reborn in the process, we might imagine that motherhood is itself her goal. And her misunderstanding has a further advantage, since it may leave the reader with the impression that her miscarriage is a rejection of the conventional world—if not by Ursula, since she does not control her own body, then by God. This idea is also suggested by the horse scene, since the visitation of those dark angels seems somehow to precipitate her illness and subsequent realization of anticommunal individuality.

In a letter Lawrence may have written the same day as the scene with the horses, he uses horses just as he does in that scene, as a symbol of self-realization through experience that is physical and procreative:

> I see Van Gogh so sadly. If he could only have set the angel of himself clear in relation to the animal of himself, clear and distinct but always truly related, in harmony and union, he need not have cut off his ear and gone mad. But he said, do you remember—about 'in the midst of an artistic life the yearning for the real life remains—*one offers no resistance, neither does one resign oneself'*—he means to the yearning to procreate oneself 'with other horses, also free.'—This is why he went mad. He should either have resigned himself and lived his animal 'other horses'—and have seen *if his art would come out of that*—or he should have resisted, like Fra Angelico. But best of all, if he could have known a great humanity where to

live one's animal would be to create oneself, *in fact, be the artist creating a man in living fact* (not like Christ, as he wrongly said)—and where the art was the final expression of the created animal or man—not the be-all and being of man—but the end, the climax. And some men would end in artistic utterance, and some men wouldn't. But each one would create the work of art, the living man, achieve that piece of supreme art, a man's life.[44]

Though the goal here is to balance the angel and animal within, "living the animal" is conducive to this recreation of the self; the animal is what has been left out, just as in "Hardy" the mental and male have overbalanced the physical and female. The solution in both cases is a plunge into the physical, but into an animal life that seems to be distinguished in Lawrence's mind from *mere* animal life because it is procreative, but not of offspring. "To procreate oneself" is a semantic double take, the only admissible object of "procreate" being some word signifying progeny; used to mean "create oneself," as he says subsequently, it is a compact version of the horse scene. Ursula has a procreative experience that results in her spiritual or psychological rebirth rather than her child's physical birth.

This idea of spiritual procreativity explains why Lawrence created an opposition between Ursula's self and her body in the end. He is not advocating a return to mindless physical being, primitive preconscious life; he wants us to know that it is possible to live in the body without being one with the divine. In fact, living entirely for the preservation of the body is the opposite of procreating oneself—in "Hardy," "begetting children" is opposed to self-preservation, as are "dancing and howling and sticking feathers in the hair." If Ursula were to marry Skrebensky, whom she no longer fears, who

44. Cambridge *Letters 2*, 298–99, tentatively dated March 1, 1915, the day before Lawrence declared himself finished with *The Rainbow* (which he then sent to the typist and subsequently revised by hand). The horse scene remained unrevised, and though he had written earlier versions of Ursula's story ("The Sisters" and "The Wedding Ring"), Lawrence apparently rewrote the entire story in this drafting, and he may well have written the short final chapter containing the horse scene on or about March 1, 1915.

is completely known, she would no longer have to risk herself, to fly the flag of herself at the extreme tip of life. Even pregnancy and birth do not necessarily open into the beyond: Ursula envisions her own motherhood as free of risk, "rich, peaceful, complete, with no beyond" (483). She thinks, "What was her flesh but for childbearing?" (485). But, like her mother, she must learn that bearing children "is not the woman's significance," though the act that begets children may be the means to bearing oneself.

The fine distinction between merely physical life and physical life opening into the beyond is one of Lawrence's major concerns in the third generation of *The Rainbow*. The distinction is made at least three times: in Ursula's miscarriage, in her rejection of Anthony Schofield, and in the transformations of Skrebensky's character, which make it possible for him to be seen as both an extreme sensualist, dangerous to the ordered world of man, and as a highly civilized builder of empire.

Anthony Schofield is an obvious foil (even in name) to Anton Skrebensky. Anthony is a farmer like the earliest Brangwens, but more clearly animal than they are: we are told repeatedly that he is like a goat and does things as an animal might. He is also like a satyr and a faun, nonhuman denizens of the animal world. He attracts Ursula sexually, but he is not frightening, as a lover opening into the beyond would be, and she has to refuse him because "he had no soul." She momentarily regrets that she has one, feeling lonely, but she realizes that she must travel onward, "seeking the goal that she knew she did draw nearer to" (416–17).

This goal will be her soul's realization and will be reached through experience in the body, yet Anthony "had no soul," even though "he was an isolated creature living in the fulfilment of his own senses." There must be a difference between animal sexuality and the leap off the cliff; Anthony clearly has no soul because he is too animal, not human enough. What is human is to see the landscape, be conscious of it as well as one with it, yet "he did not see it. He was one with it. But she saw it, and was one with it. Her seeing separated them infinitely" (416–17). The final adverb is carefully chosen. Ursula travels forward into conscious life, beyond her ancestors; therefore she cannot be herself and one with the infinite unless she sees. And the conscious life is lived in the civilized world, just as "the spoken world" exists far from the primitive physicality of the early days on Marsh farm (2).

That is why Anton Skrebensky attracts her, and the reason he appears to be the Son of God for whom Ursula is waiting is as important as why the appearance proves false. He is educated, traveled, even titled, a foreign aristocrat. He orients himself to the civilized world rather than the natural. Ursula's vision in the end is of the regeneration of all people; Skrebensky is only wrong in his conception of the problem and the solution. That is, he is wrong when he is consistent to the type of the sensual, egocentric social man. But when he comes back from Africa, he briefly understands, like Ursula in the end, the need to abolish present social structures and revere the beast within.

The horses, then, do indeed come to remind her of something she had with Skrebensky, and then lost. Even incidental details of the horse scene coincide with the passage in which they enter "the dark fields of immortality": in both scenes, there are roaring trees overhead, lights glimmering in the darkness, and "powerful, indomitable," nonhuman "presences" around—the great trees roaring, and the horses thundering by, both suggesting angels in the darkness. But what they remind her of is not male sexual potency. The difference between what the lovers experience in the dark love scenes and in the moonlit ones is not a difference in Skrebensky's potency; even late in the affair, their passion is "fierce, and extreme, and good" (471). There is indeed an "ordeal of proof" on Skrebensky in their final moonlit scene, but it is not ordinary sexual satisfaction that Ursula is trying to wrest from him. She wants to procreate herself. True, she once was fulfilled through sex with Skrebensky and is no longer. He is once again, as Lawrence said in "Hardy" of Alec d'Urberville, "in the strict though not the technical sense, impotent. . . . He was spiritually impotent in love" (*Phoenix* 489).

What Skrebensky has temporarily and then loses is not male but female: "He aroused no fruitful fecundity in her" (473), whereas once he had been "her mate, her complement, her sharer in fruition" (449). The moon has been a fertility symbol in every age, and that may be why it hangs over Ursula's unsatisfied desire when Skrebensky is spiritually barren. She longs for the moon rather than the man because the fecundity he once aroused in her is now removed from them and objectified in the sky.

But, ironically, he has left a deposit of physical fecundity in Ursula that seems to play a major role in her salvation. In "Hardy" the "Natural Law" that modern humanity has violated is not only female; Lawrence even called it "the great Law of the Womb" (482). Civilized humanity has tried to "overcome the Law in Love" (510), which means both to control the instincts with rational effort and to supplant the female part of oneself (the "Law") with the male (identified with "Love"). In doing so, "man" has "gone so far in his male conceit as to supersede the Creator, and win death as a reward" (*Phoenix* 488). Ursula and Skrebensky are both predominantly "male"—highly conscious, intellectual, educated—and they must be taught, as Ursula herself realizes earlier, that human consciousness is not the Creator. Ursula is saved while Skrebensky is lost because she is forced, in an obvious way, to recognize "the great Law of the Womb."

But Skrebensky, too, might have learned to rest in the vaster power, which is not yet "the overweening heart of the intrinsic male."[45] It will become that soon enough, in *Women in Love*, *The Captain's Doll*, and *The Fox*. But then Lawrence's definitions of "male" and "female" will have changed: those terms will simply denote the difference between the sexes, and Lawrence will advocate, not a balancing of these opposites in one being, but "polarisation," when "the man is pure

45. Sagar, "Third Generation," 67–68: "In the horses she must recognize what was not in Skrebensky to be recognized, 'the triumphant, flaming, overweening heart of the intrinsic male,' the potency of that life which is no part of her life, to which she must submit if she is ever to come into being."

man, the woman pure woman . . . each one free from any contamination of the other" (*Women in Love* 193). Maleness will have become for Lawrence an almost mystical force, and in his novels the energy of the cosmos will express itself through men's bodies more than women's. The horse that eventually appears in Lawrence's work is the stallion St. Mawr, though even he is more Pan than Priapus. In *Women in Love*, Gerald is metaphorically a stallion and the only actual horse is female, a delicate mare standing in for Gudrun, secretly relishing (according to Birkin) her subjection to the overweening Gerald (102–6, 132). In that novel, the fulfillment of women and horses is in "the last, perhaps highest, love-impulse: resign your will to the higher being" (132). But in *The Rainbow*, no one is expected to do that. In the end Ursula is the highest being in sight, a prophet vouchsafed a vision of the "living fabric of Truth" (495), waiting for a man not to lead her (or be led) but simply to match her closeness to the divine: "The man would come out of Eternity to which she herself belonged" (493).

3

The Snake's Place

In *The Rainbow*, self-realization is achieved through transcendent physical experience, usually sex between partners who fear each other as the unknown but break through their fear to a consummation that is associated with procreation, both of offspring and of the self. In the substantial philosophical essay Lawrence produced while writing *The Rainbow*, "the *via media* to being . . . is love, and love alone," and the sex act may produce children but is primarily for "leaping off into the unknown," the ego loss that allows one to bear one's new self (*Phoenix* 410, 441). In both the essay and the novel, this transcendent sexuality is distinguished from mere sensuality, which is based on ego gratification with a person who is known and not feared. Such sensual experience is destructive to self and others, because it is "spiritually impotent" and "barren." In both works the preconditions for rising above such barren experience include a new reverence for the body and the feelings (associated with "the female"), which modern humanity has undervalued in favor of mental and spiritual abstractions (associated with "the male"). Therefore *The Rainbow* celebrates the female, especially female reproductive power.

In *Women in Love*, however, self-realization is achieved through quite different means. There the transcendent experience is spiritual, based on a Taoist transcendence of desire, and its preconditions include the acceptance of corruption in the body as well as the discovery by the woman of a power in the male that seems to proceed from sources within him implicitly related to deathliness and corruption. In this novel the *via media* to being is not sex but stillness and an impersonal

bond based on recognition of the partner's unreachable otherness, whereas sex is treated as destructive of self and others. And in the version of "The Crown" Lawrence wrote
shortly before he began the major draftings of *Women in Love*,
"passion means the reacting of the sexes against one another
in a purely reducing activity" (CMS V, 3). Accordingly,
Women in Love presents active heterosexuality as a battle, as
regression into primitive or diabolic cruelty, and it treats female sexuality and procreative power as weapons in the battle
for dominance between the sexes.

In *Women in Love* and essays contemporaneous with it
(1916–19), Lawrence considered new forms of interpersonal
union that would create a wholeness of the self sufficient to
withstand modern pressures toward self-disintegration. The
usual approach to his work is to accept these proposals without examining all the components of the new relationships.
My next chapter will argue that they constitute the earliest
appearances of Lawrence's authoritarian politics and that
those politics seem to be a response to the threat of powerful
women and female sexuality as well as an acceptable means
of expressing desire for other men. In early unpublished versions of *Women in Love* and "The Crown," these fears and desires are treated openly, but in the final version of the novel
they have been transformed into essentially the same political
ideas he was then examining in nonfiction works. By 1918,
instead of arguing against sex, Lawrence was arguing for the
transcendence of desire and for female submission in passivity; instead of speaking about men who want only men rather
than women, as he did in the unpublished "Crown" and an
early version of the novel, he was arguing for a political "unison" of manhood based on love, tenderness, and the recognition of superiority in great men. That his heroic politics
have something to do with his new sexual ideas seems clear.
This chapter will examine the sexual developments, and
chapter 4 will show their intimate connection to his new political thought.

In *Women in Love*, fertility certainly lacks the positive significance that it has in *The Rainbow*. Only two characters, both

minor, are pregnant. In "A Chair," Birkin admires the ratlike youth who is being forced to marry his pregnant girlfriend, "instantly sympathising with the aloof, furtive youth, against the active, procreant female" (349). Minette/Pussum is also pregnant and finds the fact "beastly," but this reaction is not a measure of her decadence and distance from natural life. One of Halliday's West Pacific/African[1] figures is of a woman in labor, and Gerald "saw Minette in it. As in a dream, he knew her." She has "a terrible face . . . abstracted almost into meaninglessness by the weight of sensation beneath," and she represents a "culture in the . . . really ultimate *physical* consciousness, mindless, utterly sensual" (71–72). This mindless sensuality is later an important component of the African degeneracy, though Birkin logically enough seems to have a different statuette of Halliday's in mind then: the likeness of a woman in labor would hardly be the appropriate symbol of a supraphallic civilization. Such a statuette, nevertheless, is a product of that same chillingly corrupt culture, and childbirth is now a "totem" of corruption and reductive sensuality.

In the original "Crown," Lawrence reiterates in an apparently obsessive way the image of the present age as a dry, stiffened, exhausted, inflexible womb, unable to bring forth the creatures incarcerated within. The uterus is identified with the insect shell around the egocentric self, "this sack of nullity, this withered womb wherein we are enclosed . . . wherein the flux of corruption boils hotly and in supreme gratification" (CMS IV, 15–16). He also observes of the wounded soldier that "the strange abstraction of horror and death was so perfect in his face, like the horror of birth on a new-born infant" (CMS V, 9). And he comes close to declaring, as Birkin does in *Women in Love*, that "the destructive creation" is "all our reality nowadays" (164): in the original

---

1. Lawrence patchily changed the location of the corrupt culture to "West Pacific" only after the first American edition (1920) and only because of Heseltine's threatened libel suit. See Robert Chamberlain, "Pussum, Minette, and the Afro-Nordic Symbol in *Women in Love*," *PMLA* 78 (September 1963): 407–16.

"Crown" manuscript he first wrote, "All birth comes from the reduction of old tissue," then changed the "from" to "with," and left the more daring statement to Birkin (CMS V, 15).

Birkin shares Lawrence's new horror of birth: he accuses Ursula of considering herself "the perfect womb, the bath of birth" and calls her "horrible" for it (301). This repugnance surely explains Birkin's controversial stoning of an ancient fertility symbol in "Moony"; he curses "Cybele" and "Syria Dea," both fertility goddesses, while trying to obliterate the moon's reflection on the pond (238). Elsewhere, he castigates womankind for wanting to be the "Magna Mater" or "Great Mother," ostensibly because the pride of creation gives woman "the unthinkable overweening assumption of primacy." The "Mater Dolorosa" pretends to be subservient but actually claims "with horrible, insidious arrogance and female tyranny, her own again. . . . she bound her son with chains, she held him her everlasting prisoner." This mother wants "to have, to own, to control, to be dominant"—not only in relation to her own son, but to all men (192). Drawing an implicit analogy between the mother's desire to own or reabsorb her son and all women's sexual behavior, Birkin denounces "Woman, the Great Mother" because she "was always so horrible and clutching, she had such a lust for possession, a greed of self-importance in love." Because of woman's sexual greed, "the merging, the clutching, the mingling of love was become madly abhorrent to him" and "he hated sex" (191–92).

Such desires do not afflict the mothers of *The Rainbow*. There the central female characters are extremely powerful, perhaps alarmingly so, yet the struggle for marital peace is rarely described in terms of dominance or submission. In each generation the men want more attention than the women are willing to give, Lydia because of her present pregnancy and grief over the past, Anna because of her delight in homemaking and motherhood, Ursula because of her narcissism. But in every case it is the man who has to make an adjustment before the couple is fulfilled: Tom has to push through his fear of merging with Lydia, Will has to become more independent and separate, Skrebensky must relinquish his identification with social ideals and act on his own desires. Until they make these adjustments, the woman may seem to have control (Anna momentarily regrets the loss of "her old, established supremacy" 231–32), but only because she is more self-sufficient and needs less than the man. As the last chapter argued, both parties must learn to submit to something greater than the will of either, which, if anything, expresses itself more in the woman than the man. This dynamic is affirmed in letters Lawrence wrote while working on *The Rainbow*: "I think *the* one thing to do, is for men to have courage to draw nearer to women, expose themselves to them, and be altered by them: and for women to accept and admit men."[2] If anyone is doing any submitting here it is the man, as another letter suggests: "There is no getting of a vision . . . before we get our souls fertilised by the *female* . . . (not necessarily woman but most obviously woman). . . . Then the vision we're after . . . contains awe and dread and submission" to "the tremendous unknown forces of life."[3]

Of course, Ursula is horrible and clutching in her sexual greed in several scenes near the end of *The Rainbow*. But, as was previously argued, even though she is made into a harpy because of it, the error is not so much hers as Skrebensky's— and what he has failed to do is to remain spiritually fecund, a participant in the immortal sexuality that is associated with "the great Law of the Womb." Even though Ursula may be expressing a "greed of self-importance" in the moonlit love scenes, she does so not because woman's potential motherhood gives her the assumption of primacy but because she wants to participate in the mystery of creation and self-creation. In *The Rainbow* not motherhood but sterility, barrenness for both sexes (caused by the male's "spiritual impotence" in the affair between Ursula and Skrebensky), provokes wom-

2. Cambridge *Letters* 2, 181.
3. Ibid., 218.

an's "horrible and clutching" sexuality; female sexuality itself is not so characterized. It is, rather, a power that can fertilize the soul and put one in touch with "the tremendous un-known forces of life," which can be dangerous if resisted: the letter quoted earlier describes those forces as "driving us, forcing us, destroying us if we do not submit to be swept away." Skrebensky's intermittent refusal to submit to them may well explain his destruction in the moonlit scenes.

But in *Women in Love* the hero rejects all female sexuality and does so, he says, because of woman's motherhood and her consequent assumption of primacy. The negative female behavior may be the same in the two novels, but the explana-tions of it are opposed, and, consequently, so are its mean-ings. After making love to Ursula for the first time, Birkin thinks, "he would rather not live than accept the love she proffered. . . . He wanted something clearer, more open, cooler, as it were. The hot narrow intimacy between man and wife was abhorrent." He notes that "he believed in sex mar-riage," and merely wants sex "to revert to the level of the other appetites, to be regarded as a functional process, not as a fulfilment." But his hatred of it is apparent in the tone of such statements as "woman was always so horrible and clutching . . . in love" (191–92).

Though Birkin uses the word "love" in this context, the language in which he denounces it is evocative of sex (clutch-ing, hot, merging), and Lawrence often uses "love" to refer to sex, as in "Study of Thomas Hardy," in which he declares: "In love, a man, a woman flows on to the very furthest edge of known feeling, being, and out beyond the furthest edge: and taking the superb and supreme risk, deposits a security of life in the womb" (*Phoenix* 441). Even in letters he often preferred this term as a reference to sex; the meaning is clear, for in-stance, when he says that a publisher "wants the love pas-sages ton[ed] down in the novel."[4]

4. Ibid., 246.

Birkin's position is clearly a reversal of Lawrence's in "Hardy." There Lawrence laments that sex is usually only on the level of the other appetites, "only functional, a matter of relief or sensation, equivalent to eating or drinking or passing of excrement," whereas ideally a woman possesses a man's soul in sex and "procreates it and makes it big with new idea, motion" (*Phoenix* 445). And whereas Lawrence in "Hardy" sees sex as a process that separates male and female elements in an individual temporarily, the goal of the process is to make of the couple "the surpassing One," a unity (*Phoenix* 468); the most vital individuals unify both male and female in themselves. He sees Shelley as a completely male being, who, because of this denial of the female in himself, "never lived. He transcended life. But we do not want to transcend life, since we are of life." Therefore "must each body pertain both to the male and the female" (*Phoenix* 459).

Birkin, on the other hand, announces that sex produces a permanent separation of male and female elements, and that the process is now drawing to a close. Now the ideal is to be purely male or purely female, and once that purity is achieved, sex will no longer be necessary:

> We are not broken fragments of one whole. Rather we are the singling away into purity and clear being, of things that were mixed. Rather the sex is that which remains in us of the mixed, the unresolved. And passion is the further separating of this mixture, that which is manly being taken into the being of the man, that which is womanly passing to the woman, till the two are clear and whole as angels, the admixture of sex in the highest sense surpassed, leaving two single beings constellated like two stars. . . . There is now to come the new day, when we are beings each of us, fulfilled in difference. The man is pure man, the woman pure woman, they are perfectly polarised. But there is no longer any of the horrible merging, mingling self-abnegation of love.
>
> (192–93)

The novelty of this idea in Lawrence's work is clear. In "Hardy" he argues that the union of man and woman is the goal of life: a man "must know that he is half, and the woman is the other half. . . . they are two-in-one" (*Phoenix* 515). He sees the separation of male and female as a condition of earthly imperfection, which may be rectified in eternity. In life, the nearest approach to the infinite is the fusion of male and female, both in the individual and between man and woman (*Phoenix* 443–44).

It might be possible to argue that Birkin's antisexual ideal is not shared by his author and represents merely a phase in Birkin's spiritual illness, were it not for the novel's nearly consistent association of heterosexuality with destruction. In the only dramatized instance of sex between Birkin and Ursula, it is her idea, and it happens over his objections. He wants to be still and peaceful with her, but she inflames him, not understanding what he wants: "'Not this, not this,' he whimpered to himself, as the first perfect mood of softness and sleep-loveliness ebbed back away." He feels desire and takes her, but the desire is violently described ("inevitable as death, beyond question"), results in his being "satisfied and shattered, fulfilled and destroyed," and cannot entirely silence "an unyielding anguish of another thing . . . a small lament in the darkness." Though immediately afterwards Birkin feels it to be an "ultimate and triumphant experience . . . like a new spell of life. . . . yet somewhere far off and small, the other hovered" (179–80).

Most significant, the reversion from this temporary sexuality is violent. Birkin is ill for weeks afterwards, "in pure opposition to everything," especially to love and sex; his meditations on the new antisexual ideal occur during this illness. At the same time Ursula is suddenly suicidal. "Her passion seemed to bleed to death," and she muses for pages on the beauty, the joy, the cleanliness of death, sounding very much like Lawrence's letters to Forster: "How beautiful, how grand and perfect death was, how good to look forward to," she thinks, while sinking into "the unutterable anguish of dissolution, the only anguish that is too much, the far-off awful nausea of dissolution set in within the body" (183–85). When Birkin comes to call the evening after their first lovemaking, they quarrel coldly and part, after which she hates him with a hatred that is "pure and gem-like" (190). No explanation is offered for any of this, and the sequence of events suggests that sex is destructive, that the morning-after reaction includes physical and mental dissolution and division between lovers.

When next they meet, some months later, Ursula still wants to give in to "the old destructive fires," but Birkin "too had his idea and his will. He wanted only gentle communion, no other, no passion now." When she tries to interest him sexually, he says to her, "But we'll be still, shall we?" He tells her that he hates "ecstasy, Dionysic or any other kind. It's like going round in a squirrel cage." Like a Buddhist ascetic denouncing the repetitious nature of desire, Lawrence reports that it is bliss for Birkin "not to have any thoughts or any desires or any will. . . . To be content in bliss, without desire or insistence anywhere, this was heaven: to be together in happy stillness" (243–45).

Eventually he convinces Ursula of the benefits of "paradisal" asexuality. In "Excurse," when she feels "a new heaven round her," she "wished he were passionate, because in passion she was at home. But this was so still and frail, as space is more frightening than force" (303). But soon afterwards, in the tearoom scene, her conversion is complete: "she had learned at last to be still and perfect," and when she cries "I'm so glad!" it is with "a queer little crowing sound of triumph" and "unspeakable relief" (307).

Their new relationship seems to allow them to indulge in sex later in the novel, but initially it has to be excluded in order for them to accomplish their union. And when other lovers in the novel persist in giving in to passion, the terms of its description are consistent with Birkin's view of "the old destructive fires." Minette/Pussum appeals to Gerald because "he would be able to destroy her utterly in the strength of his discharge" (57–58). The morning after he sleeps with her, she has the "inchoate look of a violated slave, whose fulfilment lies in her further and further violation" (72), and the fact of her previous sexual connection with Halliday is evoked as "an unfathomable hell of knowledge" when she looks at him (58).

When Gerald and Gudrun first make love, "the terrible frictional violence of death filled her, and she received it in an ecstasy of subjection, in throes of acute, violent sensation." The language suggests that sex itself is destructive, both here and in a later lovemaking between them:

> Like a child at the breast, he cleaved intensely to her, and she could not put him away. And his seared, ruined membrane relaxed, softened, that which was seared and stiff and blasted yielded again, became soft and flexible, palpitating with new life.
>
> (338)

> So at last he was given again, warm and flexible. He turned and gathered her in his arms. And feeling her soft against him, so perfectly and wondrously soft and recipient, his arms tightened on her. She was as if crushed, powerless in him. His brain seemed hard and invincible now like a jewel, there was no resisting him.
>
> His passion was awful to her, tense and ghastly, and impersonal, like a destruction, ultimate. She felt it would kill her. She was being killed.
>
> (435)

In these passages softness and flexibility are good; hardness, stiffness, or tension, hurtful. Though Lawrence identifies Gerald's desire for sex with the infant's cleaving to the breast, these passages indicate, as Howe argues, that the novel exalts what sounds like infant-mother love while seeming to condemn genital sexuality.[5]

The novel finally implies, as Howe also suggests, that Gerald is destroyed by persisting in his heterosexuality. Toward the end of his life he describes his sex with Gudrun as follows: "it's blasting . . . it is a great experience, something final—and then—you're shrivelled as if struck by electricity."

---

5. Marguerite Beede Howe, *The Art of the Self in D. H. Lawrence* (Athens, Ohio: Ohio University Press, 1977), 52–78.

Because of this, he says, "I hate her somewhere" and "it's not finished" (431). When he plans to "do away with her . . . he trembled delicately in every limb, in anticipation, as he trembled in his most violent accesses of passionate approach to her, trembling with too much desire" (438–39). The association of sexual and murderous lust culminates in his attempt to strangle her: he reaches "at last to take the apple of his desire," and her "struggling was her reciprocal lustful passion in this embrace . . . till the zenith was reached . . . her movement became softer, appeased." Gerald walks away from this "God-given gratification," this sexual near-murder, to his own death (463).

As Howe has argued, the alternative to murderous sexuality offered by this novel seems to be an imitation of natal-family bonding. Birkin wants Ursula to be committed to him forever, but he does not want to woo her or have sex with her for most of the novel. Since, like all couples in Lawrence's fiction, they are incomplete as people until they experience self-realization together, another experience must take the place of the sexual consummations in *The Rainbow*. In *Women in Love*, the self-realizing experience seems to be comprised of the two developments in "Excurse" that were briefly discussed in chapter 1: Ursula's discovery of a superhuman, ultraphallic power in Birkin's buttocks, and the anal caress. The former is what teaches Ursula to be "still and perfect" and the latter, which occurs in Sherwood Forest after the tearoom scene, creates the "star balance" Birkin desires, the permanent bond in unbridgeable separation.

The consummation in Sherwood Forest may be, and often is, mistaken by readers for sex. Lawrence does say, "She had her desire fulfilled. He had his desire fulfilled" (312). What both now apparently desire, however, is not sex. At this point in the novel, Birkin still seems to denounce sex virulently: "Fusion, fusion, this horrible fusion of two beings, which every woman and most men insisted on, was it not nauseous and horrible anyhow, whether it was a fusion of the spirit or of the emotional body?" He rejects what he considers to be

Ursula's view, that "all men must come" to "the bath of birth" represented by her "perfect womb" (301). At the same time he is impatiently waiting for her to take of him "the dark knowledge" that he has taken of her:

> He had taken her at the roots of her darkness and shame—like a demon, laughing over the fountain of mystic corruption which was one of the sources of her being, laughing, shrugging, accepting, accepting finally. As for her, when would she so much go beyond herself as to accept him at the quick of death?
>
> (296)

And immediately before they have their "desire fulfilled," Ursula's desire is apparently to touch him in that way:

> To touch, mindlessly in darkness to come in pure touching upon the living reality of him, his suave perfect loins and thighs of darkness, this was her sustaining anticipation.
> And he too waited in the magical steadfastness of suspense for her to take this knowledge of him as he had taken it of her. He knew her darkly, with the fullness of dark knowledge. Now she would know him, and he too would be liberated.
>
> (311)

Because Ursula will be able "to take this knowledge of him as he had taken it of her," his "taking her" in the first passage does not seem to refer to sodomy. The first passage more clearly refers to the anus, and the second mentions loins and thighs instead. But Birkin's desire is the same in both passages; he wants her to return a touch he has given her, a touch that conveys "dark knowledge," and she does so just after the second passage ("she had her desire of him, she touched" 312). The coincidence of imagery implies that loins and thighs are metonymically associated with the "fountain of corruption," as they seem to be in the tearoom scene, where the buttocks ("the smitten rock of the man's body") are equated with "the strange marvellous flanks and thighs," and all together are the "strange fountains of his body" from which come "floods of ineffable darkness and ineffable riches" (306).

These floods are also electrical, "a new current of passional electric energy" that comes from "the darkest poles of his body" (305–6), and as such they evoke the electrical map of the body's power centers that Lawrence developed fully in *Fantasia of the Unconscious* (1922). There the lower posterior nerve center is associated with personal independence and with power. As we shall see in the next chapter, the original formulation of these ideas appears in his early essays on American literature, which are contemporaneous with this passage in "Excurse"; there, however, the lower power centers are situated not in nerve ganglia but in the bowels. And, as discussed earlier, the power Ursula discovers is linked imagistically with the fecal sensuality of the African process: both are dark, fluid, associated with Egypt or Africa, and "beyond the phallic." The images of strange flooding fountains of darkness and dark knowledge surely evoke the body's dark river of dissolution, the "fountain of mystic corruption" in the passage just quoted.

The reason Birkin apparently wants her to accept and laugh over his excretory function is that it will finally get them off "the emotional personal level" on which Ursula still wants to dwell, the level that includes love, desire, admiration for each other's qualities, all the things Ursula wants throughout most of the novel while Birkin wants an impersonal conjunction. "There is a real impersonal me, that is beyond love," Birkin tells Ursula, "an isolated me, that does *not* meet and mingle. . . . [and] it is there I would want to meet you" (137). They get the "star balance" only after the anal caress: "Now she would know him, and he too would be liberated. . . . They would give each other this star-equilibrium which alone is freedom" (311). The anal caress inaugurates the unbridgeable separation apparently because it is "a palpable revelation of living otherness" (312).

The source of this odd idea may lie in civilized humanity's alienation from excrement. We do not identify even with our own anuses (one of our most common obscene insults accuses the insulted of being one), and they are not usually included in the adorable parts of the beloved; we object to the fact that "Love has pitched his mansion in / The place of excrement."[6] Norman O. Brown argues that Swift antici- pated Freud in recognizing the irrationality of "the notion that there is some absolute contradiction between the state of be- ing in love and an awareness of the excremental function of the beloved."[7] In 1929, Lawrence recognized the problem in Swift while assuming that Swift did not understand it ("He couldn't even see how much worse it would be if Celia didn't shit")[8] and without recognizing that his own work, especially *Women in Love*, tended to uphold this same contradiction.

The poem "Manifesto" was written at Zennor, where Law- rence lived while writing and initially while revising *Women in Love*. In that poem, as in "Excurse," discovery of the excre- tory function in the beloved leads to recognition that hus- band and wife are separate people, not one, not mixed and merged:

VII
I want her, though, to take the same from me.
She touches me as if I were herself, her own.
She has not realised yet, that fearful thing, that I am the other,
she thinks we are all of one piece.
It is painfully untrue.
I want her to touch me at last, ah, on the root and quick of my darkness
and perish on me, as I have perished on her.

Then, we shall be two and distinct, we shall have each our separate being.
And that will be pure existence, real liberty.
Till then, we are confused, a mixture, unresolved, unextri- cated one from the other.
It is in pure, unutterable resolvedness, distinction of being, that one is free,

6. W. B. Yeats, "Crazy Jane Talks with the Bishop," *The Collected Poems of W. B. Yeats* (New York: Macmillan, 1956), 254–55.

7. Norman O. Brown, "The Excremental Vision," in his *Life Against Death: The Psychoanalytic Meaning of History* (New York: Random House, 1959), 186– 87.

8. D. H. Lawrence, "Introduction to *Pansies*," in his *Sex, Literature and Censorship*, ed. H. T. Moore (New York: Viking, 1953), 56–57.

not in mixing, merging, not in similarity.
When she has put her hand on my secret, darkest sources,
    the darkest outgoings,
when it has struck home to her, like a death, "this is *him*!"
she has no part in it, no part whatever,
it is the terrible *other*,
when she knows the fearful *other flesh*, ah, darkness unfath-
    omable and fearful, contiguous and concrete,
when she is slain against me, and lies in a heap like one out-
    side the house,
when she passes away as I have passed away,
being pressed up against the *other*,
then I shall be glad, I shall not be confused with her,
I shall be cleared, distinct, single as if burnished in silver,
having no adherence, no adhesion anywhere,
one clear, burnished, isolated being, unique,
and she also, pure, isolated, complete,
two of us, unutterably distinguished, and in unutterable
    conjunction.

Then we shall be free, freer than angels, ah, perfect.[9]

This poem distinguishes the anal caress from the sodomy it is
sometimes confused with, since the point seems to be the
discovery of a vital function that excludes the other body entirely—neither body penetrates the other, and they remain
separate. Here, as in "Excurse," this touch gets the credit for
creating the "unutterable conjunction," "this star-equilibrium
which alone is freedom," based as it is on a recognition of
separateness. Again, as in the novel, the speaker is waiting
for her to touch him, and the phrase "the darkest outgoings"
makes *where* reasonably clear.

Two short passages in "Continental" imply, surprisingly,
that once they have achieved their equilibrium, all things are
possible for Birkin and Ursula, including sex. In the first of
these instances, Birkin approaches Ursula with evident lust:
he will not speak but stares at her with "remorseless suggestivity," apparently trying to hypnotize her with his eyes. The

9. D. H. Lawrence, "Manifesto," *The Complete Poems of D. H. Lawrence*, ed. Vivian de Sola Pinto and F. Warren Roberts (New York: Viking, 1964), 266–67.

result is one of Knight's instances of sodomy, and Ursula, while wincing to remember it, exults as well: "She was free, when she knew everything, and no dark shameful things were denied her" (403).

Birkin obviously thinks he is doing something wrong here, playing with something sinister; his suggestivity is mocking, his eyelids "drooped with a faint motion of satiric contempt." This liberation through conscious indulgence in sin seems to present us with one of the novel's Romantic paradoxes: sex is destructive, but one needs to incorporate all the destructive things to be free. It might also be argued that sodomy is a special kind of sex and that, for Birkin, ordinary sexual relations are destructive, since they cause merging and mingling, as well as possible procreation and birth, while sodomy is nonreproductive and awareness of the excretory function keeps sodomy sufficiently impersonal that no merging occurs.

The antisexual theme is suddenly undercut, however, in a short, undramatized passage near the end of the novel that seems to attribute quite ordinary sexual relations to the newlyweds. Birkin is saddened because "she could not be herself, she *dared* not come forth quite nakedly to his nakedness, abandoning all adjustment, lapsing in pure faith with him. . . . they were never *quite* together, at the same moment, one was always a little left out" (426). This idea of "abandoning all adjustment, lapsing in pure faith" sounds like a version of a theme developed in *Lady Chatterley's Lover*: in that novel the woman is rewarded with a deeper satisfaction than she has ever known only when she relinquishes control of the sex act, asking for nothing, letting the man "work the business."[10] As Millett has argued, the central issue of that novel seems to be female submission to male dominance even while sex is being elaborately affirmed. It is, however, pointedly male-oriented sex that is endorsed (sodomy, which is not intended for female satisfaction, gets the highest affirmation),

10. D. H. Lawrence, *Lady Chatterley's Lover* (Florence, 1928; rpt. New York: Grove Press, 1957), 261.

and Connie's education in submission is based on her learning sexual passivity. Lawrence, like Freud, believed that the female sexual passivity endorsed by his culture actually represented a woman's biological maturity; both assumed that such passivity resulted in an orgasm different in kind from that produced by a woman's own exertions (an idea that recent research, has, of course, shown to be untrue). For Freud, this mature orgasm is vaginal (as opposed to the immature clitoral one) and results from a passive, even masochistic acceptance of male activity by the woman; for Lawrence, it is not consciously experienced by the woman and is sparked by the male orgasm.[11]

The passages from "Continental" quoted earlier seem to represent an early appearance of these ideas in Lawrence's work. Birkin initiates the sodomy on an evening when Ursula has temporarily slipped away from her submersion in him: while singing for a crowd at the hotel, she feels "full of a conceit of emotion and power, working upon all those people, and upon herself" (397). And when he makes his lustful approach, "Ursula was frightened of him, and fascinated." She wants to repel him but decides instead to submit, in spite of herself: "before the resolution had formed she had submitted again, yielded to her fear." In fact "she wanted to submit, she wanted to know," and she "gave way," let him "do as he would" (402–3). Here, as in the later novel, a woman's sexual submission frees her, and she is glad to have yielded to the man against her own wishes.

In the second passage, Birkin reflects on their sexual life after Ursula offers him a hard kiss, with her lips "gripped." He regrets that "she could not let go a certain hold over herself"; she either "abandoned herself to *him*, or she took hold of him and gathered her joy of him," striving for her own orgasm the way Bertha Coutts does with Mellors and Connie learns not to. Birkin's wish that she abandon "all adjustment, lapsing in pure faith with him . . . quite together, at the same

---

11. For a related but slightly different reading of this theme in Lawrence's work, see Kate Millett, *Sexual Politics* (New York: Doubleday, 1970), 237–93.

moment" suggests that he expects Ursula eventually to learn the new, apocryphal orgasm attributed to Connie in the later novel. Birkin's "stillness" now is apparently waiting for this development in her: "he was still and soft and patient, for the time" (426–27).

Lawrence's later works storm against the sexual demands of women who are assertive or who have "sex in the head." Although he occasionally notes that in men, too, "the passions or desires which are thought-born are deadly," he says plainly that "it is much more true for women," ostensibly because it perverts their "natural emotional positivity," which is yielding, passive, submissive. Ideally a woman does not assert herself sexually: "The real desirable wife-spirit . . . the quiescent, flowering love of a mature woman" manifests itself in "sexually asking nothing, asking nothing of the beloved, save that he shall be himself, and that for his living he shall accept the gift of her love." But Lawrence makes clear that in his experience modern women are not sexually submissive: "At the very *âge dangereuse*, when a woman should be accomplishing her own fulfilment into maturity and rich quiescence, she turns rabidly to seek a new lover." Instead of quiescence, she asks "for more excitements." The solution is for the husband "to withdraw into his own stillness and singleness, and put the wife under the spell of his fulfilled decision" (as Birkin does Ursula); otherwise, "the unhappy woman beats about for her insatiable satisfaction, seeking whom she may devour." Like Gudrun, such a woman, unrestrained, will be not only unfaithful, but lethal: "Ultimately, she tears him to bits."[12]

In *Women in Love* and the later works, sexual quiescence must be taught to women by men, and it is contrary to what they initially want. The necessity of their instruction and submission is a reversal of the precondition for sexual fulfillment in *The Rainbow*, but it bears a significant resemblance to a theme

12. D. H. Lawrence, *Psychoanalysis and the Unconscious/Fantasia of the Unconscious* (New York: Viking, 1960), 121, 132–35, 156–59.

in Lawrence's earlier fiction. One of the constants in his work is the rejection of what modern life has done to women. In *The Rainbow*, an overly mental modern woman destroys a man in sex while trying to achieve the regenerative consummation she had with him earlier, which did not require her to be passive ("She had taken him, they had been together" 451). In *Women in Love*, overly mental modern women enjoy sex and need to be taught to accept nonsexual sensuality (and sex that is not conducive to female satisfaction). Conscious modern womanhood is equally destructive in Lawrence's earlier fiction; but in all novels and stories before the Brangwen-saga, such women destroy men in their *refusal* to have sex.

In *Sons and Lovers*, Miriam's nunlike chastity blights Paul's young life, and he is revived by Clara's robust sexual response. When a moon rises over a beach in that novel, it inflames the man rather than the woman, and her shrinking "in her convulsed, coiled torture" from the thought of sex "prevented even their first love-kiss." Later "she lay to be sacrificed for him because she loved him so much," but her obvious lack of desire makes the experience deathly: "Why did the thought of death, the after-life, seem so sweet and consoling?" Paul wonders afterwards.[13]

The Trespasser (1912) and the early story "Witch à la Mode" concern similar destruction of males by sexless women, in whom "passion exhausts itself at the mouth."[14] And in Lawrence's first novel, *The White Peacock* (1911), the gamekeeper's former wife, Lady Crystabel, rejects childbearing and, therefore, sex with her husband; because of this denial of his body, she is compared to a peacock defecating on the statue of an angel. She is "a woman to the end . . . all vanity and screech and defilement."[15] Hilary Simpson analyzes the appearance of the "'dreaming,' 'spiritual' or 'Pre-Raphaelite' woman" in

13. D. H. Lawrence, *Sons and Lovers* (1913; rpt. New York: Penguin, 1976), 290.
14. D. H. Lawrence, *The Trespasser* (1912; rpt. Cambridge: Cambridge University Press, 1981), 64.
15. D. H. Lawrence, *The White Peacock* (1911; rpt. Carbondale: Southern Illinois University Press, 1966), 92.

Lawrence's early work. In discussing Lady Crystabel, Simpson supplies the helpful information that the "manuscript version of the novel is more explicit about the peacock image; a woman defiles the 'angel' in a man by refusing to recognise his sexual need."[16]

Simpson traces the image of this spiritual woman only as far as Hermione in the "Prologue" to *Women in Love,* and for good reason. No such asexual women appear in Lawrence's later works, and in the final version of *Women in Love* even Hermione is revoltingly libidinous, like most of the other grown female characters: she watches her "naked animal actions in mirrors" (36), Minette seeks defilement as a sexual slave, Gudrun plans to reap "unthinkable subtleties of sensation" (443) before she dies. The next gamekeeper's ex-wife (Bertha Coutts in *Lady Chatterley's Lover*) will also defile and endanger men, but not because she refuses to have sex; rather because she demands to be sexually satisfied. The later characters are more clearly "New Women" than Pre-Raphaelite dreamers, and their succession to the position of representing destructive modern womanhood in Lawrence's work is dramatic and significant. The earlier image implies that female desire is a good too often denied to men, the later one that it is an evil often forced upon them.

The reversal in Lawrence's feelings about women and sexuality is also evident in the difference between what we know of the earliest drafts and the final version of *Women in Love.* Two fragments survive of the earliest versions of "The Sisters," apparently written in 1913. One includes a scene between Birkin and Ursula, who was then called Ella. The second contains the confrontation scene between Gerald, Loerke, and Gudrun (in her lodgings in Beldover) and is apparently from near the end of that draft. Both fragments concern rather conventional romantic difficulties: Ella is incompletely healed from her earlier love affair (with Ben Templeman, the Anton Skrebensky of this version, which covered

---

16. Hilary Simpson, *D. H. Lawrence and Feminism* (De Kalb: Northern Illinois University Press, 1982), 46, 52.

the events of the last generation in *The Rainbow* as well as the material of *Women in Love*), and she finds Birkin's approach a trifle cool and unromantic. Gerald has been toying with Gudrun and realizes almost too late that he loves her, by which time Loerke has arrived from Germany to marry her, since she is pregnant with Gerald's child. The scenes are realistically presented, closer to the mode of *Sons and Lovers* than to the intensely symbolic dramatization of *The Rainbow* and *Women in Love*. And, apart from the fact that most of them have evidently had premarital sex, the characters seem quite conventional, with no bohemian touches and no demonic desires; they are all rather drawing-room proper, and even Loerke behaves and is treated like "a decent fellow," as Gerald calls him.[17]

Most to the point here, in this earliest version Birkin desires Ella sexually, and that urge is not associated with destructive fires; Birkin's desire is merely too strong for her at first. In one of the surviving scenes, he calls to find her alone and touches her, apparently for the first time. She feels he is "strange" and "cold," perhaps because he does not speak but simply holds her "tight, hard, compressing her. . . . the quivering man stiffened with desire was strange and horrible to her." She tries to leave the room, but collapses in agony, "crying like some wild animal in pain," until she overcomes the grief. When Birkin recovers from the shock of watching her, he stammers out that he loves her, and then they are interrupted by Gudrun's return.

Alone with Gudrun, Ella tells her, "He proposed to me." Two days later she and Gudrun leave to join the rest of the family at the seaside, and Ella writes to Birkin in the train, explaining that "it takes us a long time to get rid of the old things." She says, "I love you," in a rather buried way: "In a way I love you because I can make a fool of myself before you, and you don't mind." The reply Birkin sends her she finds

17. The holograph fragments of "The Sisters" (1913), numbered 291–96 and 373–80, are in the Humanities Research Center, the University of Texas at Austin.

"queer and abstract . . . as if he stated his love in algebraic terms." Then Gudrun and Ella see Ben Templeman as they walk on a rock causeway and Ella realizes "he had still power over her: he was still Man to her."

In this version of the Birkin-Ursula story, male love and desire encounter female reticence, which is based here not on prudery or overrefined spirituality but on an old wound; Birkin, too, admits: "my own feelings are always so mixed, and I can never get them straight." He writes to her that "everything has come toppling down, like an earthquake, since I have known you," and he plans to come to her in a few days. And though she is still in Templeman's power, she realizes that "her fate was bringing her closer and closer into connection" with Birkin.

The romantic seriousness of Birkin and Ella is apparently what has been missing from the story's other love plot. Gerald realizes that he wants to marry Gudrun only when Loerke has arrived to do so himself; as they confront each other, Gudrun says to Gerald, "You pretend *now* you want to marry me—" and "you have treated me like the cheapest thing." When pressed for the motive of his change of heart—"You trust to your position to play with her," Loerke says—Gerald "flung up his face blindly, crying stubborn with misery: 'I didn't know.'" Loerke then leaves, and though Gudrun continues to resist him mistrustfully, Gerald discovers the "complete tenderness of love" in comforting her: "he had got something he pretended to disbelieve in. . . . he knew this was his life's fulfilment."

Some bitterness lingers, and the terms in which it is expressed bear an ironic relation to the published novel: "Sometimes I could have strangled you as you lay asleep," Gudrun says, remembering how she felt going away with him when he didn't love her. And Gerald, hearing her, realizes that "something in her had shut up, or had gone frozen, during that time, and was now unresponsive to him." But "he would get it all right" by submitting "to suffering. In his new conversion, he had almost a passion for submission. . . . But he would never submit to fail in getting her love."

Though Gudrun clearly has resorted to taking another lover, she seems to be entirely a victim in this scene, a loving woman mistreated by a playboy who happily experiences a last-minute conversion to love. As mentioned in the last chapter, Gerald is uneasy with her feeling for the child but recognizes that he has made it his rival for her affections: he asks if she "thought only of the child" when she discovered her pregnancy, and she answers, "When I saw how you were. . . . I do love you. . . . But you killed a lot of it." He sees that "she came to him as the father of her child, not as to a lover, a husband" and regrets that "he had had a chance, and lost it. He had been a fool. . . . it hurt that she did not seem to want him very much." But the fragment, which must be nearly if not the very last scene of their story,[18] ends with Gudrun murmuring, as so many of Lawrence's heroines do, "My love!"

As far as one can tell from these fragments, in the early versions of what would be *Women in Love*, males might feel more desire than women and might treat them unkindly or be unloved by them, but procreative sexual love itself is a tender fulfillment. Such it always is, in fact, in Lawrence's early works, including *The Rainbow*, so long as both lovers give themselves up to it.

In *Women in Love*, on the other hand, it is nearly true, as Howe argues, that "sex literally annihilates being." Howe thinks this change represents a refinement of Lawrence's ego psychology, his series of recommendations designed to protect the weak ego from destruction either through merging with another or through isolation. She argues that, in this novel, sex "is corrupt because it is a separation from primal unity," which can only be achieved in Birkin and Ursula's imitation of infant-mother love. According to Howe, Birkin requires a permanent union with a man also, because Ursula's being is subsumed in "star balance" and Birkin then has no one to assert himself against, which is also a requirement of whole being.

18. See chapter 2, n. 42.

This reading may attest to Lawrence's affinities with existential psychology, but it cannot explain the sudden appearance of these new ideas in his work. For one thing, *Blutbrüderschaft* (blood brotherhood) is a requirement of Birkin's from the start, well before Ursula's capitulation: "the problem of love and eternal conjunction between two men," he realizes in "Man to Man" (long before "Excurse"), "had been a necessity inside himself all his life" (198). This necessity is an absolute in the novel, not dependent on the state of Birkin's ego, and as such it is certainly a new idea in Lawrence's work.

Howe sees Lawrence's sudden advocacy of blood brotherhood as an attempt to rehabilitate maleness in a form acceptable to a matriarchal culture. Lawrence came from a mother-dominated family and was therefore, in Howe's view, subject to feelings of "oedipal guilt": "In this situation the only permissible sexuality is feminine. Hence *The Rainbow* brims with life because the first principle is the divine feminine, and that is an acceptable form of sexuality. *Women in Love* is primarily about heterosexuality, and is consequently full of retributive death."[19] This analysis is illogical on its own grounds because all healthy sex is heterosexual in *The Rainbow* (and an all-female sexual relationship is seen as destructive). It also ignores the negative charge suddenly given to female sexuality, procreation, and birth in *Women in Love*, as well as the sudden emergence of anal eroticism as a necessity of wholeness. A more logical conclusion would be that, for some reason during the interval between the two books, Lawrence began to view sex with women as destructive. At the same time he became extremely interested in both erotic and nonerotic forms of male bonding, and, perhaps not coincidentally, he began to embody new positive values in imagery associated with the bowels.

This complex of new ideas first appears in largely unpublished works from the years 1915–17, including the original "Crown," "The Reality of Peace," and the first complete post-

19. Marguerite Beede Howe, *Art of the Self in D. H. Lawrence*, 64, 71, 78.

"Sisters" draft of *Women in Love*. This draft, which was written between April and December 1916, survives as the typed portion of the definitive typescript in the Humanities Research Center.[20] The typing is massively crossed out and replaced with interlinear holograph revisions throughout in various inks and pen tips representing several clearly distinguishable periods of revision, but, like the lowest stratum of an archeological dig, it remains legible. This 1916 stratum is vastly different from the novel we know today as *Women in Love*. Like "The Sisters" fragments, it lacks the imagistic tension of the final version; technically it is close to the flat realism and flaccid autobiography of Lawrence's next novel, *Aaron's Rod*.

The action of this draft is likewise not exactly that of the published version. Relevant to the point here is the fact that Birkin is utterly and openly opposed to sex. In the tearoom scene of the original "Excurse," Birkin feels "the old madness of lust coming up again," but "it was not this, not this he wanted with her—not the poignant ecstasies of sex passion. . . . the desire seemed like death to him." He wants "a new sort of love . . . that was gentle and still and so happy, it was chastity and innocence itself" (WLTS 505). Though he calls it "a new sort of intercourse," he makes clear to Ursula that he does not want sexual intercourse at all: much to her dismay, he declares, "I don't want to take you as a mistress—never—not even once" (WLTS 507). He says he has had enough of passion with other women and that he hopes she has had it with other men, because he is "tired of l'amour" and does not want it anymore (WLTS 506).

It might be objected that Birkin is simply opposed to sex outside marriage because he does not want to take her as a *mistress*. But the fact that he says "never," when he intends shortly to marry her, argues against that interpretation. And, as noted earlier, Lawrence rarely refers explicitly to sexual

---

20. From the definitive typescript, Humanities Research Center, University of Texas at Austin. The typescript portion of this holograph-corrected manuscript will be cited in the text and identified as WLTS. See chapter 1, n. 15.

intercourse; his characters especially are much more likely to say "love" or "passion" when they mean sex. As the conversation continues, it becomes clear that Birkin is proposing abstinence. When Ursula assures him that she does not want to be taken "as a mistress," Birkin replies, "Nay, are you sure? . . . Don't you want passion?" She says one can't decide such things deliberately, and he replies, "Yes—the very choice 'happens'—when one has had enough—more than enough." She asks what he has had enough of, and he says, "Of physical passion—you know—the top note of joy-in-voluptuousness, animal ecstasy—call it what you like." Like Lawrence in the original "Crown," he calls passion "a reduction one against the other" (WLTS 509). And like the explicitly homoerotic Birkin of the "Prologue," who loves women as sisters but cannot physically desire them, Birkin here clearly distinguishes the love he feels for Ursula from physical passion: "I've been in love hard enough before—but not this—always desire, always passion.—And now, it isn't that" (WLTS 510).

Some of the terms he uses, in fact, seem to reveal what sounds like an infantile fear of sex and desire for comfort: "It only hurts one, that old way.—One should be soft, and all gentle, and so near, so near." As Birkin says this he is "like an infant crying in the night" (WLTS 507). But Lawrence's recognition of the infant in this fear is not judgmental: he seems to be thoroughly with Birkin here, since he gives Ursula a perspective that supports Birkin's rather than undercuts it. She is shocked and disappointed that he does not intend to have sex with her. But when he does offer to give her "the extremities of passion" if she still wants them, then she looks at him "almost aghast"—not because he has revealed an aversion to sex, but because he has startled her into reflection on the "evil," the "sinister and marvellous serpent" of sexuality. Suddenly she shows a view of sex identical to Birkin's:

> To be gone with him in that violent conflict of sensual ecstasy—ah, her nerves quivered with keen desirous bliss at the suggestion. But having seen his face, having seen so plainly

the torment, the twisting of evil, the sinister and marvellous serpent glide from his mouth, she was shocked, startled into reflection. She would have to choose now, and choose deliberately.

(WLTS 507)

Neither she nor Birkin is contemplating the excesses of the Marquis de Sade, though that is what it sounds like. They are talking about Birkin's taking her "as a mistress . . . even once," the implication being that any sexual intercourse is evil, that there is no middle ground in sexuality: all passion is violent. "I am frightened of passion, of that sort of love," Birkin cries in distress. "It is a friction, a breaking down, a destruction." And the horror of the Great War suddenly looms up in the next line as a sort of explanation: "There is enough of breaking down and destruction—let it be something else" (WLTS 506).

What the "something else" is remains unclear in the earliest "Excurse." The old way is renounced, and Birkin finds "peace, peace of soul—only peace," but Ursula is not with him. The chapter ends when Birkin asks, "And the peace is the greatest reality, even if we make war—isn't it?" She does not answer, and "her eyes were full of sad tears" (WLTS 510). She does not discover the marvelous richness at the back and base of his loins, the fluid Egyptian power that makes him one of the Sons of God and potent as a pharaoh; all that is added in the interlinear holograph revision, replacing Birkin's honest cry of distress against sex.

This version of the novel also states explicitly that the feeling between Birkin and Gerald is homosexual, as does the "Prologue" to *Women in Love*; the latter (published by Ford in 1963 and reprinted in *Phoenix 2*) is one of two chapters Lawrence wrote apparently in the spring of 1916 before producing the definitive typescript draft.[21] In the "Prologue," Birkin rec-

---

21. "Prologue to *Women in Love*," ed. George Ford, *Texas Quarterly* (Spring 1963): 98–111. See also Charles Ross, *The Composition of* The Rainbow *and* Women in Love: *A History* (Charlottesville: University Press of Virginia, 1979), 97–114.

ognizes his own homosexuality: "it was for men that he felt the hot, flushing, roused attraction which a man is supposed to feel for the other sex." He feels it particularly for "men of no very great intelligence, but of pleasant appearance: ruddy, well-nourished fellows, good-natured and easy." Though he wills himself to desire women, he is only able to suppress the desire he does feel for men. He loves Hermione with his soul but not his body, and he longs "to be able to love completely, in one and the same act: both body and soul at once, struck into a complete oneness in contact with a complete woman" (*Phoenix 2* 103–4).

This explicitly homosexual Birkin would probably still have found his consummation with Ursula, since that is what he desired. The opening movements of the finished novel are shaped already, with Birkin moving away from Hermione and becoming ready for Ursula, though he only loves Gerald. In the great tradition of love stories, however, Birkin's unrequited passion for Gerald is sympathetically realized in the "Prologue." The novel that followed this opening would have to resolve the romantic tension created there, either casting Gerald into Birkin's arms or climaxing in the tragic death of Gerald and thus ending that possibility—which is of course what happens in all surviving versions.

The ending of the completed 1916 draft is a protracted plaint by Birkin over Gerald's death, entirely excluding Ursula, as if the central movement of the novel were in the male love story. Ursula does not enter to argue against his need for Gerald, and the closing pages of the novel are soaked with Birkin's tears; he even sounds as if he wants to join Gerald in death. This is the very end of the 1916 draft:

> "At any rate, you sleep," he said, through his tears and pain. "At any rate you sleep now: we needn't grieve for you anymore. We will cover you over, and leave you—and you will be warm in death. We will love you—you won't be cold."
> Then again his face broke with tears.
> "But it was horrible for you," he cried. "And then—nothing—nothing—never to struggle clear—never to struggle clear—Gerald—"

He could not bear it. His heart seemed to be torn in his chest.

"But even then," he strove to say, "we needn't all be like that. All is not lost, because many are lost.—I am not afraid or ashamed to die and be dead."[22]

Understandably, Lawrence muted the homosexual theme in subsequent drafts. Few writers in his time dared to publish on this subject, no matter how committed to it they were in private. The fiction published in E. M. Forster's lifetime contains no hint of his sexual orientation, and his homoerotic love story *Maurice*, written in 1913–14, was not published until after his death in 1970. In 1911, André Gide privately printed twelve copies of *Corydon*, a dialogue in defense of male homosexuality, but kept the copies in a drawer; when he released it for wider publication in 1924, he attached a preface indicating his awareness of the risk he was taking. That risk appears to have been greater in England than it was in France: when Radclyffe Hall followed her highly acclaimed novel *Adam's Breed* (1926) with a sympathetic portrait of sapphism in *The Well of Loneliness* (1928), the latter was immediately suppressed in England but continued to be available in an English edition published in Paris.[23]

Lawrence was a courageous writer, more than willing to offend the sensibilities of conventional English readers, but his feelings about homosexuality were extremely mixed. Like Birkin in the "Prologue," "he never really faced the question. He never accepted the desire, and received it as part of himself. He always tried to keep it expelled from him" (*Phoenix 2*

22. Contrary to his usual practice of revising by hand on the definitive typescript, Lawrence discarded the last few typed pages and wrote out the ending as we know it longhand on blank sheets (in the spidery brown ink of the last revision, 1919). Therefore I had to take this ending from an earlier typescript, made by Lawrence's agent in 1916; it is one of two copies on which Lawrence made revisions before the definitive typescript was produced. See Ross, *Composition*, 103–8. The copy of the penultimate typescript from which I took this 1916 ending is in the Humanities Research Center, the University of Texas at Austin.

23. Lovat Dickson, *Radclyffe Hall at the Well of Loneliness: A Sapphic Chronicle* (London, Toronto: Collins, 1975), 14.

107). For a few years around the time that he wrote these lines, however, Lawrence was obviously conscious of such a desire in himself and attempting to understand it, and during those years he wrote about it in works intended for publication.

He deleted all mention of homosexuality when he rewrote "The Crown" for publication in *Reflections on the Death of a Porcupine* in 1925. But in 1915, in the unpublished chapters of the original essay, he openly recoils from heterosexuality and all but admits his own homoeroticism. He asserts that "passion means the reacting of the sexes against one another in a purely reducing activity" (CMS V, 3). A man going to a woman no longer seeks "a consummation of himself with that which is not himself. . . . he seeks not a consummation in union, but a consummation in reduction. He seeks to plunge his compound flesh into the cold acid that will reduce him, in supreme sensual experience, down to his parts" (CMS IV, 8). This joy in self-disintegration is sick, but it is the only pleasure that sex affords in this sick age. And for some men, sex no longer offers even that dubious benefit:

> It is only coarse, insensitive men who can obtain the prime gratification of reduction in physical connection with a woman. . . . The sensitive man, caught within the flux of reduction, seeking a woman, knows the destruction of some basic self in him, while the complexity and unity of his consciousness remains intact above the reduction. Which gives him jangled horror. . . . he has got only a wound in his unified soul, a sort of maiming. He is horrified at his own mangled, maimed condition. . . . So that a woman becomes repulsive to him, in the thought of connection with her. It is too gross, almost horrible.
>
> (CMS IV, 10–11)

This sensitive man can obtain "the gratification of self-reduction," which everyone now seeks, only in "mental or conscious contacts," and "in physical contact he seeks another outlet. He loves men, really." Like the eponymous character in Forster's *Maurice*, he loves the gamekeeper: "a man who is to a certain degree less developed than himself," because "his ideal, his basic desire, will be to get *back* to a state which he has long surpassed"(CMS IV, 10–11).

Though the sensitive man, too, "is given up to the flux of reduction, his mouth is upon the mouth of corruption" (CMS IV, 11), Lawrence seems sympathetic to his dilemma, to his horror of heterosexuality and his regressive attraction to a warm, unthinking male. There is no horror or maiming in the homosexual desire, and it is not coarse, chilling, or gross. The description of the sensitive man must in fact remind us of Lawrence himself, who (as we shall see) objected to serving in the army on the same grounds as the sensitive man:

> There are the men who are too fine for the mere sensual grati-
> fication of the reduction with women, and too conscious, too
> much aware of their own individuality to become soldiers, to
> merge into a mass feeling. These remain active in thought and
> mental analysis, they are the men with ideas. And these men
> have very little connection with women, their love is almost
> purely for men.
>
> (CMS IV, 13–14)

In the published version of *Women in Love*, Loerke is a sensitive, intellectual homosexual, but also a repulsive "sewer rat," who clearly has his whole body in the river of dissolution. But the "Crown" description of the sensitive man could also apply to Birkin, with his horror of mass feeling and merging, his strong sense of individuality, and his vocation for ideas. This sensitive man also echoes the Birkin of the "Prologue" in his attraction to "men of no very great intelligence."

Lawrence's letters make clear that he was more or less aware of a homoerotic or bisexual orientation in himself. He had been thinking of himself for some time as a genius when, in December 1913, he wrote to a friend asking

> why nearly every man that approaches greatness tends to ho-
> mosexuality, whether he admits it or not: so that he loves the
> *body* of a man better than the body of a woman. . . . he can
> always get satisfaction from a man, but it is the hardest thing
> in life to get one's soul and body satisfied from a woman, so
> that one is free from oneself. And one is kept by all tradition
> and instinct from loving men, or a man—for it means just ex-
> tinction of all the purposive influences. And one doesn't be-

144 · *The Snake's Place*

lieve in one's power to find and to form the woman in whom one can be free—and one shoots oneself, if one is vital and feels powerfully and down to the core.

Although Lawrence ends this passage, "Again I don't know what I'm talking about," he certainly seems to.[24] He also sounds authoritative, writing to Russell in February 1915, when he gives the following analysis of sodomy, by which he means "the man goes to the man": "Sodomy only means that a man knows he is chained to the rock, so he will try to get the finest possible sensation out of himself."[25]

As has often been observed, homoeroticism is a buried theme in all Lawrence's work. In *The White Peacock*, two young men rub each other down after a swim and nearly bring their mutual attraction to consciousness but fail at the last moment. In *Sons and Lovers*, the fight between Paul and Baxter has erotic undertones: Paul's "body, hard and wonderful in itself, cleaved against the struggling body of the other man. . . . It was the other man's mouth he was dying to get at," and when he does, "he shivered with pleasure."[26] Ursula has a lesbian affair in *The Rainbow*. And though Birkin declines merging with Ursula, he seems to want it with Gerald in the wrestling scene: "They seemed to drive their white flesh deeper and deeper against each other, as if they would break into a oneness . . . two bodies clinched into oneness" (262–63). In *Aaron's Rod* (1922), Lilly massages Aaron tenderly, bringing him back to life, and in *Kangaroo* (1923), Somers regrets his failure to speak his love for the eponymous character at the latter's deathbed.

Lawrence's paintings show uninhibited appreciation for the male body, and one of the watercolors is frankly homoerotic in subject. In *Spring*, six naked men dance together,

---

24. Cambridge *Letters* 2, 115–16. For Lawrence's self-assessment as a genius, see, for instance, the testimony of William Edward Hopkin, in *D. H. Lawrence: A Composite Biography*, ed. Edward Nehls (Madison: The University of Wisconsin Press, 1957), vol. 1, 70–75.
25. Cambridge *Letters* 2, 285.
26. Lawrence, *Sons and Lovers*, 365–66.

kissing and hugging on a grassy knoll. The odd *Singing of Swans* features four figures (all apparently male, three with visible male genitalia), two lying on the ground in attitudes of sleep or abandon, two engaging in fisticuffs, while two swans rise toward the sun in the upper lefthand corner. In all, eight of the twenty-six paintings published in 1929 are of exclusively male groups, and (as is true of many of his paintings) all of the figures in these groups are naked, sometimes anomalously so, as in *Accident in a Mine*.[27]

Lawrence's evidently constant interest in homoeroticism was, however, never greater than in the years when he was writing *Women in Love*. In addition to works already mentioned, he wrote another draft of his philosophy in the winter of 1916, just before writing the "Prologue" to *Women in Love*. Cecil Gray, who read the lost opus *Goats and Compasses*, reports that it was "a bombastic, pseudo-mystical, psycho-philosophical treatise dealing largely with homosexuality."[28] This work and the 1915 "Crown" and the 1916 drafts of *Women in Love* represent a stage in Lawrence's response to his apparent sexual crisis of those years; he spoke more openly of homosexuality in these works than at any other time in his life. He also expressed misogyny with a directness not found in works from other years. For instance, whereas in the published novel Birkin meditates on woman's dominating greed in love, in the 1916 draft he simply feels hostility toward Ursula and love for Gerald: "There was the love between him and Gerald and the other was denied, all other was denied." Even though homosexual love is "ultimately death," it is all Birkin and Gerald can feel, and it is "a love which was complemented by the hatred for women" (WLTS 320–24). The final version allows Birkin to "believe in sex marriage" and desire simply something he says is beyond it, though he also hates and denounces sex. Therefore it seems that he does not

27. *The Paintings of D. H. Lawrence*, privately printed for subscribers only (n.p.: The Mandrake Press, 1929).
28. Nehls, ed., *Composite Biography*, vol. 1, 582.

reject sex or women but merely women's desire to dominate (a desire that somehow leads to loss of identity in love and the view of sex as a fulfillment). And the issue is similarly complicated in the novel as a whole.

The paradoxical treatment of sensuality in *Women in Love* is strongly reinforced in works from the same period. While revising that novel (1917–19), Lawrence began to imagine a new political utopia that may have answered his need to limit the power of frightening females and to come into some kind of "unison" with other men. He also created a philosophical system that would, perhaps, allow him to sanction desires that he felt to be destructive. The various philosophical works from this period show a progression similar in some respects to that visible in the drafts of the novels. Taken by themselves, the April 1915 revisions to *The Rainbow* suggest that heterosexuality is deathly but that death itself is a source of life. The 1915 version of "The Crown" and the 1916 *Women in Love* are both negative about heterosexuality, biased toward homosexuality, and convinced of the decadence of both desires. Perhaps as a solution, both offer decadence itself as redemptive. Later works, corresponding in time to the major revisions of *Women in Love*, develop the notion that all desire can be transcended (as it seems to be by Birkin and Ursula in the final version) if creative and destructive desires are joined.

In the original "Crown," passion is "a purely reducing activity," but reduction is splendid, a means to fulfillment. That essay is an argument for the Heraclitean war of contraries as the essence of life, partaking of divinity: "it is the fight of opposites which is holy."[29] As Stephen J. Miko points out, "The Crown" signals a change in Lawrence's metaphysical system: whereas the creative principle was eternal in "Hardy," in "The Crown" Lawrence "places both his creative

---

29. D. H. Lawrence, "The Crown," *The Signature* 1 (4 October 1915): 14.

and destructive forces in a world of flux and reserves his most ultimate realm for the 'perfect relation.'"[30] In "Hardy," there is only one eternity, the creative unknown or source of life, which is associated with darkness and passion in *The Rainbow*. But in "The Crown" there are two eternities, one ahead of us (the "goal") and one behind (the "source"), and God exists not in either but only in the perfect relation between the two, which transcends both.

The ramifications of this shift are considerable, since what was eternity itself in Lawrence's *Rainbow* period has now been shrunk to approximately the status of the "Law" in "Hardy." In "The Crown," the eternity of the "source" is identifiable with the source of life, but also with past time, pagan attitudes, selfishness, and the feudal aristocracy as well as sensuality. The eternity of the "goal," on the other hand, is the one toward which the Christian era has striven: it is identified with spirituality, unselfishness, democracy, and the reward after death. So long as eternity is identifiable with the source of life, sex and physical being are center stage, but in the new system death rivals the source of life in its divinity. The only approach to the divine is through some ritual that celebrates both eternities equally and transcends both, since eternity itself is now a relative matter and God subsists only in the relation between the two. Whereas "self was a oneness with the infinite" in *The Rainbow* and "Hardy," it is only a oneness with a relative eternity in "The Crown," and the divine state is transcendent above a union of self and not-self:

> Immortality is not a question of time, of everlasting life. It is a question of consummate being. . . . it is a question of submitting to the divine grace, in suffering and self-obliteration, and it is a question of conquering the Divine Grace, as the tiger leaps on the trembling deer, in utter satisfaction of the Self, in complete fulfilment of desire. The fulfilment is dual.
>
> (CMS VI, 3–4)

---

30. Stephen J. Miko, *Towards* Women in Love (New Haven: Yale University Press, 1971), 209–14.

In *The Rainbow* the lovers are fulfilled as tigers taking their desire, and Lawrence's ideal community of the same period (February 1915) would be based on "not self-sacrifice, but . . . fulfilment in the flesh of all strong desire." But a few months later this satisfaction is exactly half the requirement for immortality, the other half being submission to something that negates and denies the self's desire, "submitting to the divine grace, in suffering and self-obliteration."

Lawrence seems to have modeled this new duality on the works of Heraclitus, as presented by John Burnet. Heraclitus' metaphysics are based on a belief that the world is made of fire, which is constantly being transmuted into water and earth: "Everything is either mounting upwards to serve as fuel, or sinking downwards after having nourished the flame. It follows that the whole of reality is an ever-flowing stream."[31] Sinking downwards, matter becomes water, then earth. This sinking is a necessity, for the upward and downward motions are perpetual and dependent on each other: fire consumes its fuel and requires the rising of matter from earth, into water, to be exhaled as fuel for the fire. If there were no corresponding sinkage of the consumed fuel into water and earth, then water and earth would soon be consumed in the fire, and the creation would end. Therefore, neither motion is better than the other; in fact, "the way up and the way down are one and the same" (Burnet 151–52).

These opposing paths exist not simply in the natural world but have their correlatives in human conduct. Heraclitus identifies fire with life, wisdom, and the soul, water with pleasure and death (Burnet 171–72). But neither life nor death is better: "To God all things are fair and good and right, but men hold some things wrong and some right." Therefore, even though "the dry soul is wisest and best," some people will inevitably have wet ones. For one thing, "it is pleasure to

31. John Burnet, *Early Greek Philosophy* (London: Adam and Charles Black, 1908), 162. Hereafter this work will be cited in the text and identified as Burnet.

souls to become moist"; becoming moist seems to include getting drunk, falling asleep, and wantonness (Burnet 152, 171, 191). Furthermore, both upward and downward processes go on simultaneously in humans: "the fire in us is perpetually becoming water, and the water earth" (Burnet 169). Though too much water in a soul is death, as is too much fire, either death is only temporary: "The soul that has died from excess of moisture sinks down to earth; but from earth comes water, and from water is once more exhaled a soul." The only state that is a bad idea is stasis (Burnet 172–73).

Accordingly, in "The Crown" reduction is one path to the infinite, and "corruption, like creation, is only divine when all is given up to it. If it be allowed as a controlled activity within an intact whole, this is vile," because it is then static, not part of a continuous flowing in both directions (CMS V, 11). The horror of his age for Lawrence was that he saw corruption taking place within the fixed form of things as they were. What was wrong was the "null envelope" of the conventional form, not corruption itself. "This is utter evil, this secret, silent worship of the null envelope that preserves us intact for our gratification with the flux of corruption"; it is worshiped because of the intense sensual pleasure of the downward process (CMS IV, 8).

This null envelope is the same as the hard shell of the ego around the mechanized characters in *Women in Love*, and Lawrence's association of water with dissolution in that novel is obviously Heraclitean. Birkin even quotes Heraclitus in "Water-Party": "You know Herakleitos says 'a dry soul is best.'" Birkin also asks, "But why isn't the end of the world as good as the beginning?" Ursula thinks of herself as "a rose of happiness," what Birkin calls a "flamy" rose, a creature of fire. But Birkin feels that he and Ursula are doomed like the rest to the downward process, fire sinking into water and then earth (164–65). Whereas the rest damn themselves by adhering to the old way of life, however, Birkin and Ursula are willing to give up the old form in all its incarnations— including the human race, the world of things, England, conventional marriage, and sex seen as a fulfillment. But their life outside the confines will not be only upward; they will not simply "blast through degradation to new health," as Knight says. They will be constantly in flux, their life combining both upward and downward ways, both corruption and creation, water and fire, but primarily transcending both.

Here Lawrence goes beyond Heraclitus to an idea that seems primarily Taoist: for his God in "The Crown" is not a balance of opposites so much as a relation between them, a transcendent third thing. The two eternities "flow together, and they flow apart," and "God is not the one infinite, nor the other. . . . God is the utter relation between the two eternities, he is in the flowing together and the flowing apart" (CMS VI, 2). Similarly, though what Birkin and Ursula achieve is at the same time sensual and spiritual, corrupt and vital, incorporating imagery from traditions both Christian (Son of God, New Jerusalem) and pagan (scarab beetles, Egyptian pharaohs), their fulfillment is meant to transcend these oppositions.

Lawrence makes the transcendent nature of the third state explicit in "The Reality of Peace" (1917), written the same year he made the major revisions to *Women in Love*. There he advocates acceptance of corruption as a necessary component of life:

> We are not only creatures of light and virtue. We are also alive in corruption and death. It is necessary to balance the dark against the light if we are ever going to be free. We must know that we, ourselves, are the living stream of seething corruption, this also, all the while, as well as the bright river of life. We must recover our balance to be free. From our bodies comes the issue of corruption as well as the issue of creation. We must have our being in both, our knowledge must consist in both.
>
> (*Phoenix* 676)

"Knowledge such as the beetles have" is a necessity, and freedom comes from acknowledging the corruption within. He does not mean only moral corruption or the blood lust he thought his contemporaries felt during the war:

> Within our bowels flows the slow stream of corruption, to the issue of corruption. This is one direction. Within our veins flows the stream of life, towards the issue of pure creation. This is the other direction. We are of both. . . . If we shrink from some sickening issue of ourselves, instead of recoiling and rising above ourselves, let us go down into ourselves, enter the hell of corruption and putrescence, and rise again, not fouled, but fulfilled and free.
>
> (*Phoenix* 677)

Written the same year as "Excurse" and "Moony" as we know them, this passage alone should assure us that Lawrence *intended* to make Birkin and Ursula find freedom through incorporation of what was shameful and horrible to them. The logic of this descent into hell is that one cannot change the self:

> If there is a serpent of secret and shameful desire in my soul, let me not beat it out of my consciousness with sticks. . . . There is no hope in exclusion. For whatsoever limbo we cast our devils into will receive us ourselves at last. . . .
>
> I must make my peace with the serpent of abhorrence that is within me. I must own my most secret shame and my most secret shameful desire.
>
> (*Phoenix* 677–78)

This serpent of shameful desire he associates with his bowels: "There is no killing the serpent. . . . his principle moves slowly in my belly; I must disembowel myself to get rid of him." In Lawrentian logic, emotions and spiritual states are physical, conditions of flesh, blood, and bone; and shame, as a spiritual state, naturally has its home in the body. The bowels are also the obvious site of Heraclitus' downward way in the body, where water sinks to earth.

The serpent, the desire, the bowels are not euphemized or made more pleasant; they remain shameful, corrupt, putrescent, hellish. Instead, Lawrence proclaims, like Heraclitus, that the opposite of corruption requires it: "Life feeds death,

death feeds life." If either "the desire for creation or the desire for dissolution" is denied, "then neither is fulfilled." The logic again relies on the futility of fighting the undesirable half: "We can never conquer death; that is folly." Therefore, we must affirm both, and thereby transcend both: "For there are ultimately only two desires, the desire of life and the desire of death. Beyond these is pure being, where I am absolved from desire and made perfect." Perfection is not to desire life but to desire both life and death, and, therefore, neither; to have no desires, to transcend desire and be "perfect and time-less . . . timeless as a jewel" (*Phoenix* 679–81).

This Taoist transcendence of desire seems to be what Lawrence has in mind for Birkin and Ursula. They must incorporate paired desires, for sex and against, for corruption and against; then they transcend, into the "paradisal" realm of stillness, where they want neither. Or so it seems in theory, though of course, in practice, when this state is dramatized in the novel, it sounds remarkably like a retreat from sexuality.

In a letter from April 1915 Lawrence condemns himself and his contemporaries, saying: "we refuse to acknowledge the passionate evil that is in us. This makes us secret and rotten."[32] Though he made philosophical matter out of it, the impetus behind his Heraclitean and Taoist strategies in "The Crown" and "The Reality of Peace" may have lain in the need to deal somehow with what he called "my most secret and shameful desire." Lawrence does not identify that urge. His association of it with the bowels may suggest that it is for (heterosexual) sodomy, but that predilection is not a great secret nor hard to accept in his novels; as Knight has shown, many of Lawrence's couples indulge in it.

The truly secret, unacceptable desire in Lawrence's work is Birkin's in the "Prologue." (His homoerotic desire is "the one and only secret he kept to himself" *Phoenix* 2, 107.) The bowels would also be an appropriate symbolic site for repressed

32. Cambridge *Letters* 2, 315.

homosexual passion not only because, culturally, the desire is taboo and decadent (having to do with decay) but also because of homosexual anal eroticism. The association seems clear in Lawrence's mind: images of corruption, putrescence, and dissolution abound whenever he speaks directly about homosexuality, and the beetles swarming in the April 1915 letters about his horror of "men lovers of men" are probably meant to be dung-rolling scarab beetles, as Delany suggests.[33] The large intestine, like shameful desire, is a part of the self that can neither be accepted nor killed.

Ford points out that the biblical analogue attached to the African process is Sodom, and that the sin of Sodom, for which the city was destroyed, was homosexuality; he suggests that homosexuality is the horror excoriated in the "obscene religious mystery" of the Africans.[34] And Scott Sanders, looking at quite different evidence, plots *Women in Love* as a symbolic exorcism of Lawrence's homosexual desire.[35] Like Sanders, David Cavitch also sees Lawrence as transferring his own feelings to Gudrun and suggests that "her responses give evidence of Lawrence's shame and anxiety over such desires."[36] But since the African process is not finally excoriated, and the secret hiding place of sin is glorified in "Excurse" as "the source of the deepest life force," *Women in Love* may be, as Meyers suggests, not so much an exorcism as a celebration of hidden homosexuality incorporated into an overtly heterosexual relationship.[37] It may be that the sin of Sodom, the snake of the bowels, is part of Birkin, and that is why his initial choices seem limited to two kinds of anal eroticism (the

---

33. Paul Delany, *D. H. Lawrence's Nightmare: The Writer and His Circle in the Years of the Great War* (New York: Basic Books, 1978), 89.

34. George Ford, *Double Measure: A Study of the Novels and Stories of D. H. Lawrence* (New York: Holt, Rinehart and Winston, 1965), 198.

35. Scott Sanders, *D. H. Lawrence: The World of the Five Major Novels* (New York: Viking, 1973), 129–32.

36. David Cavitch, *D. H. Lawrence and the New World* (New York: Oxford University Press, 1969), 67.

37. Jeffrey Meyers, "D. H. Lawrence and Homosexuality," in *D. H. Lawrence: Novelist, Poet, Prophet*, ed. Stephen Spender (London: Weidenfeld and Nicolson, 1973), 145–46.

African process versus the "paradisal" way, initiated by the anal caress). The movement toward regeneration is one not of exclusion but of inclusion, giving the snake his place in the sun.

Before he reached the paradoxical resolutions described here, however, Lawrence's crisis of 1915–17 had made him irascible on the whole subject of sex. In his works from the late war years, he was obviously arguing with himself about sexuality, and he invested emotional energy on all sides of the argument. In these pieces it is sometimes difficult to sort out consistently what Lawrence means; he often seems drawn to what he condemns, and both the repulsion and the attraction are violently stated. One such piece is *Twilight in Italy*, which was written between the original "Crown" and the 1916 *Women in Love*.[38]

Late in his life, in such novels as *Lady Chatterley's Lover* and *The Man Who Died*, Lawrence returned to a glorification of sexuality, though not to the female-centric birth worship of *The Rainbow*. Later works deify the phallus; late in his authoritarian period it is the totem of the hierarchy of manhood, and in all his last works it is the godhead in the flesh. *Twilight in Italy* is as far from *Lady Chatterley's Lover* in some ways as Lawrence's work gets. In *Twilight in Italy*, Lawrence condemns the phallus, the body, the blood; he also reserves a special loathing for those who hate the body, as well as for those who consciously enjoy it. Anything connected with sex seems to enrage him. At the same time, as demonstrated in letters from the same period, he seems simply fed up with everyone

38. Keith Sagar, *D. H. Lawrence: A Calendar of His Works* (Austin: University of Texas Press, 1979), 63–64. Lawrence rewrote several sections of *Twilight in Italy* in July, August, and September 1915 (including "Crucifix Across the Mountains," "The Spinner and the Monks," "Lemon Gardens," "The Theatre," and "San Gaudenzio"), and these versions are quite different from those written and published (in *The English Review*) in 1913. Yet Sagar, in his *Life of D. H. Lawrence* (New York: Pantheon Books, 1980), gives 1913 as the date of composition for *Twilight in Italy*, when (as his own *Calendar* indicates) the appropriate date is 1915 or even 1916, since Lawrence corrected proofs for it in 1916, possibly revising at the same time (see Sagar's *Calendar*, 68).

and everything. Again and again he condemns the human race wholesale, declaring it to be, in fact, "inhuman."

But unlike the letters from the same period, *Twilight in Italy* is a revision of an earlier work and therefore dramatically reveals the new developments in Lawrence's thought and temperament. The original versions of the Italian sketches were first published in the *English Review* in 1913; Lawrence revised them between the summer of 1915 and winter of 1916. The 1913 version is a realistic travelogue, the only philosophy in it having to do with the difference between the Italian and the English national characters.[39]

In both versions, the Italians are more physical, less spiritual than the English. In the original version, however, the Italians seem if anything to benefit from this characteristic, whereas in *Twilight in Italy* Lawrence sees them being destroyed by "phallic worship," a form of subjugation to women and a denial of the "male spirit, which would subdue the immediate flesh to some conscious or social purpose."[40] The Italians' error is to see the phallus as divine, since it produces children, and the mind of man as nothing; this arrangement lets "the women triumph. . . . the woman in her maternity is . . . the supreme authority." Therefore the men must go to America, not for money, but "to recover some dignity as men, as producers, as workers, as creators from the spirit, not only from the flesh. It is a profound desire to get away from women altogether, the terrible subjugation to sex, to phallic worship" (*TI* 104–5).

This "terrible subjugation to sex" destroys the men who remain, because "there is no synthetic love between men and women, there is only passion, and passion is fundamental hatred, the act of love is a fight." What is missing is "spiritual love"; there is "no happiness of being together, only the

---

39. For a rather slight analysis of the difference between the styles of the two versions, see Jeanie Wagner, "D. H. Lawrence's Neglected Italian Studies," *D. H. Lawrence Review* 13 (Fall 1980): 260–74.

40. D. H. Lawrence, *Twilight in Italy* (London: Duckworth, 1916), 104. Hereafter this work will be cited in the text and identified as *TI*.

roused excitement which is based on a fundamental hostility." There exists between the men and women, therefore, "a condition of battle" that the women habitually win because the men cannot shake their addiction to sex (*TI* 102–3). Consequently the women are "vindictive" (*TI* 101), and "they seem like weapons, dangerous." "At the worst" the women show "a yellow poisonous bitterness of the flesh that is like a narcotic" (*TI* 104).

Nothing comparable appears in the 1913 version. Lawrence reports that there is "no comradeship" and "little courting" between the sexes, but in the original version the men do not need to go to America. In a letter Lawrence wrote while actually in Italy, he says the Italians leave home because they can make more money in America, and "it is a queer business altogether" that "they leave their wives for seven years at a time."[41] And in the 1913 version of the essays sex is certainly not viewed as a battle or as "fundamental hatred." The Italians are unhappy because passionate, but only because "passion is an instrument, a means; and to mistake the means for the end is to leave oneself at last empty." In the original version Lawrence gives us a reflection of his early marital happiness when he contrasts this Italian passion with that of the English:

> The northern races are the really passionate people, because theirs is a passion that persists and achieves . . . that intimacy between a man and a woman which is the fruit of passion, and which is rarely seen here: the love, the knowledge, the simplicity, and the absence of shame, that one sometimes sees in English eyes, and which is the flower of civilisation.[42]

Nothing so positive on any subject, and certainly not about his countrymen, sex, or women, appears in *Twilight in Italy*.

And the terms are different in the later work. Once again Lawrence condemns a certain kind of sexuality, "the senses

---

41. Cambridge *Letters 2*, 149.
42. D. H. Lawrence, "Italian Studies," *The English Review* 15 (September 1913), 212. Hereafter these essays will be cited in the text and identified as *ER*.

conscious and crying out in their consciousness in the pangs of the enjoyment." He associates this sex-in-the-head with Aphrodite, who has suddenly become "goddess of destruction, her white, cold fire consumes and does not create" (*TI* 60). This portrait of Aphrodite is new: in "Hardy" she is associated with "the female," which he also calls "the great, unknown Positive, towards which all must flow" (*Phoenix* 457). But Lawrence's feelings toward females changed, especially toward the Aphroditean kind, and therefore this goddess has become "the flowering mystery of the death-process. . . . born in the first spasm of universal dissolution" (*Women in Love* 164).

In the original essays on Italy, the Italians worship a different god, and though they look empty to the spiritual Englishman, the Italians are certainly not being consumed:

> The man seems not to be able to believe in himself till he has a child. . . . That he is himself, is nothing. For his soul is nothing to him.
> Which is why he can move so gracefully, hang like a bird in the olive trees, row down the lake standing in the boat and swinging forward, rhythmic as the ripples under him. An Englishman walks as if he must brave it out: as if it were a chagrin to him to be forced to acknowledge his legs and arms in public. For he considers that in him is Almighty God, cumbered here in the flesh. But the Italian feels, no matter what he believes, that he is made in the image of God, and in this image of flesh is his godliness, and with its defacement and crumbling, crumbles himself.
>
> (*ER* 215)

In the 1913 version Lawrence the Englishman sees the limitations of the Italian mode, but he would rather live in Italy than in England. His sympathies are more on the side of the godhead in the flesh than with the stilted spiritual Englishman; when he admires the English, it is for something they have achieved through passion. Thinking of the productions in the theater of his Italian village, he imagines that "everybody hates Ibsen" because Ibsen "denied the universality of the blood, of which we are all cups. . . . Then he showed how the mind is overthrown at any moment by the body. But why shouldn't it be?" (*ER* 224). He condemned Hamlet because "he could not love, he could only judge. . . . He had no feelings. He never had any." In 1913 Lawrence felt a tremendous sympathy for Ophelia and thought, "What a miserable creature Hamlet was, behaving in his indirect, indecent, dirty fashion to the girl. . . . It was enough to send any girl crazy, to have given her love to a phosphorescent thing like Hamlet." Phosphorescence is always an image of decay in Lawrence's work, and, because of Hamlet's lack of feeling, Lawrence saw the whole play as "a gleam of decay" (*ER* 229–31).

In 1915–16, however, Lawrence's view of *Hamlet* changed; it was not just about lack of feeling but was "the tragedy of the convulsed reaction of the mind from the flesh, of the spirit from the self, the reaction from the great aristocratic to the great democratic principle" (*TI* 124). How exactly Lawrence felt about these respective principles is unclear, since by this time he seemed equally unsympathetic to all characters in the play and merely reported that the peasants had sympathy for Ophelia. And Ibsen remained hateful, but for quite a different reason than before: not because he denied the blood, but because he had it in his head, was "fingering with the mind the secret places and sources of the blood, impertinent, irreverent, nasty." This nastiness is "a sort of phallic worship" and, like the Italians', it is "mental and perverted: the phallus is the real fetish, but it is the source of uncleanliness and corruption and death, it is the Moloch, worshipped in obscenity" (*TI* 108–9).

The exact implications of this denunciation are difficult to determine, since in *Twilight in Italy* Lawrence finds any sort of phallic worship destructive. Ironically enough, in view of Lawrence's later works, in *Twilight in Italy* a man who worships the phallus denies the male spirit "of outgoing, of uniting, of making order out of chaos, in the outer world." Looking at the Italian actor who played Hamlet, Lawrence thought, "His real man's soul, the soul that goes forth and builds up a new world out of the void, was ineffectual. It could only revert to the senses." Therefore "his divinity was the phallic divinity." The repression of his "real man's soul" was what had made him such a sensualist: his unused male spirit "cried out helplessly in him through the insistent, inflammable flesh." The actor was "beaten by his own flesh" (*TI* 108–9).

There is a clue to what may lie behind this violent denunciation of the flesh in a passage that was deleted in revision. In the 1913 essays, Lawrence finds it curious that the Italian considers his manhood to be contingent on fatherhood; but even as he does so, he reveals himself to be a man who fully expects to be a father. Objecting to the bleakness of Ibsen's *Ghosts*, Lawrence says,

> I am sorry for the son of Ghosts, as if I had lost my left hand. But because I lost my left hand, it is not finished with me. There are many more left hands even within my living flesh: for if I have a son, he will be born with both hands. . . . We are tired of going rigid with grief, or insane, over a little spilt life. The sun will lick it up.
>
> (*ER* 224)

Not only this passage, but this sanguine spirit is missing from the revised version. One cannot help wondering if Lawrence's own failure to become a father contributed to the embitterment between himself and his wife, which was surely either a cause or an effect of this change in Lawrence's thought. Their publicly admitted item of contention was his wife's grief over the loss of her three children; with the courts and post-Victorian public outrage on his side, her first husband successfully removed her children from her life when she ran away with Lawrence. Perhaps she wanted to have another child; Lawrence certainly wanted to have one with her (he wrote to her, in their earliest weeks together, that he would be glad if she were pregnant already),[43] and they failed. Then in 1915–16, he jeered at the Italians for their enslavement to woman's maternity and asserted that true manhood was antithetical to matters phallic—while just a year before he had seen sexual fulfillment with a woman as a nec-

43. Cambridge *Letters 1*, 402–3.

essary prerequisite to the achievement of manhood. In a letter he connects Forster's homosexuality to his assumption that social action is futile: "Forster knows that his implicit manhood is to be satisfied by nothing but immediate physical action," meaning a revolution to help those oppressed by "the fetters of this money." But a first requirement for such social action is sexual fulfillment with a woman: "But why can't he act? Why can't he take a woman and fight clear to his own basic, primal being? . . . For I go to a woman to know myself, and to know her. And I want to know myself, that I may know how to act for humanity."[44]

Lest we think he condemns it entirely, Lawrence explains in *Twilight in Italy* that "the phallus is a symbol of creative divinity. But it represents only part of creative divinity" (*TI* 109). Yet repeated and ferocious denunciations are more audible than such calm disclaimers, and there are no happy couples in *Twilight in Italy* comparable to the passionate English people in the original version to give us a normative model and some sense that sex is ever a good idea. Furthermore, his desideratum is no longer for "that intimacy between a man and woman which is the fruit of passion." In the later version it is for a solitary, transcendent ecstasy, in which, not lovers, but parts of the self embrace: "where in mankind is the ecstasy of light and dark together, the supreme transcendence of the afterglow . . . which makes . . . single abandon of the single body and soul also an ecstasy . . . beyond the range of loneliness or solitude?" (*TI* 53).

Again, as in other works from the *Women in Love* period, the rejection of sex and the desire for transcendence appear alongside evidence of homosexual feeling. The only people Lawrence seems to like in all of *Twilight in Italy* are several young men, and he records, with no apparent modesty, their attraction to him. His contacts with women, on the other hand, are all presented as cool; the various landladies are incomprehensible creatures he does not admire. Most of all he

---

44. Cambridge *Letters* 2, 283–84.

likes the sixteen-year-old Giovanni, who is beautiful and says to Lawrence as they dance together, "'It's better like this, two men?' . . . his blue eyes hot, his face curiously tender" (*TI* 177). Lawrence explains at length that their sort of folk dancing is utterly erotic, climbing "always nearer, nearer, always to a more perfect climax. . . . there was a moment when the dance passed into a possession" (*TI* 179). Though at this point he is ostensibly describing the two male-female couples present, he also asserts that the Italians "love even better to dance with men, with a dear blood-friend, than with women" (*TI* 176–77).

The second half of *Twilight in Italy* covers previously unpublished material, so we cannot compare Lawrence's views of the young men and the dance in the two versions. Lawrence may well have liked Giovanni as much in the original, since latent homoeroticism is a constant feature in his work. The idea that all-male contact might be preferable or superior to the love of women, however, is first openly expressed in his works from the late war period and, as the next chapter argues, lies at the heart of his new political thought.

How are we to view the concurrence between Lawrence's surge of interest in the homoerotic and his rejection of women, birth, and heterosexuality? Lawrence himself seems to have seen nothing illogical in the idea that love between men is "complemented by the hatred for women," as he says in the 1916 *Women in Love*. In "The Crown," the sensitive men have "very little connection with women, their love is almost purely for men"; though they also "seek" women, they are "maimed" by having sex with them. Something in the "men with ideas," like Lawrence himself, who are "too much aware of their own individuality to become soldiers, to merge into a mass feeling," makes them open to "the destruction of some basic self" in themselves if they go to a woman (CMS IV, 10–14). Such feelings were obviously Lawrence's own, at least for a time. He had been living with Frieda for three years when he wrote "The Crown"; in his work from the earlier part of their relationship, sensitive young men fear powerful women (as Tom fears Lydia) but they are made whole in merging with them and do not seem to desire men. The crisis that caused this change will probably always be obscure, but Lawrence's works provide evidence for a reconstruction of its nature.

From the point of view of clinical psychology, Lawrence's eventual feelings of revulsion toward women may have been predictable from the oedipal attachment obvious in *Sons and Lovers*; women in his works are always enormously powerful, and therefore potentially threatening. Certainly Lawrence's personal psychology was profoundly affected by this tie, and much of his work does seem to be a symbolic attempt to re-establish what Howe calls "the perfect equilibrium between mother and infant."[45] Even the method he invents for enforcing separateness between husband and wife is curiously related to infant-mother interaction: mothers not only accept a child's excretory function, they give authorized anal caresses while bathing and cleaning babies.

Yet however much consistency Lawrence's psyche may display at the deepest level, it appears quite volatile closer to the surface, and its metamorphoses are always directly reflected in his work. Cavitch suggests that Lawrence was all his life in quest of the happy family he finally created in *The Plumed Serpent*, at the end of which Kate, Don Ramon, and Don Cipriano are pledged to one another like mother, father, son.[46] Certainly this is the desired family constellation in Lawrence's work from *Women in Love* onward. But in *The Rainbow* the male-female dyad is all that life requires, and in "Hardy" it seems almost the source of life: "when the two clasp hands, a moment, male and female . . . the gay poppy flies into flower again" (*Phoenix* 516). Neither "Hardy" nor *The Rainbow* implies the need for a third (male) party. Something important seems to have happened to Lawrence between the two Brangwen novels.

The portraits of Birkin in the "Prologue" to *Women in Love* and of the "sensitive man" in the original "Crown" suggest

---

45. Howe, *Art of the Self in D. H. Lawrence*, 21.
46. Cavitch, *Lawrence and the New World*, 188.

that Lawrence's sexual orientation was primarily homoerotic but that he was unable to accept it. He probably felt he had resolved this tension after eloping with a mother of three, older than himself; his early years with Frieda may be seen as a symbolic fulfillment of the oedipal son's dream and *The Rainbow* as a hymn to that idyll. But Frieda may have asked too much of him, in an unmotherly fashion, making him feel threatened and smothered. For some reason, at least, he was jarred into recognition of homoerotic desires in himself after a period of marital happiness, and the same works that imply this recognition denounce the sexual demands of independent women.

That the Lawrences were happy in the early years of their marriage is not open to much doubt. About the penultimate draft of *The Rainbow*, Lawrence wrote to Garnett in April 1914: "I am sure of this now, this novel. It is a big and beautiful work. Before, I could not get my soul into it. That was because of the struggle and the resistance between Frieda and me. Now you will find her and me in the novel, I think, and the work is of both of us."[47] In this period he was so far from the idea of a further "unison" of manhood, beyond marriage, that he made sex the source of a man's action: "The man embraces in the woman all that is not himself, and from that one resultant, from that embrace, comes every new action."[48] The man's action is not the important result, toward which all is aimed, but simply a fringe benefit. Although the "peace and inner security" that come from love "will leave you free to act and produce your own work,"

> you mustn't think that your desire or your fundamental need is to make a good career, or to fill your life with activity, or even to provide for your family materially. It isn't. Your most vital necessity in this life is that you shall love your wife completely and implicitly and in entire nakedness of body and spirit.[49]

47. Cambridge *Letters* 2, 164.
48. Ibid., 294.
49. Ibid., 191.

Lawrence wrote this letter in the summer of 1914, before beginning the final draft of *The Rainbow*.

But not long after he finished that novel, he told a friend that Frieda was taking rooms in Hampstead and that they were going to live apart: "I wish she would have her rooms in Hampstead and leave me alone," he wrote in May 1915.[50] They apparently did not separate for long, though Lawrence announced several other imminent ruptures in the next few years. In 1917, as he revised the poems about his early married life for publication in *Look! We Have Come Through!*, he made clear that he considered these poems, with their title proclaiming his marital happiness, to represent a superseded part of his life: "As a sort of last work, I have gathered and shaped my last poems into a book," he wrote in what must have been a suicidal mood. "It is a sort of final conclusion of the old life in me—'And now farewell' is really the motto."[51]

What might have caused this marital reversal? In 1915, Lawrence attributed their difficulties to Frieda's "thinking herself a wronged, injured and aggrieved person, because of the children, and because she is a German."[52] But this first separation followed hard upon Lawrence's visit to Cambridge in March 1915, which initiated the severe depression that precipitated early changes in his thinking. As discussed earlier, Lawrence was evidently plunged into despair simply because of the homosexuality he observed at Cambridge. In succeeding years, he tried in his life as well as in his work to find an acceptable form of union with other men: he proposed blood brotherhood to Murry and Russell, among others. (Both turned him down.) At the height of the marital crisis, Lawrence may even have had a homoerotic love affair. In *Kangaroo*, much of which is simply autobiography with the names changed, Richard and Harriet Somers are estranged in Cornwall over Somers's friendship with a young farmer. Lawrence actually calls the farmer "John Thomas," the name he later bestows on Mellors's penis in *Lady Chatterley's Lover*: "Poor

50. Ibid., 343.
51. Cambridge *Letters* 3, 87.
52. Cambridge *Letters* 2, 343.

Harriet spent many lonely days in the cottage. Richard was not interested in her now. He was only interested in John Thomas and the farm people. . . . even he neglected and hated her," preferring instead to "linger" with John Thomas, "lying in the bracken or on the heather as they waited for a wain."[53] After Somers and Harriet have been forced to leave Cornwall, "he craved to be back, his soul was there. He wrote passionately to John Thomas."[54]

Delany explores the evidence for Lawrence's affair with a young Cornish farmer, the best of which is Frieda's letter to Murry, which specifies no time: "I think the homosexuality in him was a short phase out of misery—I fought him and won."[55] Delany concludes that Lawrence may have tried, with William Henry Hocking, "to achieve a homoerotic solution to the painful and exhausting conflicts of his sexual life," but that the attempt was a failure, and he "would never be so close to a man again."[56]

Lawrence's own explanations of what happened to his marriage in these years exclude all mention of homosexuality, but they are consistent with his "Crown" portrait of the "overly sensitive" man "with ideas" who only desires men and is therefore "maimed" by going to a woman, even while he overtly blames the woman's overweening motherliness. Though he objected to Freud's emphasis on the erotic nature of the oedipal tie, Lawrence embraced the idea that all of his own ills stemmed from mother-son attachment, perhaps because it allowed him a self-explanation that ignored his homoerotic orientation. He wrote to Katherine Mansfield in 1918 that

> at certain periods the man has a desire and a tendency to re-
> turn unto the woman, make her his goal and end, find his
> justification in her. In this way he casts himself as it were into
> her womb, and she, the Magna Mater, receives him with grat-

53. D. H. Lawrence, *Kangaroo* (1923; rpt. New York: Viking, 1960), 241–43.

54. Ibid., 253.

55. *Frieda Lawrence: The Memoirs and Correspondence*, ed. E. W. Tedlock, Jr. (New York: Knopf, 1964), 360.

56. Delany, *Lawrence's Nightmare*, 309–15.

ification. This is a kind of incest. . . . I have done it, and now
struggle all my might to get out. In a way, Frieda is the devouring mother.—It is awfully hard, once the sex relation has gone
this way, to recover. If we don't recover, we die.

In this letter the destructive process begins when the man
makes the woman "his goal and end," as Lawrence did in the
period of "Hardy" and *The Rainbow;* in the letter just quoted
he may be attempting to make sense of his own progression
from uxoriousness to gynephobia. He believed that the solution to the problem, however, would be in his wife's relinquishing her self-assertion. The letter continues, without so
much as a paragraph break: "But Frieda says I am antedilu-
vian in my positive attitude. I do think a woman must yield
some sort of precedence to a man, and he must take this precedence. . . . I believe this. Frieda doesn't. Hence our fight."[57]

What sort of submission Lawrence expected from his wife
is suggested in his contemporaneous essay on Hawthorne
(written in 1917–18). There he asserts that Hester seduced
Dimmesdale against his will, thereby becoming his lethal
mother. "When woman is the leader or dominant in the sex
relationship," Lawrence explains, "then the activity of mankind is an activity of disintegration and undoing." The sexually dominant woman becomes a man's smothering mother,
who destroys him while trying to revive him. She exerts a
"malevolent force . . . pressing, sapping, shattering life unknowably at its very sources."

A dominant woman finds this destruction especially easy
if she and the man are socially isolated, as the Lawrences
were during their years in Cornwall:

> If Dimmesdale had fled with Hester they would have felt
> themselves social outcasts. And then they would have had to
> live in secret hatred of mankind, like criminal accomplices; or
> they would have felt isolated, cut off, two lost creatures, a man
> meaningless except as the agent, or tool, or creature of the
> possessive woman; and when a man loses his meaning, the
> woman one way or other destroys him. She kills him by her

57. Cambridge *Letters* 3, 301–2.

very possessive love itself. It would have been necessary for Dimmesdale in some way to conquer society with a new spirit and a new idea.

Lawrence certainly seems to be talking about himself and Frieda here. Their frequent moves and lack of a supportive community must have made them excessively dependent on one another. But Lawrence seems most of all to blame the woman's use of the man (he is her "agent, or tool, or creature") in "love" (which, as discussed earlier, is often his term for sexual activity): "She kills him by her very possessive love itself," and the "Age of Woman" is "the age of fatal, suffocating love, love which kills like a Laocoon snake." This love destroys "the flow, the very life itself" at "the centres of primary life in a man."[58]

In these passages Lawrence seems to be blaming his wife for making him ill and, possibly, for making him impotent. Though Lawrence never admitted to having tuberculosis, his biographers have found evidence that it was diagnosed early in the war; Harry T. Moore suggests that Lawrence's outbursts of violent rage in Cornwall are a symptom of the advancing disease.[59] Lawrence's pantheistic world view did not allow him to see any illness as meaningless, and he needed a reason to explain why that force was directed at him. His wife was the only person close to him during the years in question, and she was apparently asserting herself at home and abroad in ways that would have been particularly threatening to a man who was both ill and unsure of his sexual orientation.

In *The Plumed Serpent*, Kate Leslie realizes that she killed her intellectual, sensitive, Lawrence-like husband by refusing to submit to him passively as Teresa does to Ramon;[60] in *Fan-*

---

58. D. H. Lawrence, *The Symbolic Meaning: The Uncollected Versions of Studies in Classic American Literature*, ed. Armin Arnold (New York: Viking, 1964), 132–34.

59. Harry T. Moore, *The Intelligent Heart* (1954; rpt. New York: Penguin, 1960), 470.

60. D. H. Lawrence, *The Plumed Serpent* (1926; rpt. Vintage Books, 1956), 438.

tasia, Lawrence asserts that promiscuous, demanding wives tear their husbands to shreds; in *Women in Love,* promiscuous, seductive Gudrun kills Gerald spiritually, and Birkin finds Ursula perfect when she is perfectly still. Such protests can scarcely lack a source in Lawrence's marriage. His illness may have depleted his already uncertain sexual energy; though Murry probably overstates the influence of sexual failure on Lawrence's work, he can claim some credibility on the question of its existence, since he and Katherine Mansfield lived briefly with the Lawrences in Cornwall and witnessed their fights.[61] Frieda apparently aggravated this already painful situation by having affairs.[62]

His wife believed that Lawrence's homoeroticism was temporary, the result of "misery," by which she may have meant their marital dilemma. Lawrence's own view may be closer to the truth when he says that a man who wants only other men will feel "maimed" going to a woman; he evidently felt that his wife's love was killing him. Perhaps the mystery is that he did experience a period of happiness early in their marriage. That he forced himself to persist after becoming aware of contrary desires, with a debilitating illness and a wife who was more ready to challenge than to support his sense of himself, surely explains the simultaneous appearance of gynephobia and homoeroticism in his work.

The two were in any case connected for Lawrence: in *Fantasia*, he blames female assertiveness for male homosexuality itself. When man is given up to "the service of emotional and procreative woman," then woman becomes "a fearsome tyrant," usurping the active male role. And when "the old poles" are thus reversed, "man begins to have all the feelings of woman," including "the peculiarly strong passive sex desire, the desire to be taken."[63] Lawrence never considered the

61. See Delany, *Lawrence's Nightmare*, 229–30, for a previously unpublished letter from Katherine Mansfield describing a horrific fight between the Lawrences in Cornwall.

62. Ibid., 311, 331–33.

63. Lawrence, *Psychoanalysis/Fantasia*, 134.

possibility that such desire in a male was anything but path-
ological, and he constructed political and social schemes designed to combat the forces that he saw creating homoeroticism while allowing for its expression in nonthreatening,
socially constructive ways.

4

Surpassing the Love of Women

The shift in Lawrence's thought from the glorification of pro-creative sexuality toward the transcendence of desire has political as well as private implications in *Women in Love* and the works contemporaneous with it. With his changed view of heterosexuality, Lawrence in the same works displays a new attitude toward women, often manifested as revulsion toward their sexual desire (which may be rebuffed by the male characters, as Birkin does Ursula's). The terms in which Lawrence describes women's sexuality reveal that he now understands it not only as a private but also as a political phenomenon: in *Women in Love*, Birkin rejects "the merging, the clutching, the mingling of love" because "woman was always so horrible and clutching. . . . She wanted to have, to own, to control, to be dominant" (191–92).

At the same time, in essays contemporaneous with that novel, Lawrence argues for a social system based on attraction between men, and he does so as if it were a purely political idea: he proposes a hierarchical, authoritarian political organization composed entirely of males, to be based on a pledge of love from each man to his chosen leader. Each man, having pledged himself to his superior, would march away from his woman with other men. This male organization Lawrence calls a "sensual" and "culminating" hierarchy, though it is not sexual. The use of "sensual" imagery to describe this political idea seems to be an inversion of the phenomenon noted earlier: at the same time that he is translating sexual behavior into political terms, Lawrence also appropriates sexual images to describe political phenomena. This conflation may in fact be covertly appropriate, since his new political ideas are related to the sexual discomfort examined in the last chapter. Lawrence was not allowing himself openly to express gynephobia and homoeroticism, either in his life or in his work, and certain political ideas became vehicles for the expression of those feelings.

The same ideas appear both in *Women in Love* and in the essays contemporaneous with it, but ideas asserted in the essays are debated in the novel. In the essays, Lawrence proclaims that "the future of mankind depends" on the establishment of a relationship between men that will be as eternal and as socially entrenched as marriage already is. This male marriage is to be not a sexual union but an impersonal conjunction similar to the one Birkin and Ursula establish in *Women in Love*—though, in the essays in which the manhood cult is described, no such conjunction seems possible between men and women: the latter are simply to be taught submission and left behind. The novelistic treatment of the idea, then, is different from that given it in the essays, and the difference may again suggest that the apparently heterosexual relationship between Birkin and Ursula incorporates intrinsically homoerotic elements. The confusion created by this incorporation, and by Lawrence's ambivalence toward the homoerotic, helps to explain some of the ambiguity and felt complexity of that work. But some of that complexity proceeds from a desire on Lawrence's part to discuss the political ideas with himself, to make of the novels what W. B. Yeats calls the poetry created in argument with oneself, rather than the rhetoric used to convince others.[1] Whereas the essays argue energetically for Lawrence's new political ideas, *Women in Love* poses serious opposition to them as well.

The political shift followed the same chronological ordering as the related changes. Embryonic evidence of it appeared in the April 1915 revisions to *The Rainbow*, and essays written during the composition of *Women in Love* expanded and modified the new ideas where *Women in Love* itself gave them am-

1. W. B. Yeats, "Per Amica Silentia Lunae," *Mythologies* (New York: Macmillan, 1959), 331.

biguous treatment. In this chapter we shall examine the vague but discernible politics of Lawrence's *Rainbow* period before proceeding to the essays contemporaneous with *Women in Love*, which present the new ideas in their clearest form. We shall then consider the artistically complex appearance of these notions in *Women in Love* but will end by arguing that certain contemporaneous essays allow us to see clear political underpinnings beneath the poetry of that novel. In particular, the climax of Birkin and Ursula's struggle, the tearoom scene, can be read in the light of the essays as an intersection of Lawrence's authoritarian politics with latent homosexuality and antifeminism.

The social vision of *The Rainbow* is the subject of some dispute; many critics feel that the ending, with its utopian vision of a better life in the future, bears little relation to the novel as a whole. Miko, for instance, thinks that Ursula's final vision asserts unsuccessfully the religious dimension of social problems and their religious solution. He argues that Lawrence in *The Rainbow* is "trying to find a viable social mode of fulfillment but keeps being overcome by a repulsion to everything beyond the personal and religious searching of the first two generations."[2] Sanders agrees, arguing that nature always overwhelms society in this work, and that "collective, purposive human effort, wherever it appears in the novel, is destructive."[3] On the other hand, Eugene Goodheart finds that, in all of Lawrence's work (as, clearly, in *Fantasia of the Unconscious*), "activity in 'the daylight world' . . . is purposive and selfless, a spontaneous giving up of oneself to the life of the community" and "the great purpose of manhood."[4]

Some of this critical disagreement stems from the April 1915 revisions. Before those changes, no positive collective

2. Stephen J. Miko, *Towards* Women in Love (New Haven: Yale University Press, 1971), 167.

3. Scott Sanders, *D. H. Lawrence: The World of the Five Major Novels* (New York: Viking, 1973), 87.

4. Eugene Goodheart, *The Utopian Vision of D. H. Lawrence* (Chicago: University of Chicago Press, 1963), 13–14.

activity appeared in the novel: none of the early Brangwens identify with groups larger than their families, Ursula is disillusioned with movements and institutions, and when Skrebensky participates selflessly in warfare and empire, he fails to realize "that the highest good of the community as it stands is no longer the highest good of even the average individual" (327). As discussed earlier, Skrebensky's adherence to abstractions instead of "his own intrinsic life" (326) makes him look "like nothing" to Ursula (309) and leaves him open to being destroyed by her desire to "procreate" herself. And originally even Will's accession to public life was not a particularly positive development: whereas in the final version his sensuality "set another man in him free," in the typescript it is presented only as "leaving a superficial man in him disengaged," and he merely acquires a "public self" instead of a "purposive" one (RTS 354, *Rainbow* 235).

In the new ending to "The Child," however, Will goes out "to be unanimous with the whole of purposive mankind" in what is not his nullification or a hobby for his superficial self, but "a supremely desirable thing to be doing" that puts his family "in connection with the great human endeavor at last. It gained new vigour thereby" (235–36). Because Anna stays home, this revision represents an adjusted view not only of collective activity but also of gender roles; it is the first appearance in Lawrence's work of the idea that men should have a further life, apart from women. Even so, it is not yet a "purpose of manhood," as it will be in *Fantasia* and other works from the leadership period; the term "manhood" is scarcely invoked in *The Rainbow*. No one would be likely to identify it as such, in fact, without hindsight from the later works, since, as Goodheart himself observes, in *The Rainbow* it is the women who feel the greatest need for a further life, beyond the home, whereas the men seem to live for sexual fulfillment.[5]

The April revisions, then, show the start of what would

5. Goodheart, *Utopian Vision*, 118.

become essential elements of Lawrence's leadership politics. The rest of the novel, however, insofar as it is political, favors anarchy rather than leadership, and sexual equality rather than male dominance; letters from the same period concur. In the last paragraph of the novel a female prophet predicts the achievement of heaven on earth, which will happen when people are freed from their artificial shells. She has gone ahead to this release already, and her rebirth makes clear that the "shell" consists of attachment to "the world of things" and conventional social relations ("all the vast encumbrances of the world that was in contact with her . . . her father, and her mother, and her lover, and all her acquaintance" 491–92). She foresees a divine world "built up in a living fabric of Truth, fitting to the over-arching heaven" when "houses and factories" are "swept away" (495). This vision in fact makes sense in relation to the rest of the novel: if fangs are identifiable with angels' swords, then there must be a divine order that will establish itself when the conventional order is removed. The implication is that the godliness in each noble savage needs only to be freed to express itself.

Writing to Lady Ottoline Morrell in February 1915, Lawrence described his Rananim as just such an anarchic utopia. He considered himself and Lady Ottoline to be planning the actual establishment of this heaven on earth:

> I hold this the most sacred duty—the gathering together of a number of people who shall so agree to live by the *best* they know, that they shall be *free* to live by the best they know. The ideal, the religion, must now be *lived, practiced.* . . .
>
> Every strong soul must put off its connection with this society, its vanity and chiefly its fear, and go naked with its fellows, weaponless, armourless, without shield or spear, but only with naked hands and open eyes. Not self-sacrifice, but fulfilment, the flesh and the spirit in league together, not in arms against one another. And each man shall know that he is part of the greater body, each man shall submit that his own soul is not supreme even to himself. To be or not to be is no longer the question. The question now, is how shall we fulfil our declaration, 'God is'. For all our life is now based on the assumption that God is not—or except on rare occasions.

The belief that "God is not" expresses itself in contemporary society in "a myriad contrivances for preventing us from being let down by the meanness in ourselves or in our neighbors," and such precautions inadvertently inhibit the flowering of individual life, which needs freedom and fulfillment "in the flesh of all strong desire . . . not on heaven but on earth." Like Gandhi, Lawrence thought that going weaponless in the world would put an end to the need for weapons, and his economics were similarly based on faith in innate human virtue: the economy of heaven on earth will be "communism based, not on poverty, but on riches," and the inhabitants will be "not bent on getting and having, because we know we inherit all things."[6]

Lawrence was poor all his life, and he never stopped hoping for a system that would eliminate the need to struggle for a living. He always felt that the unequal distribution of money prevented people from concentrating on what really mattered: "It is no use saying a man's soul should be free, if his boots hurt him so much he can't walk." In February 1915 he wrote to Russell that the "modern industrial capitalistic system" must be broken, that "there must be a revolution in the state. It shall begin by the nationalising of all industries and means of communication, and of the land—in one fell blow. Then a man shall have his wages whether he is sick or well or old."[7] He hoped to form "a little colony where there shall be no money but a sort of communism as far as necessaries of life go, and some real decency." With competition for material goods removed, the community would be "established upon the assumption of goodness in the members, instead of the assumption of badness."[8]

Innately good, economically satisfied humans do not have much use for government, and at this time Lawrence saw no intrinsic need for people even to organize politically, far less

6. Cambridge *Letters* 2, 271–73.
7. Ibid., 282–83.
8. Ibid., 259.

to lead or be led. Yet in the letter just quoted, in which Lawrence sketches the lineaments of his Rananim, he sounds suddenly authoritarian on the subject of those who might oppose its establishment:

> We will be aristocrats, and as wise as the serpent in dealing with the mob. For the mob shall not crush us nor starve us nor cry us to death. We will deal cunningly with the mob, the greedy soul, we will gradually bring it to subjection.[9]

Clearly, his utopia is to be elitist, a solution for the few. But this assertion of a need to subject the mob is not authoritarian in the sense that it will be in his later work. The subjection is not for its own sake, as a desirable political principle, nor is it seen as a permanent arrangement for the good of the race; it is more a matter of self-defense, for the purpose of protecting the members of utopia from the threat of being subjected *by* the mob, which seems to want to "crush" or "starve" or "cry to death" those who hope to live differently.

Similarly, in *The Rainbow* Ursula is elitist without being authoritarian. She objects to the idea that other people are equal to her when they have the same amount of money, and on those grounds she dislikes democracy. In the original typescript, however, she does not even object to democracy; the April revisions also adjusted Ursula's attitude in the direction of leadership politics. In the original, Ursula implicitly endorses democracy by criticizing the system around her as "a false democracy," but in April Lawrence revised the passage as follows. [Brackets] indicate what he deleted and ⟨angle brackets⟩ enclose the new material:

> "Everything is so meagre and paltry, it is so unspiritual—[a false] ⟨I hate⟩ democracy."
> "What do you mean," he asked her, hostile, "[by a false] ⟨why do you hate⟩ democracy?"
> "[Every pursy little man, as soon as he gets a bit of money, shoving himself forward and becoming a voice, putting his finger in the pie, no matter what voice of a fool he's got, nor

9. Ibid., 273.

what dirty finger.] ⟨Only the greedy and ugly people come to the top in a democracy," she said, "because they're the only people who will push themselves there. Only degenerate people are democratic.⟩"

The original implies that in a *true* democracy those who are worthy to be heard will be, regardless of their social position, whereas the revision condemns democracy wholesale. And Ursula does not say, "I *know* I am better than all of them," asserting herself as a superior being, until the April revision (RTS 688, *Rainbow* 461).

Lawrence's Rananim might have been elitist, but he believed that his "aristocrats" would desire neither money nor power, but the common good, defined in a new way: "this shall be the new hope: that there shall be a life wherein the struggle shall not be for money or for power, but for individual freedom and common effort towards good." This new hope even sounds at times as if it were for everyone and not just for the anarchic aristocrats. The need for a "new hope" is explained in this way: "After the war, the soul of the people will be so maimed and so injured that it is horrible to think of." And when he widens this vision to make it a "revolution in the state," he clearly thinks it will be a liberation for all. Yet he does not seem to think that it will need to be imposed on anyone; "subjection" seems to be reserved for the greedy few who seek to destroy the new hope by enforcing conformity. In fact, in the same letter, practically in the same breath in which he speaks of subjecting the greedy mob, Lawrence declares that

> the great serpent to destroy, is the Will to Power: the desire for one man to have some dominion over his fellow man. Let us have *no* personal influence, if possible—nor personal magnetism, as they used to call it, nor persuasion—no 'Follow me'—but only 'Behold.'[10]

Inconsistent and politically naive this vision may certainly be. Lawrence may even have had an unconscious or unadmitted

10. Ibid., 272.

image of himself leading others toward this humble 'Behold.' But insofar as it is a conscious political vision, it is of a new organization that transcends considerations of power.

The utopia outlined here further distinguishes itself from Lawrence's later political thought by including women and not requiring their submission to males. In this period Lawrence seems especially concerned that women take their place as free and self-responsible individuals in his religious community. He designated "the germ" of "The Sisters" as "woman becoming individual, self-responsible, taking her own initiative,"[11] and he seems to approve of the idea, both in that letter and in *The Rainbow*, where his heroine achieves individuality and self-responsibility in the end.

True, Ursula dreams of a man who will be a "Son of God," for whom she will be merely a "daughter of men"; that sounds like a hierarchical relationship and may indicate that certain preconceptions about male dominance exist beneath the surface of *The Rainbow*. As noted earlier, however, the way Lawrence uses "Son of God" in his *Rainbow* period does not always have gender connotations. In a contemporaneous letter he uses the phrase to refer to a person of either sex who knows how to live, how to shrug off economic motives and live from the soul. Writing to the woman who was to have an equal share in establishing his Rananim, Lawrence says, "I want you to form the nucleus of a new community which shall start a new life amongst us. . . . We will be Sons of God who walk here on earth."[12] And Ursula's desire for a Son of God may not finally imply a distinction between herself and him. The phrase is not used at the end of the novel, and the man she awaits will only be God's son in the sense that he will be "a man created by God" (rather than by herself). But in that she will be his equal: "The man would come out of Eternity to which she herself belonged" (493).

Earlier, as a young man in Eastwood, Lawrence had asso-

11. Ibid., 165.
12. Ibid., 271–73.

ciated with feminists, though in the novelistic reflection of his
Eastwood years the autobiographical hero has a stereotypi-
cally Victorian male's view of what women can do: "work *can*
be nearly everything to a man," Paul Morel argues, "but a
woman only works with a part of herself. The real and vital
part is covered up."[13] The fulfillment of this vital self, however, is not in service and obedience; rather it is in the joint
submission by both members of the couple to the impersonal
forces that sweep through them in sex, just as it is in *The
Rainbow*. And by the time he wrote *The Rainbow*, Lawrence
had lost the idea that work could be everything to a person of
either sex.

Though Ursula cannot find fulfillment in work, the reason
lies not in her gender but in the nature of the work available.
Her struggle for a "place in the working world . . . with full
rights there" is beneficial to her: "Her real, individual self
drew together and became more coherent during these two
years of teaching. . . . her wild, chaotic, soul became hard
and independent" (407–11). But she moves on to prophesy a
revolution that will sweep away the present industrial system, because she has experienced it as a violation of her
being. Watching a successful teacher, she thinks, "The man
was become a mechanism working on and on and on. But the
personal man was in subdued friction all the time." Work is
not everything, or even nearly everything, to this man, and
the same work dehumanizes Ursula identically despite the
difference in their genders:

> She must become the same—put away the personal self, be-
> come an instrument, an abstraction, working upon a certain
> material, the class, to achieve a set purpose of making them
> know so much each day. And she could not submit. Yet grad-
> ually she felt the invincible iron closing upon her.
>
> (383)

13. D. H. Lawrence, *Sons and Lovers* (1913; rpt. New York: Penguin, 1976),
416. See Hilary Simpson, *D. H. Lawrence and Feminism* (De Kalb: Northern
Illinois University Press, 1982), 19–60, for a discussion of Lawrence's early
relationship with the movement.

Each generation in *The Rainbow* finds its remunerative labor more barren and mechanical than did the last, and this jaundiced view of the job persists in *Women in Love*, where Birkin and Ursula defect from the educational system. The vision of *Women in Love* is not of a better world in which men work and women stay home, but of one in which no one works.

Clearly, equal treatment of the sexes on this issue should not block the perception that by the time he finished *Women in Love* Lawrence had changed his mind about the self-responsibility of women. In 1917–18, he declared, "When man falls before woman, and she must become alone and self-responsible, she goes on and on in destruction, till all is death or till man can rise anew and take his place."[14] It might be argued that Skrebensky falls before Ursula; but he was not leading her when he fell, and she does not need him to stop her destructive career. She rises on her own, having been renewed by direct contact with the divine power in the horses; and horses, as we saw in chapter 2, have little to do with maleness in this phase of Lawrence's thinking. The fact that *The Rainbow*'s prophet is a woman indicates how much more Lawrence thought of women's potential in early 1915 than he would when he was revising *Women in Love*—for in 1917–18 he also said that "woman cannot take the creative lead" and "what woman knows, she knows because man has taught it her" (*SM* 133).

While writing *The Rainbow*, Lawrence declared in "Study of Thomas Hardy" that "men have kept their women tightly in bondage" only "because they were afraid of the unknown, and because they wanted to retain the full-veined gratification of self-pleasure," which was a form of mechanical "reaction upon" themselves (Lawrence's euphemism for masturbation). A man can only come to "the full consummation" if he has "intense fear and reverence of the female, as of the

14. D. H. Lawrence, *The Symbolic Meaning: The Uncollected Versions of Studies in Classic American Literature*, ed. Armin Arnold (New York: Viking, 1964), 131. Hereafter this work will be cited in the text and identified as *SM*.

unknown." He must leave her free of his domination if he is to gain "a sense of richness and oneness with all life, as if, by being part of life, he were infinitely rich. Which is different from the sense of power, of dominating life. The *Wille zur Macht* is a spurious feeling" (*Phoenix* 491–93).

The couples in *The Rainbow*, accordingly, find fulfillment without any sort of submission on the woman's part; when they falter on the way, the woman's lack of submission is not the problem. This difference is clearly visible in the contrasting connotations of two otherwise similar scenes in *The Rainbow* and in *Women in Love*. In a climactic moment of the second novel, Ursula recognizes Birkin as a superior being when she crouches before him, stroking his buttocks and the backs of his thighs: "It was here she discovered him one of the sons of God such as were in the beginning of the world, not a man, something other, something more" (305). Because of this recognition, she abruptly accepts the relationship he has wanted all along.

But the scene almost exactly like it in *The Rainbow* has nothing to do with power. Lydia embraces Tom's buttocks and crouches, looking up at him the way Ursula looks up at Birkin, but Lydia is not making a discovery. The embrace is frankly sexual and uncomplicated, though Lawrence made it less so in the April revisions. Originally, "she put her arms round him as he stood before her, round his thighs, pressing his loins against her breast." Lawrence later substituted "him" for "his loins," but the frontal pressing is still the important motion. And though this touch reveals to Tom "the mould of his own nakedness" and he finds himself "passionately lovely," he is not powerful and Lydia's attitude toward him does not change. The issue in this scene is whether or not Tom will be able to go forth into "the awful unknown" that he perceives her to be, and that going forth is characterized as "yielding to her . . . relaxing towards her . . . mingling with her" (RTS 142–43, *Rainbow* 90).

A similar scene may have occurred between the Lawrences early in their marriage, and he interpreted its significance differently in the two novels because his ideas changed. In the earlier novel, regeneration comes through submission to a procreative divinity that is essentially female and revealed in the bodies of women; therefore the emphasis is on Tom's terrified yielding to the unknown in his wife. In the second novel, power is male and woman's place is not to mingle with it but to revere it and leave it alone.

Between 1922 and 1926, Lawrence published the three books usually referred to as his leadership novels (*Aaron's Rod, Kangaroo,* and *The Plumed Serpent*). In these works he explores the doctrine expounded in *Psychoanalysis and the Unconscious* (1921) and *Fantasia of the Unconscious* (1922). *Fantasia* in particular calls for the establishment of a hierarchical "unison of manhood": "Men have got to choose their leaders, and obey them to the death. And it must be a system of culminating aristocracy, society tapering like a pyramid to the supreme leader." Women will not be a part of this political organization based on "a relationship of men towards men in a spirit of unfathomable trust and responsibility, service and leadership, obedience and pure authority." Though he assumes that men will continue to be married, Lawrence exhorts them to "go on alone, ahead of the woman . . . and never look back." "Husbands, don't love your wives any more," he says; "combat her in her sexual pertinacity"; and "look round for the man your heart will point out to you. And follow . . ." Though he insists that "the great collective passion of belief which brings men together . . . is not a sex passion," it sounds like a sanitized substitute or rationalization for homoerotic desire: "The intense, passionate yearning of the soul towards the soul of a stronger, greater individual, and the passionate blood-belief in the fulfilment of this yearning will give men the next motive for life." This male cult is also designed to teach women "wife-submission," which is based on "sexually asking nothing"; a husband can only hope to inspire this submission if he has "the courage to withdraw into his own stillness and singleness, and put the wife under the spell of his fulfilled decision." If the husband does not insist on the "divinity" of "*non-domestic, male* action, which is not devoted to the increase of the female," then "ultimately she tears him to bits."[15]

Lawrence is generally believed to have developed these views after the war, when authoritarian political thought became popular all over Europe. He was certainly a visible part of that reactionary surge. In addition to the three leadership novels and the two major polemics mentioned earlier, he also wrote a history textbook for Oxford University Press that ends with the following idea:

> A great united Europe of productive working-people, all materially equal, will never be able to continue and remain firm unless it unites also round one great chosen figure, some hero who can lead a great war, as well as administer a wide peace. It all depends on the will of the people. But the will of the people must concentrate in one figure, who is also supreme over the will of the people. He must be chosen, but responsible to God alone.[16]

Movements in European History was not a success with the educational establishment; it was in print from 1921 to 1944 but sold only 15,000 copies. Those copies, however, were indeed used to teach history to school children in England and Ireland, a fact that indicates how acceptable such views were at least to some of Lawrence's contemporaries.[17]

But Lawrence does not seem to have been influenced in his political thinking by the postwar reactionary movements. Unlike some other modernist authoritarian writers, he was critical of the fascists from the time he became aware of them, despite parallels between his thinking and theirs. In his "Epilogue" to *Movements in European History* (written for the 1924 edition but rejected by the press), he derides fascism in Italy as "only another kind of bullying." Nevertheless, he calls for

---

15. D. H. Lawrence, *Psychoanalysis and the Unconscious/Fantasia of the Unconscious* (New York: Viking, 1960), 210, 218, 177, 145, 211, 157–59, 134–35.

16. D. H. Lawrence, *Movements in European History* (1921; rpt. ed. James T. Boulton, London: Oxford University Press, 1971), 306.

17. James T. Boulton, "Introduction to the New Edition," *Movements in European History*, xii–xvii.

the investment of unquestioned authority in a leader whose "natural nobility" is "given by God or the Unknown" rather than by a self-interested electorate, which chooses leaders "without a spark of true power" to be their "mere tools." He even briefly adopts the condemnation of big capital that led Ezra Pound to work for Mussolini: the "Force of Finance" is "a great Secret Society . . . a great irresponsible Force which has escaped from the control of true human power, and which is likely to work enormous evil."[18]

In some of his writings from this period Lawrence was also anti-Semitic. For instance in his earliest essay on James Fenimore Cooper (which the *English Review* did not hesitate to publish in 1919), he asserts that "as long as we believe in Equality, so long shall we grind mechanically till, like most Jews, we have no living soul, no living self, but only a super-machine faculty which will coin money" (*SM* 79); and in *Kangaroo* he opines that "if a man is to be brought to any heel, better a spurred heel than the heel of a Jewish financier."[19]

He does not object to fascism itself, in fact, but only to some of its methods. The fascists shot the mayor of Fiesole for being a socialist; therefore fascism equals bullying, while his own leadership politics do not. He goes on to assert that "we *must* have authority, and there *must* be power," but "the forcing of one man's will over another man is bullying." Instead, people are to recognize the superiority of the leader and follow voluntarily: each person is "to care supremely for nothing but the spark of *noblesse* that is in him and in her, and to follow only the leader who is a star of the new, natural *Noblesse*."[20]

These views were not only compatible in the main with those of the fascists, they were also obviously shaped in part by Lawrence's reading of sources, especially Nietzsche, that helped to create the climate for fascism;[21] but they became a

18. Lawrence, *Movements in European History*, 317–21.
19. D. H. Lawrence, *Kangaroo* (1923; rpt. New York: Viking, 1960), 217.
20. Lawrence, *Movements in European History*, 317–20.
21. See Emile Delavenay, *D. H. Lawrence: The Man and His Work*, trans. Katharine M. Delavenay (Carbondale: Southern Illinois University Press,

part of his thinking well before the postwar rise of that movement. The politics of dominance began to appear in Lawrence's letters in June 1915, soon after his reading of Heraclitus (who was also an important source for Nietzsche). He wrote to Russell: "There must be an aristocracy of people who have wisdom, and there must be a Ruler: A Kaiser: no Presidents and democracies. . . . You must have a government based upon good, better and best." In one of these letters he quoted three Heraclitean fragments, one against war, one against the mob, and the last for a single ruler: "And it is law, too, to obey the counsel of one."[22]

Lawrence's anarchic utopia of a few months before had relied implicitly on a belief in the innate goodness of humanity, but he lost that faith between March and April 1915. In April he wanted to rewrite his "philosophy": "I will not tell the people this time that they are angels in disguise. Curse them, I will tell them they are dogs and swine, bloodsuckers."[23] The year before he had declared, "I like people as people anywhere,"[24] and in February 1915 that he was "ashamed to write any real writing of passionate love to my fellow men" until after the revolution;[25] but in April 1915 he felt that "it would do me so much good if I could kill a few people."[26] From here it is a short way to Lawrence's general misanthropy of February 1916 ("People are so self-important. Let them die, silly blighters, fools, and twopenny knaves").[27]

Fools and knaves need to be either avoided or led, and the

1972), 298–303 and passim. Delavenay argues that Lawrence was influenced by Houston Chamberlain and other racist thinkers important to early fascism, but the circumstantial evidence he accumulates is not convincing. Lawrence's copious correspondence is full of references to writers that interested him, but he does not mention Chamberlain or Delavenay's other candidates even once, nor do such writers appear on the lists of Lawrence's reading left by the women who were close to him.

22. Cambridge *Letters 2*, 364, 366.
23. Ibid., 313.
24. Ibid., 149.
25. Ibid., 283.
26. Ibid., 313.
27. Ibid., 537.

two impulses of alienation and leadership shaped Lawrence's political thought of the next few years. Most critics have been reluctant to recognize that Lawrence's next novel was moving in the direction of the leadership politics, and they have justified their reluctance on the grounds that *Women in Love* was written in 1916, predating the leadership novels and essays that were written after the war. But the same year Lawrence evidently made the reddish brown revisions to *Women in Love*, he also finished the first draft of *Aaron's Rod*.[28] That novel as we know it ends with Lilly telling Aaron that he will know when he has found his leader. Lilly, who appears to be one of Lawrence's many self-portraits, clearly has himself in mind for the position: he lectures Aaron, who is powerfully drawn to Lilly while resisting him. The first draft of *Aaron's Rod* does not survive, and it is impossible, therefore, to tell what Lawrence changed when he revised it in 1920–21. But even the final composition of *Aaron's Rod* followed that of *Women in Love* by no more than two years, and Lawrence worked on both novels in 1917 and 1919.

Furthermore, there is no doubt that Lawrence extensively revised *Women in Love* in 1917, the year he also began the first full philosophical treatment of his leadership politics. Written between September 1917 and June 1918,[29] the original versions of Lawrence's essays on American literature are considerably different from those published later as *Studies in Classic American Literature* (1923); they first appeared in the *English Review* between November 1918 and June 1919, and in 1964 they were collected and published by Armin Arnold as *The Symbolic Meaning*. These essays anticipate *Fantasia* in nearly every particular, calling for a hierarchical political structure based on a "unison of manhood" and showing signs of a fear of sex and women. They also link power, sexuality, and the bowels in a way that is peculiar to this period of his thinking and that illuminates "Excurse" while clearly indicating that

28. Keith Sagar, *D. H. Lawrence: A Calendar of His Works* (Austin: University of Texas Press, 1979), 96–97.
29. Sagar, *Calendar*, 79–81, 84–86.

Lawrence's turn toward leadership politics was motivated at least in part by private emotional reasons.

The social theory proposed in these essays centers on the idea of innate inequality among men: "Some men are born from the mystery of creation, to know, to lead, and to command. And some are born to listen, to follow, to obey" (*SM* 78). The inequality resides not in heredity or possessions, but in "the inmost sincere soul" (*SM* 79). His basic political idea continued to be that the social and the private solutions were identical. But by 1917 the private self-realization had a more distinctly political dimension: "Let every man learn to be himself, and in so being to give reverence and obedience where such is due, and to take command and authority where these are due. Let this be done spontaneously, from the living, real self" (*SM* 80).

Lawrence used American literature in this political polemic because he found under its surface a dual impulse, one side of which was Calvinist repression, "a deep lust for vindictive power over the life-issue," and the other side, the motion of life itself toward a new creation, a "mystic transubstantiation" to a new form of living. The repressive side in America has led to "the utter subjection of the living, spontaneous being to the fixed, mechanical, ultimately insane *will*"; the political form of this subjection is "this mechanical democracy . . . this vast mechanical concord of innumerable machine-parts" (*SM* 25–31).

Because it necessitates the suppression of impulse, democracy represents for Lawrence a denial of the "sensual or passional self," yet he is not retailing the stereotypical view that Puritan culture was sexually repressive. The coming regeneration is imaged in these essays as the liberation of a political rather than a sexual impulse, though it will be satisfied in passionate friendship between men, replacing and surpassing sex with women. The prototype of this friendship occurs between Bumppo and Chingachgook in Cooper's "Leatherstocking" novels. Lawrence sees it as "this perfect relationship, this last abstract love"; the two are "balanced in unspeakable conjunction," as Birkin wants to be with Ursula, "without contact of word or touch." This asexual union is "the inception of a new psyche, a new race-soul," and Lawrence uses fertility metaphors (flower and seed) to characterize the spiritual mating of the two men, from which will somehow spring a new race (*SM* 95, 102–3, 106).

For Lawrence this all-male friendship will renew the white race because it represents a new union of opposites: Bumppo, the white man, "sees the Red man, the sensual being which for ages he has been destroying or fleeing from. And that which he has most perfectly destroyed he now most perfectly accepts across the gulf" (*SM* 102). Bumppo needs this abstract, sexless communion with someone who only symbolically represents sensual being because, like the race of sensation seekers in "The Crown," he has come to the end of one line of experience and can go no further in it. Bumppo's only physical consummation is in fear and death:

> He has a passion for the experience of danger and death. No woman could give him the sheer flame of sensation he feels when the hand of a hostile Indian is laid on him as he lies in his canoe believing himself to be far out on the water. . . . He has come to the end of his journey, and before him lies the leap into space, into oblivion, into death.
>
> (*SM* 102)

But that which lies ahead is not simply death: it is also Chingachgook, and here, as elsewhere in Lawrence's work, the association between death and comradeship is not accidental.

The 1917–18 version of the essay on Whitman was never published and has unfortunately been lost; but there does survive a version Lawrence wrote in 1920, which is quite different from the essay published in *Studies in Classic American Literature* (1923). The 1920 essay on Whitman is largely a celebration of "the love of comrades," which is superior to and surpasses marriage. Lawrence exhorts his readers to move on from marriage and "establish the love of comrades, as marriage is really established now. . . . the future of mankind depends on the way in which this relationship is entered upon by us" (*SM* 239). He felt a similar urgency about the need for this new relationship in "The Education of the People" (begun in 1918 and extended in 1920). In this essay Lawrence exhorts men to "go always ahead of their women . . . all the time hovering at the tip of life and on the verge of death, the men, the leaders," pledged to one another: "Let there be again the old passion of deathless friendship between man and man. Humanity can never advance into the new regions of unexplored futurity otherwise" (*Phoenix* 665).

The logic of this necessity in part resembles Lawrence's argument in "The Crown": we have reached such a state of development as a race that we need to incorporate the death with the life in us, to become whole. "Creative life must come near to death, to link up the mystic circuit" (*SM* 238), and "manly love" is a development in death, or on the brink of death:

> In its beauty, the ultimate comradeship flowers on the brink of death. But it flowers from the root of all life upon the blossoming tree of life.
> The life circuit now depends entirely upon the sex-unison of marriage. This circuit must never be broken. But it must be still surpassed. We cannot help the laws of life. . . . If marriage is eternal, the great bond of life, how much more is this bond eternal, being the great life-circuit which borders on death in all its round.
>
> (*SM* 239)

The superior eternality of this bond proceeds from the kind of transcendence described in "The Reality of Peace": when the life flow and the death flow unite, we become a lark in song, a rose of all the world, a pure gem of transcendence. "The ultimate comradeship" links life and death and is therefore "the last seedless flower of pure beauty, beyond purpose."

Here, Lawrence significantly alters the terms he employed in "Hardy." In the earlier essay, the flowering into being in sex between man and woman had no purpose but might incidentally leave offspring behind, and the ultimate flowering of life was presumably near to death because it was "at the extreme tip of life" (*Phoenix* 406–9). In the "Hardy" version of the soul's flowering, women flowered as well as men; it was a woman's responsibility to "bear herself" just as it was a man's to bear himself. But in the Whitman essay the flowering of comradeship that "is the soul's last and most vivid responsibility" not only occurs without women, women are excluded from it; and it is nonsexual. Apparently there are "centres" of life within a man more profound than those related to sex:

> Acting from the last and profoundest centres, man acts womanless. It is no longer a question of race continuance. It is a question of sheer, ultimate being, the perfection of life, nearest to death. Acting from these centres, man is an extreme being, the unthinkable warrior, creator, mover, and maker.
> And the polarity is between man and man.
>
> (*SM* 236–37)

Not male friendship but heterosexual love was Lawrence's original dynamic of life, and accordingly, in 1913, he declared Whitman's poetry to be "neither art nor religion nor truth: Just a self revelation of a man who could not live." Whitman failed at life because "he never fought with another person"; he was not engaged in the struggle to "come through" with a woman, as Lawrence was.[30] But by 1920, Whitman had become for Lawrence "the greatest modern poet," who "alone of all moderns has known . . . the last dynamic truth of life . . . the mystery of manly love" (*SM* 240, 237).

As in the original version of "The Crown," and perhaps in "The Reality of Peace," in the Whitman essay Lawrence connects love between men with death but also glorifies it. Although he speaks openly of homosexual passion in the original "Crown" and in "The Reality of Peace" of secret shameful desire, his comradely love of 1920 is not overtly sexual, and "if it destroys marriage it makes itself purely deathly" (*SM* 239). The new love is a communion transcending "word or touch," and such it will remain throughout Lawrence's leadership period. The comrades-in-arms of *Kangaroo* and *The*

---

30. Cambridge *Letters* 2, 130. Lawrence used the phrase "come through" to characterize what he thought was the end of his marital struggle when he was writing the poems collected in *Look! We Have Come Through!* (published in 1917 but written earlier).

Plumed Serpent are married men who yet have a further life with the other warriors, and the closest they come to each other is when one nurses the other in illness, as Lilly does Aaron in *Aaron's Rod*.

The works written in Lawrence's traditionally recognized leadership period, however, seem to represent in some ways a political sublimation of ideas he expressed more openly during the war years. By 1919 Lawrence had dropped the explicitly homosexual prologue to *Women in Love* and made Birkin's original renunciation of sex ambiguous; and the 1920 essay on Whitman places manly love beyond sex and patronizes marriage. Some readers in Lawrence's time may, however, have recognized the homoerotic origins of his "comradely love": John Edge points out that "the word 'comradeship' was used before and during the period when Lawrence wrote his major novels as a synonym for homosexual emotion and behaviour."[31]

There are also suggestions of the homoerotic, not only in the further life with men, but in Lawrence's apparent desire to be himself one of the supreme leaders. In *Fantasia*, he asks if "President Wilson, or Karl Marx, or Bernard Shaw ever felt one hot blood-pulse of love for the working man." Possibly some of this hot love is nostalgia for the working-class roots he severed in his education and marriage. But what he wants from the working man is not friendship in equality but paternalistic power, with suggestions of passionate longing in his yearning to wield it. Speaking in his own voice, he says he would like the working man to

> give me back the responsibility for general affairs, a responsibility which he can't acquit, and which saps his life. I would like him to give me back the responsibility for the future. I would like him to give me back the responsibility for thought, for direction. . . .

31. John Edge, "D. H. Lawrence and the Theme of Comradeship," *Southern Review* (Adelaide, Australia) 9 (1976): 34. Edge cites Timothy d'Arch Smith, *Love in Earnest* (London: Routledge & Kegan Paul, 1970) and Brian Reade, *Sexual Heretics: Male Homosexuality in English Literature from 1850–1900* (London: Routledge & Kegan Paul, 1970).

He says it is his "passionate instinct" to try to "save" the working man, "alive, in his living, spontaneous, original being." He wants not to take but to be given the responsibility for thinking, reading, making decisions. In turn, he will "give" back to the working man "his old insouciance, and rich, original spontaneity and fullness of life," which has been "sapped" by his attempt to direct "general affairs" ("a responsibility he can't acquit"). This exchange Lawrence calls taking "hope and belief together."[32]

This vision of communion with the working man is compatible with certain statements Lawrence made before his politics became hierarchical, but he seems to have been almost consciously repressing homoerotic desire in his democratic period before his politics gave him a safe way to express it.[33] In the letter to Russell from February 1915 quoted earlier, Lawrence says, "I am ashamed to write any real writing of passionate love to my fellow men" until after the revolution. He modulates from the need for revolution to Forster's homosexuality, then back to revolution. The logic of the connection is that homosexuality results from "the fetters of this money." He invokes the image of "Titan nailed on the rock of the modern industrial capitalistic system," calls it "too shameful," and then reasons that a man who feels helpless to rip himself and others off the rock will not be able to go to a woman either: "But if I am aware that I cannot act for humanity?—Then I dare not go to a woman." As a result, "there is always Sodomy. The man goes to the man to repeat this reaction upon himself. . . . Sodomy only means that a man

---

32. Lawrence, *Psychoanalysis/Fantasia*, 149.
33. John Edge argues that Lawrence's homoerotic themes glorify male power throughout his work in a way that is suggestive of protofascist thinking. But though it is true, for instance, that in the bathing scene in *The White Peacock* Cyril feels like a woman in the arms of his male friend, this feeling is only an indication of homoerotic desire and not of a wish to lead or be led. And *The Rainbow* undermines the notion that "Lawrence's sense . . . of the male as the source of power and value is constant" (Edge, "Lawrence and the Theme of Comradeship," 43).

knows he is chained to the rock, so he will try to get the finest possible sensation out of himself."[34]

In this letter, Lawrence seems to be blaming his own homoerotic urges on "the industrial capitalistic system," and the logic of the letter suggests that his socialist revolutionizing was an attempt to remove the conditions responsible for that desire. Later he sanitizes his unacceptable desires by viewing them not as erotic urges but as spiritual promptings directed toward regeneration of the white races. Yet, oddly enough, he speaks of them as if they were sexual, asserting that the desire to master or submit is so intrinsic to the "spontaneous" self that it is a sensual urge:

> In the sensual mystery . . . there is the impulse of the lesser sensual psyche to yield itself, where it trusts and believes, to the greater psyche, yielding in the great culminating process which unifies all life in one gesture of magnificence. In this way we have acquired the domestic animals. . . . It is necessary, before men can unite in one great living gesture, that this impulse towards the mystic sensual yielding and culminating shall find expression. In the modern spirit of equality, we can get tremendous concerted action, really machine action, but no culminating living oneness, no great gesture of a creative people.
>
> (*SM* 56–57)

This essay was first published in January 1919; Lawrence's use of "sensual mystery" to mean the urge to lead or be led should give pause to those who think he is talking about sex in the "Foreword" to *Women in Love* (apparently written in September 1919)[35] when he cries, "Let us hesitate no longer to announce that the sensual passions and mysteries are equally sacred with the spiritual mysteries and passions." His insistence that the yielding of precedence is sensual, and his quasi-sexual use of "culminating" to describe the whole process, ostensibly proceed from a desire to distinguish this

---

34. Cambridge *Letters* 2, 283–85.
35. Sagar, *Calendar*, 80, 96.

"natural" harmony from unification enforced by an idea, contrary to the impulses of the unified.

But what is obvious is that these usages are also rhetorical appropriations of sexual imagery to characterize a purely political process. Furthermore, the consistent appearance of an inverse appropriation makes the conflation of sex and politics complete: not only does he speak of power relationships between men as if everyone understood them to be sensual, he also describes sexual affairs between men and women as if they were struggles for power. This conflation may be an attempt to demote sex by engulfing it in power; it is also a means to reject heterosexuality on acceptable grounds.

Lawrence analyzes the heterosexual relationships in American literature as if the lovers want only to consume or dominate each other, and he often sees the result as being lethal to the male. In *The Blithedale Romance*, for instance,

> Zenobia would outmatch Hollingsworth in the sensual conflict. . . . The serpent in her is stronger than the serpent in him. And for this he hates her. He needs to be predominant, because, actually, he is the sensual-subjugate being, and he craves to arrogate.
>
> (*SM* 143)

On the other hand, Priscilla destroys men not by fighting them but by being, like Minette/Pussum in *Women in Love*, passive and utterly subjugate, thereby sapping the man's vitality:

> She is the only being who will so submit to them, as to give them the last horrible thrills of sensual experience, in the direct *destruction* of the sensual body, pure prostitution. . . . she so draws the vital electricity from the male, in a horrible sensual-disintegrative flow, that she destroys his being as by magic.
>
> (*SM* 145–46)

In *The Blithedale Romance*, Priscilla appears to be a virgin, yet Lawrence speaks of her giving men "the last horrible thrills of sensual experience." The sensual experience here derives from her "unutterable passivity" and "destructive submission," which destroy both her being and the man's: Priscilla, too, "has no being," having "forfeited existence" in her passivity (*SM* 144–45). Though Lawrence is in favor of female submission during this period, he distinguishes it from such slavelike subjection, in comparison to which Zenobia's resistance seems less destructive, perhaps because a self in resistance remains intact. Her "sensual conflict" appears healthy compared to the merging of selves Lawrence sees in Poe's work, where "love is purely a frictional, destructive force. . . . The one life draws the other life with a terrible pressure. Each presses on the other intolerably till one is bound to disappear: one or both" (*SM* 108–9).

In these essays, Lawrence explains what becomes in *Women in Love* an apparently reflexive use of star imagery whenever he speaks of the need for single being, and he creates an image that symbolically presents the role darkness or "dark knowledge" plays for him in preserving individuality: a true self is so separate from other creatures that it is "like a star which must preserve the circumambient darkness which gives to it its distinction and uniqueness." "None the less," Lawrence notes, "in the sensual mystery there is that impulse to trust or love which leads to worship or empire" (*SM* 56). Singleness of being, he furthermore asserts, is best served through pledging one's will to a higher creature. Whereas "slavery is an avowed obliteration of the singleness of being," voluntary servitude is not, perhaps because Lawrence thinks it proceeds from an innate desire, and a pledge freely given presupposes a self to give it (*SM* 120). Yet the pledge is not always freely given, even within "the sensual mystery"; sometimes it must be forcibly wrested from the lower being. Lawrence notes that a kingbird chasing a crow flies on "the dark wings of the sensual ascendency" and that the Aztecs, who were "confirmed in blood-sacrifice," could see "the pure, tender trust which leads to culmination, and the frantic struggles for the enforcing of this culmination" in the natural world (*SM* 57–58).

The association of singleness of being with sensuality and hierarchical politics seems to proceed less from logic than from obsession; the need for personal separateness is so much a part of Lawrence's thinking in 1917 that whatever he approves of is declared both to reinforce and to proceed from it. The isolation on which he insists in 1917 is, furthermore, considerably more violent than the absolute self of *The Rainbow*; the new individual is a self in revolt from its environment, especially from connection to others. In 1917, Lawrence admires "the pride, the recoil, the jewel-like isolation of the vivid self" so thoroughly that he applies the idea even to chemical matter. Imagining that the creation of a new kind of live creature forces the creation also of a new chemical element, he says, "Another singleness is born, another creation takes place, new matter." And the new creature itself is first and foremost "the perfect and indescribable singleness" (*SM* 57, 163).

Lawrence so wants to emphasize the naturalness of the desire for isolation that he even speaks of blood knowledge as "knowledge in separation . . . the deep, tender recognition of the life-reality of the *other*, the other creature which exists not in union with the immediate self, but in dark juxtaposition" (*SM* 60). This idea is both new since *The Rainbow* and strained. If there were such a thing as blood knowledge, it would surely be easier to imagine it being gained through unison, as it is in *The Rainbow*, where "the pulse of the blood of the teats of the cows beat into the pulse of the hands of the men" (2) and where Ursula and Anton's "blood ran together as one stream" (447).

But, as argued earlier, such merging of selves has become repulsive to Lawrence, and therefore even sex belongs to an outmoded world cycle. The loss of singleness is not the only grounds for condemning heterosexual relationships in these essays. Often Lawrence does not offer grounds but simply attaches derogatory adjectives to his descriptions, and his condemnation is no respecter of circumstances. When Cooper's Hetty Hutter, the "White Lily" and "child of immaculate love," falls in love with the roughneck woodsman Hurry Harry, we might expect Lawrence's approval of this chance for her to be awakened to her sensual nature; later, Lawrence himself wrote tales of superior women who find themselves through love of undomesticated masculinity (*Lady Chatterley's Lover*, *The Lost Girl*, *The Plumed Serpent*, *St. Mawr*). But Lawrence calls the Hetty Hutter–Hurry Harry affair "the malignant mockery of imbecility" because "she herself longs to defile that which she most purely is. . . . she longs to prostitute herself to the mongrel embrace of Hurry Harry." And Harry "loves Judith, not with any intensity or real discrimination, but with prostituting appetite" (*SM* 100–101).

Lawrence's reading of *The Scarlet Letter*, furthermore, seems distinctly bent by fear of sex and women. Dimmesdale is for Lawrence "so spiritual and refined that he becomes impossible," and he preys on Hester's greater life so long as she is merely his spiritual devotee. But she gets her revenge by seducing him, and she kills him in the sexual act: "She seduces the saint, and the saint is seduced. Mystically, he is killed, as he must be killed." Her seduction of Dimmesdale is "the beginning of the end" of the old era, because it represents the revolt of "the sensual psyche" against the "man, the leader" who "has been slaying the dragon of the primary self" for two thousand years (*SM* 130–31).

So far it sounds as if Lawrence holds the stereotypical view of early life in America and believes that Dimmesdale represents Puritan sexual repression and that his death through sexuality signals the start of a "mystic transubstantiation" to something better. But Hester is not heroic for her sexual revolt. On the contrary, she is destructive and nihilistic, because she has changed the dynamic between the sexes. Her supposed seduction of Dimmesdale elicits this meditation from Lawrence:

> Man must either lead or be destroyed. Woman cannot lead. She can only be at one with man in the creative union, whilst he leads; or, failing this, she can destroy by undermining, by striking the heel of the male. . . . Whatever the outward profession and action may be, when woman is the leader or dominant in the sex relationship, and in the human progress, then the activity of mankind is an activity of disintegration and undoing. And it is woman who gives the first suggestion, starts the first impulse of the undoing.
>
> (*SM* 131)

Though Dimmesdale is wrong to suppress the sensual psyche in favor of the spirit, a woman's attempt to lead is more
wrong; not his error, but her assertion is the start of their
undoing.

When woman tries to lead, even in a worthy cause, man
becomes "like a child" to her, while she is his lethal mother, who "only further saps the root of life" in the man while
trying to revive him. She suffocates him with love, and thereby only makes him weaker, "destroys him, and drives him
into an insanity of self-destruction." The "Age of Woman" is
"the age of fatal, suffocating love, love which kills like a Laocoon snake" (*SM* 132). When a woman asserts herself, her
very love can be "a tremendous invisible destructive influence," a "malevolent force" that "can invisibly press upon the
sources of life" in the man, "pressing, sapping, shattering life
unknowably at its very sources" (*SM* 134).

That is what happens to Dimmesdale in Lawrence's 1917
reading of *The Scarlet Letter*: Chillingworth has no part in the
matter, and Dimmesdale is simply killed by Hester. Lawrence's misreading of the story and of Hester's character is
revealing. In his view, she is not a woman wronged by Puritan repression of the sensual psyche; neither is she an un-
thanked angel of mercy, reviled out of bigoted fear of her sin
and the pact with the devil supposedly betokened by it. Instead she is herself "a centre of mystic obstruction to the creative activity of all life" (*SM* 134). Lawrence claims that the
poor who are served by Hester revile her because of her secret
hatred of them. And he invokes the sanction of myth to bol-
ster his assertion that the mother principle, woman as nur-
turer and creator of life, is actually a destructive influence.
Though "the Astarte or Hecate principle . . . worships procreative child-birth, in its productive mood," it also "has in it
a necessary antagonism to life itself, the very issue of life: it
contains the element of blood sacrifice of children, in its
darker, destructive mood." The procreative impulse is transformed into child murder simply through "a progression in
intensity: intensity reached either through triumph and over-

weening, as in the old religions, or through opposition and repression, as in modern life" (*SM* 135).

Similar rejections of motherhood and female sexuality appear throughout Lawrence's political thought in this period. "Education of the People" (1918–20) maps out a utopia in which the supreme ruler would be "the most perfect utterer." He believes that "coal-miners are consummated in a Parnell, and Parnells are consummated in a Shelley. . . . In its living periods mankind accumulates upwards, through the zones of life-expression and passionate consciousness, upwards to the supreme utterer, or utterers" (*Phoenix* 609). In "Hardy," Lawrence saw Shelley as being completely outside of life because he denied the physical and "female" in himself (*Phoenix* 459), but now, no more than six years later, he sees Shelley as a superior being because of his transcendent mentality. A man becomes an "utterer" because of "his soul-strength and his soul-wisdom, which cause him to be a natural master of life." As such, he would be in Lawrence's utopia one of "the small class of the supreme judges: not merely legal judges, but judges of the destiny of the nation," having "the power for the directing of life itself" (*Phoenix* 607).

This writer-ruled state would be the antidote to the decline of Western civilization, which Lawrence attributes to the influence of mother love, the pernicious emotion disconnecting children from their natural impulses, making them spiritual and therefore susceptible to mechanization and the urges for democracy and money. In Lawrence's new utopia, children would be taken away from their mothers at birth and "given, not to yearning and maternal old maids, but to rather stupid fat women who can't be bothered with them. . . . all the germs in the list of bacteriology are not so dangerous for a child as mother-love" (*Phoenix* 621).

Lawrence blames women, then, for the state of the world, asserting that the manifestations of the cultural decline caused by mother love are "ten times" worse in women than in men: "Woman as the goddess in the machine of the human psyche is a heroine who will drive us, like a female chauffeur, through all the avenues of hell, till she pitches us eventually down the bottomless pit." Women are dangerous drivers here because while men get only "aeroplane thrills and political thrills" out of self-mechanization, women get "soul-thrills and sexual thrills, they float and squirm on clouds of self-glorification" (*Phoenix* 630–31). The "squirming" sexual thrill of women is evidently what bothers Lawrence here, even though he again, as in *Women in Love*, calls what he objects to by names that obscure it as well as characterize it: "self-glorification" or "self-importance in love." He fulminates for pages in "The Education of the People" about "insatiable self-conscious woman . . . grinding all her sensations from her head . . . all her physical churnings ground exceedingly small in the hateful self-conscious mills of her female mind . . . like so many little barrel-organs grinding their own sensations" (*Phoenix* 631–33)—rather than, one assumes, "letting the man work the business," as he says in *Lady Chatterley's Lover*. Lawrence asserts, therefore, that men must beat their women out of consciousness ("back she must go, to the old mindlessness, the old unconsciousness," *Phoenix* 623), the nature of the solution suggesting, again, that modern woman's sexual satisfaction is all in her head.

What Lawrence calls here woman's "self-glorification" or "self-importance," as well as her squirming, grinding, writhing, churning, insatiable hunger for sensation, he calls at about the same time in *Women in Love* her "clutching . . . lust for possession, a greed of self-importance in love . . . to have, to own, to control, to be dominant" (192). The contexts of such formulas eventually make their meanings for Lawrence apparent. These phrases are protectively vague, written by a man who had suffered greatly from censorship of his work. But they have the virtue of designating what Lawrence felt to be the spiritual or psychological significance of the physical event: here, as in *Lady Chatterley's Lover*, a woman's insistence on sexual satisfaction actually means that she wants to dominate her man. Because she is lethal, like Hester Prynne, when she does so, "back she must go, to the old mindlessness," and her man must undertake to force her back to it. The sexual assertion of modern woman necessitates her political submission.

Male dominance is traditionally justified on the basis of man's superior mind, and Lawrence endorsed this idea: "What woman *knows*, she knows because man has taught it her. . . . She can never give expression to the profound movements of her own being. These movements can only find an expression through a man. Man is the utterer, woman is the first cause" (*SM* 132–33). But Lawrence's primary doctrine was always a distrust of the mind. To build an ideological cage for womankind, therefore, he needed to center his thinking on a principle other than sex that was yet nonmental and expressed in physical being. Best of all would be a force that expressed itself better in men than women and that could trump woman's obvious connection to the divine as the source of new life.

This idea was of course power, and in Lawrence's thinking it replaced sex as the ultimate motivation of human behavior. Hints about the origin of this idea, however, continue to be in evidence; the works that argue for the "unison of manhood" and the superiority of male power consistently view women's maternity as a destructive force. Occasionally they even seem to deny its existence. In *Fantasia*, Lawrence's "account of the creation" begins with a birth, apparently accomplished, alone, by a male: "In the very beginning of all things . . . was a little living creature. . . . This little creature died. . . . But not before it had had young ones." When the "Daddy creature" dies, the young ones cling to it "because they must cling to something," and they have nothing else (that is, no mother). Lawrence calls this male progenitor "the first little master" and sees the universe being created from the disintegration of his body.[36] This casual display of womb envy attributes sole procreative power to the male, not calling attention to the procedure but leaving the suggestion of the male as the original source of life.

36. Lawrence, *Psychoanalysis/Fantasia*, 63.

This new glorification of the masculine and denigration of the feminine affirms that bonding with other men surpasses the love of women, and any erotic elements in the desire for such bonding are rendered acceptable through the conflation of sex and politics. Deerslayer (Bumppo, the white man) represents the leading tip of his race, ready to go beyond the love of woman to something greater:

> Deerslayer will not be sensually possessed by any woman. He is the spiritual type. He would melt like wax in the hot, possessive passion of Judith; she would absorb him, envelop him utterly. . . . She would be fulfilled and suffused with him, and he would be gone, merged, consumed into the woman, having no being of his own apart from her. . . . He sticks to his own singleness. A race falls when men begin to worship the Great Mother, when they are enveloped within the woman, as a child in the womb. And Deerslayer represents the heroic spirit of his race passing in singleness and perfection . . . a delicate hero, frail like an autumn crocus, and as deathly, but perfect.
>
> (*SM* 100–101)

Like Birkin and the sensitive man of the original "Crown," this delicate male wants nothing sensual to do with the devouring mother or Magna Mater (as Birkin calls Ursula while rejecting sex, 191–92).

But this very rejection is the start of the "mystic transubstantiation," which Lawrence describes in terms that echo Birkin's desire for a soft, asexual and floral stillness, as opposed to Gerald's hard, metallic sexuality and "mechanical democracy": "We wait for the miracle, for the new soft wind. Even the buds of iron break into soft little flames of issue. . . . It only wants the miracle, the new soft, creative wind" (*SM* 30). When Bumppo falters on the way to Chingachgook, falling in love with a woman, Lawrence condemns him as "shrinking from the sheer communion in isolation, which lies ahead, the mystic consummating of the White soul with the Red. It is the inevitable denial of the extreme mystic impulse." But luckily Bumppo realizes his error and leaves the woman; then "he has got back to the right track. . . . we draw a free breath. It is all over." His desire for the woman is "ugly—a

quality of roused function and of *fear* rather than of deep desire" (*SM* 97).

A similar reading of American literature has been popular-
ized in recent times by Leslie Fiedler, but the difference between Lawrence's and Fiedler's perspectives is instructive.
Fiedler argues that

> our great novelists, though experts on indignity and assault,
> on loneliness and terror, tend to avoid treating the passionate
> encounter of a man and woman, which we expect at the center
> of a novel. Indeed, they rather shy away from permitting in
> their fictions the presence of any full-fledged, mature women,
> giving us instead monsters of virtue or bitchery, symbols of the
> rejection or fear of sexuality. . . . the typical male protagonist
> of our fiction has been a man on the run, harried into the forest
> and out to sea, down the river or into combat—anywhere to
> avoid "civilization," which is to say, the confrontation of a man
> and woman which leads to the fall to sex, marriage, and
> responsibility.[37]

Such themes are for Fiedler, as Frederick Crews puts it,
"marks of a condition that might yet be rectified."[38]

Clearly, though Lawrence too uncovers "symbols of the rejection or fear of sexuality" in American literature, they strike
him not as symptoms to treat but as harbingers to welcome.
That a critic as canny as Fiedler acknowledges a debt to Lawrence rather than classing him as another "immature" writer
of the American stamp probably proceeds from his use of the
final versions of *Studies in Classic American Literature*; for, as
Lawrence revised the essays, he softened and finally dis-
guised the gynephobia. The 1920 version of the essay on
Hawthorne is no longer about lethal females and murderous
mother love. Chillingworth, who scarcely appears in the original, now has a hand in Dimmesdale's decline. And though
the final published version, written in 1922, argues shrilly
that women must submit to men, it assigns the blame for

37. Leslie A. Fiedler, *Love and Death in the American Novel*, rev. ed. (New
York: Stein and Day, 1966), 24, 26.
38. Frederick Crews, "Pop Goes the Critic," *The New Criterion* (February
1983): 8.

Dimmesdale's death to the victim himself: "he dodges into death" after having avenged himself somewhat on Hester and Chillingworth, who collaborate in exposing "the spiritual saint."

Most important, the final version may be read as attacking post-Puritan democracy for being sexually repressive. When revising the essays in 1922, Lawrence did not change his assessment of the American scene in any significant way. But he did identify the new era to come, as well as the male leadership that would make it possible, with something so blatantly sexual that no one could accuse him of shrinking from sex or women: man's "masterhood" has become "ithyphallic" (having to do with the erect penis), and woman must learn to worship "the ithyphallic gods."[39] Having decided to challenge the divinity of female fecundity on its own ground, Lawrence asserted the erect penis as a superior mystery, and such it would remain through his last novels. In *Lady Chatterley's Lover*, Connie learns to recognize the lordliness of a man's penis, after which she understands "why men are so overbearing" and feels humbly honored that the penis "comes to" her.[40]

In that novel, however, the erect penis clearly has something to do with actual sex. By the time of *Lady Chatterley's Lover*, Lawrence has renounced his leadership politics, declaring, in a letter from 1928, that "when you get down to the basis of life, to the depth of the warm creative stir, there is no power." He hopes for a new system, "based on reciprocity of tenderness."[41] *Lady Chatterley's Lover* was originally called "Tenderness," and it does not argue for a new social order culminating in a supreme leader. The last avatar of the erect phallus in Lawrence's work is as the provider of tenderness and peace, and on the surface it is devoid of political signifi-

39. D. H. Lawrence, *Studies in Classic American Literature* (1923; rpt. New York: Viking, 1964), 91, 95, 98.

40. D. H. Lawrence, *Lady Chatterley's Lover* (Florence, 1928; rpt. New York: Grove Press, 1957), 252.

41. *The Letters of D. H. Lawrence*, ed. Aldous Huxley (London: William Heinemann, 1932), 705.

cance: "the peace that comes of fucking" finally replaces the perfect asexual stillness of *Women in Love*.[42] It might seem, therefore, that Lawrence was cured concurrently of gynephobia and authoritarianism late in life, as indicated by his ceasing to use the erect penis as an emblem of power and his beginning to employ its more ordinary association with sexuality.

As Millett has shown, however, the sexuality of *Lady Chatterley's Lover* is deeply concerned with male power and female subjection, just as are the sexual relations of his most authoritarian novel, *The Plumed Serpent* (1926), in which the ithyphallic gods have much more to do with blood sacrifice than with sexuality.[43] There Kate Leslie, representative of Western womankind, learns to submerge her will in that of her lordly husband, who is in turn pledged in love and fealty to the supreme leader, Don Ramón. These warriors consider themselves to be reincarnations of Aztec gods, and they deal death through the countryside in order to establish a hierarchical social order, based on a pledge among men. Kate learns that sex is for her husband's benefit only, a form of her worship for him as "a dark column of blood," the phrase used throughout the novel to describe the source of the leaders' power. Therefore, Kate learns to condemn her own desire for orgasm and gives it up.

In other words, even though Lawrence's leadership politics initially seem linked with a desire to control women, that desire survives the end of his wider political authoritarianism. And the ithyphallus, from the moment Lawrence invokes it in a political context until the end of his life, is an image of male power, whether it is used sexually or not. It is always an instrument or an emblem of male domination over the female, though it has wider political significance in the works concerned with establishing a hierarchical structure among men (as well as between men and women). The ithyphallus emerges in the last revision of the essays on American

---

42. Lawrence, *Lady Chatterley's Lover*, 364.
43. Kate Millett, *Sexual Politics* (New York: Doubleday, 1970), 237–45.

literature to characterize what was at first simply male dominance. In the original surviving versions, however, male comradeship is associated with death as a life-giving force, and
the source of male power is not the phallus, as we shall see,
but the life-giving deathliness of the bowels.

Except for the lack of these ithyphallic gods, the 1917–18 versions of the essays on American literature could be the philosophical statement behind *The Plumed Serpent*, though in fact
they represent Lawrence's philosophy at the time he made
the most significant revisions to *Women in Love*. In regard to
the relationship between his fiction and his philosophy, Lawrence claimed that the novels came first, "unwatched out of
one's pen," and that his "pseudo-philosophy" was "deduced
from" them.[44] That sequence is not slavishly accurate. "The
Crown" is a systematic formulation of an idea that appears
full-blown only in Lawrence's next novel (*Women in Love*),
though it was born, perhaps, in the April 1915 revisions of
The Rainbow, which immediately preceded "The Crown"; and
"Hardy," which does correspond philosophically with *The
Rainbow*, was finished months before Lawrence completed
that novel. But whether he abstracted the philosophy before,
after, or while rendering it in fiction, in the case of his great
novels the separation of roles is largely accurate: philosophical ideas may be deduced from the novels but they are seldom
preached there, as they are in the essays. The novels tend
more to argue with themselves, and the debate in *Women in
Love* addresses the doctrine presented in the early versions of
the essays on American literature.

The first time Ursula speaks to him alone, Birkin is patch-
ing up a boat. He says, "I'll try it and you can watch what
happens. Then if it carries, I'll take you over to the island"
(116). Once there, they talk about death and the decline of the
human race and argue about love. Then Birkin floats some
daisies on the water, and Ursula is "strongly and mystically"

---

44. Lawrence, *Psychoanalysis/Fantasia*, 57.

moved by this; she feels "some sort of control . . . being put on her" (123).

Though the scene is vividly visualized and realistic, nearly every line of it is symbolic. Symbolically, Birkin is building an ark to save himself and Ursula from the flood that is destroying mankind, and their trip to the island presages the major features of their actual journey together. They do not quite escape getting wet, being involved in the general decline along the way: "The boat leaks a little," and their island is covered with "rank plants . . . evil-smelling figwort and hemlock." Birkin takes a daisy and makes it float "like a little water-lily," a flower of decay (116, 122).

Throughout this symbolic journey, Birkin is Ursula's leader, as he will be in most of their story. He is ahead of her in exploring into the rank plants, while she shrinks from them, as he is ahead of her in spiritual degradation. And just as he makes the boat, and rows it, and invites her to come along to the island, leaving behind the rest of the world, he will convince her in the course of the novel to adopt his misanthropy, leave the life she has known, and join with him in a rootless existence and a marriage based not on love and sex but on stillness and impersonal conjunction.

Never mind that at the end of *The Rainbow* Ursula was already prepared to renounce the whole "world of things," leave all she has ever known. At the start of *Women in Love*, she does not feel that way; she is deeply embedded in and claims to like her old life, which includes Beldover, Nottingham, England, and family, nearly everything she renounced in her rebirth at the end of *The Rainbow*. Ursula actually has to learn again, from Birkin, things she learned on her own in *The Rainbow*; she is still attached to "the world of things," thinks "life is *awfully* jolly," and objects to Birkin that "there's only this world" (117, 349). Perhaps because *The Rainbow* was banned and out of print until after *Women in Love* was published, Lawrence felt free to make Ursula's character inconsistent between the two books.

But Ursula's regression is not simply a matter of one character's inconsistency. Barbara Hardy argues that Ursula "became more orthodox, less introspective, forgot some of her past, changed to become more conventionally in need of an education from the man" only because "Lawrence moves from Ursula to Birkin" in his sympathies.[45] But that very shift in sympathy is part of the change in Lawrence's politics, a symptom of his new beliefs in male dominance over women, the political leadership of wise men, and the establishment of "the love of comrades, as marriage is really established now"—the last being apparently the most important, since "the future of mankind depends on the way in which this relation is entered upon by us" (*SM* 239). Nevertheless, these ideas, dear as they were to Lawrence at the time, appear in the novel not as self-evident truths but as propositions being tested under stress. Ursula resists Birkin's ideas, and her opposition provides much of the tension that gives *Women in Love* the texture of poetry rather than of rhetoric. The two remain locked together in opposition like balanced contraries, even at the book's end.

On some issues, Ursula does submit her will to Birkin's in the course of the book, and since they are the normative pair, the couple for whom the ending is happy, this submission seems to be a novelistic idea. But even that idea receives serious opposition in the parallel story of Gerald and his lovers, who toy destructively with power, and those relationships tend to refine this novel's notion of necessary female submission. Similarly, the idea of manly love, represented in this novel by Birkin's desire for blood brotherhood, is reasonably and sympathetically opposed by Gerald, who with Birkin is the party most concerned in the matter, and less sympathetically but still vehemently rejected by Ursula. One way of reading the end of the novel implies that Birkin is right to desire this new relationship with another man, and I think Birkin does finally have the edge in that intellectual contest, as in most of the others. Yet the novel ends without demon-

---

45. Barbara Hardy, "Women in D. H. Lawrence's Works," in *D. H. Lawrence: Novelist, Poet, Prophet*, ed. Stephen Spender (London: Weidenfeld and Nicolson, 1973), 118.

strating the positive effects of blood brotherhood, since Birkin does not get his wish, and its closing words consist of an unresolved argument between Birkin and Ursula on the subject.

Though *Women in Love* contains some ideas, therefore, the experience of reading it is not like being preached at or even like reading rhetorical argument. While it is being read, its effect is, as Clarke says, "to discourage in the reader any tendency to reach a single and ready-defined judgment."[46] Nevertheless, one can construct the *conclusions* of *Women in Love*, regarded as a poetic debate, as encouraging the making of judgments, albeit dual and original ones. Lawrence seems always, in his fiction, to hold the view of the novel's usefulness that he expresses in *Lady Chatterley's Lover*: it can cause the sympathy of the reader to flow toward new ideas and behaviors, and to recoil from "things gone dead."[47]

And, in the main, the conclusions the reader is encouraged to make in *Women in Love* coincide with Birkin's. Often those conclusions agree with Birkin's judgments as refined by Ursula, but just as often that is not the case—and the reverse is never true. Birkin's side of the argument is often the one Ursula knows or comes to know in her heart to be true, and the novel several times demonstrates Birkin's insights to be prophetic. In "Moony," Birkin predicts Gerald's death by freezing. He sees that the white races "would fulfil a mystery of ice-destructive knowledge, snow-abstract annihilation" and that Gerald "was one of these strange white wonderful demons from the north, fulfilled in the destructive frost mystery. And was he fated to pass away in this knowledge, this one process of frost-knowledge, death by perfect cold?" (246–47). Birkin also explains to Ursula that Gerald and Gudrun are "born in the process of destructive creation" like "marsh-flowers," lilies with their roots in the cold mud of dissolution (164), while elsewhere Gudrun identifies with waterplants, sees Gerald's hand "coming straight forward like a stem"

46. Colin Clarke, *River of Dissolution: D. H. Lawrence and English Romanticism* (London: Routledge and Kegan Paul, 1969), 50.
47. Lawrence, *Lady Chatterley's Lover*, 117.

across the water, and thinks "he started out of the mud" (111–13). Birkin tells Ursula that they and their contemporaries are rotted "apples of Sodom," because "they won't fall off the tree when they're ripe. They hang on to their old positions when the position is overpast." She resists him, crying, "Where are *you* right?" and Birkin modestly says, "I'm not right" (118). Soon, however, Ursula herself realizes that "she was fulfilled in a kind of bitter ripeness, there remained only to fall from the tree into death . . . as a bitter fruit plunges in its ripeness downwards" (183).

The other characters often ridicule Birkin's insights, but even as they laugh they never lose a pointed interest in what he thinks. To the extent that Birkin is subtly presented as a seer to whom the scoffers might well listen, his characterization is the first evidence in Lawrence's fiction that "some men are born from the mystery of creation, to know, to lead, and to command. And some are born to listen, to follow, to obey" (*SM* 78).

The narrative voice of the novel, in a purely editorial passage not associated with any character's consciousness, essentially affirms this idea: "In function and process, one man, one part, must of necessity be subordinate to another," and "mechanical equality" expresses "the instinct for chaos" (218–19). The idea that "there must arise a man who will give new values to things, give us new truths" is introduced into the novel as a newspaper article, to which both Birkin and Gerald respond skeptically at first. But Birkin subtly endorses this "new gospel," as Gerald calls it, or "new religion" (Birkin), because of the necessity to "stare straight at this life that we've brought upon ourselves and rejected, absolutely smash up the old idols" (47).

Hierarchical politics are not preached in the novel, but they can be discerned in the working out of themes closely associated with leadership in the contemporaneous essays: in the arguments concerning female submission, love between men, and single being as opposed to the merging of sexual love. Birkin is proven generally correct in his analysis of Gerald and what he needs, as well as in his assessment of what will make

Ursula and himself happy. And because his analyses of Gerald and of his own love choices are linked in his meditations to the largest possible public issues, such as the decline of Western civilization, Birkin seems to know, finally, where his race has gone wrong and how some (if not all) might save themselves from destruction.

Symbolically isolated on their island and "looking at the pond" (that is, observing the flood around them, 116), Birkin and Ursula write off the rest of the human race. But Ursula is not at first inclined to do so; only after arguing with Birkin does she begin to consider how "*really* desirable" would be "a clean, lovely, humanless world" (119). She becomes deeply pleased with the fantasy, apparently having forgotten her previous vision, which sounded like a prophecy, at the end of *The Rainbow*. At that time she saw that the people of the earth were living still and that they would issue forth to a new germination and would build a new heaven on earth. Now, instead, she sees that they are in a slow, obscene, and endless decline, like what Birkin calls "the African process":

> She herself knew too well the actuality of humanity, its hideous actuality. She knew it could not disappear so cleanly and conveniently. It had a long way to go yet, a long and hideous way. Her subtle, feminine, demoniacal soul knew it well.
>
> (120)

Ursula's soul does not believe this in *The Rainbow*, and she does not know it with her mind in *Women in Love* until Birkin suggests it to her, a sequence that seems to reflect Lawrence's contemporaneous pronouncement that "what woman *knows*, she knows because man has taught it her" (*SM* 133).

Early in their conversation on the island, when she says, "But *I'm* happy—I think life is *awfully* jolly," Lawrence labels this "her own self-deception . . . an instinct in her, to deceive herself" (117). She stops doing so after hearing a sermon from Birkin, during which she ostensibly opposes him, but in an odd way. She never says he is wrong, or argues with him; she simply keeps asking him "Why?" and becomes increasingly upset. Her replies are not arguments but vehement assertions of a contrary opinion, like her protest that "there *are* good people" (118), or jeers, like her mocking question, "What *do* you believe in? . . . Simply in the end of the world, and grass?" (121). Neither do Birkin's replies often constitute logical argumentation; to her assertion that there are some good people, for instance, he winningly rejoins, "Good enough for the life of to-day. But mankind is a dead tree, covered with fine brilliant galls of people." To this she implicitly capitulates, since she replies, "And if it is so, *why* is it?" (118). Apparently the lack of logic in Birkin's argument is no hindrance to its effectiveness, both because Ursula is not herself perfectly logical and because her soul agrees with him. Because it does, and because Ursula eventually does too, Birkin appears to be something of a prophet, a teller of truth that others know in their hearts but dare not speak.

Though Ursula often opposes him, sometimes with a reasonable case on her side, her objections seldom constitute the best that might be brought against Birkin; sometimes they even serve to suggest that he is a prophet. After he delivers such proclamations as "man is a mistake, he must go," Ursula does not think to herself that he is a pompous crank; instead she realizes "that, all the while, in spite of himself, he would have to be trying to save the world." Her objection to him as savior of the world is not based on his lack of aptitude for the part but on her own petty possessiveness: "She wanted him to herself, she hated the Salvator Mundi touch." Here Lawrence makes her contribute to the glorification of Birkin: her attack is against not his pretentiousness but his hypocrisy, which covers nothing to his discredit. She accuses him of actually loving humanity, and, Christlike, he is forced to admit to that flaw ("If I do love it, it is my disease" 120–21).

Elsewhere Ursula appears unreasonable and hysterical for her objections, as in "Mino," in which Birkin uses his male cat and its mate as models in arguing with Ursula about "star balance." Ursula's most logical points include such remarks as "tell it to the Horse Marines," and even the cat "glanced at Birkin in disdain of the noisy woman." Birkin counsels the cat to do what he himself obviously intends: "Keep your male dignity, and your higher understanding" (141). Birkin also looks rather ridiculous here for his assumption of superiority, but in the course of the novel Ursula converts to his "star balance," thereby intrinsically vindicating him for having considered himself to have a higher understanding. Originally, Ursula wants love, whereas Birkin wants something so impersonal that it is "quite inhuman" (138). But eventually she announces to Gudrun that "love is too human and little. I believe in something inhuman. . . . it is something infinitely more than love" (429). Ursula seems to have become Birkin's mouthpiece, and she is completely happy now that she and Birkin have achieved the "superfine stability" that the cat Mino was working for by cuffing the stray female.

Despite Birkin's disclaimer that both he and the cat want only stability, not the subjection of the female, it is difficult to see the difference between the relationship of satellite to planet, which is how Ursula originally sees "star balance," and the equilibrium that Birkin and Ursula eventually achieve. For one thing, Birkin makes it clear elsewhere that he finds the subjection of women natural and desirable: "woman is the same as horses," he declares. Both feel "the last, perhaps highest, love-impulse: resign your will to the higher being." But woman, like a horse, also feels an opposing will "to bolt, and pitch her rider to perdition" (132).

True, much of the novel is devoted to Ursula and Birkin's conflict and argument, which gives the book a great deal of its dramatic life; and the fulfillment they achieve together consequently seems based on the necessity of conflict, as if affirmation can only come through serious opposition. Yet Ursula's opposition is gradually, in the course of the book, subsumed. Birkin's comparison of women and horses is hard to ignore here, for along the way Ursula does exhibit precisely the "two wills" or urges Birkin claims both have. She is eventually domesticated at least to the point that she no longer threatens to pitch Birkin to perdition. "It's a dangerous thing to domesticate even horses, let alone women," Birkin says (132). But he is apparently rewarded for braving that danger: by the end of the novel Ursula has submerged her life in his and accepted all his ideas, with the sole exception of blood brotherhood, for which reservation she is made to look a bit selfish and conventional.

Throughout the novel images of dangerous female independence reinforce the benefits of domesticating women. Hermione, Gudrun, and Diana Crich all recoil from male leadership, and all are lethal. Diana, named for the goddess of female independence, drinks champagne against Gerald's orders (22), and, under a bright moon, drowns the young man who attempts to save her from another folly. "Di—Di—Di—" her sister shrieks eerily, revealing the deathliness in the moon goddess's name (171). Hermione needs to bully males: "It was always the same, this joy in power she manifested, peculiarly in power over any male being" (292). She tries to control Birkin, as she does the stag in her park: "He was male, so she must exert some kind of power over him" (80). Birkin resists her violently, and she tries to smash his head, in order to "break him down before her" (98).

Gudrun, too, asserts her dangerous freedom from Gerald: she correctly predicts that she will strike the last blow as well as the first (162, 463). She bullies Gerald the way Hermione does the cat, forcing him to admit one minute that he never will love her, the next that he always will. In the midst of this sport she pities him, like a mother comforting a child, but her pity is motivated by hate and "fear of his power over her, which she must always counterfoil" (434). In a symbolic moment, Gerald runs after her in the snow, "overtaking her, but not gaining any power over her" (388); she soon flaunts his influence to the point of openly taking another lover from among the other guests in the hotel where they are staying.

When Gerald climbs to his death under "a small bright moon . . . a painful brilliant thing that was always there, unremitting, from which there was no escape," he is climbing toward the Marienhütte (464–65). Mary is the "Mater Dolorosa," whom Birkin identifies with the Magna Mater, "the awful, arrogant queen of life" who "wanted to have, to own, to control, to be dominant," viewing men as her sons and holding them "her everlasting prisoner" (192). When Gerald sees the image of Mary's murdered son (in a mountain crucifix), "he could feel the blow descending, he knew he was murdered" (465)—presumably by his own domineering woman. Birkin's analyses again seem vindicated: Gudrun will mother a man only to dominate and destroy him, and she will be "promiscuous as the wind," like the female cat, until she recognizes a male as her superior and therefore her fate (141).

Even so, *Women in Love* is not on the side of every sort of female submission. The novel's second love story also helps to refine the notion of female passivity that is made sympathetic in this novel, especially in the light of Lawrence's original essays on American literature. Gudrun enjoys being "subject" to Gerald as well as dominant over him; she experiences their lovemaking as "an ecstasy of subjection" (337). His beauty "compels" and "subjugates" her (341), and her relationship with him is a "contest":

> Sometimes it was he who seemed strongest, whilst she was almost gone, creeping near the earth like a spent wind; sometimes it was the reverse. But always it was this eternal see-saw, one destroyed that the other might exist, one ratified because the other was nulled.
>
> (436)

Minette even more than Gudrun desires to be dominated by Gerald and is even more "disintegrated" because of it: she has the "look of a violated slave, whose fulfilment lies in her further and further violation." When she is with Gerald, "his was the only will, she was the passive substance of his will" (72), and Gerald relishes the somatic sense of power this gives him: "Her being suffused into his veins like a magnetic darkness, and concentrated at the base of his spine like a fearful source of power" (65). Gerald is healthy enough to resist this destructive symbiosis, though he finds Gudrun's less abject subjection irresistible. What he recognizes in Gudrun that first attracts him is "her sullen passion of cruelty" (232), which corresponds to his own. Gerald's emotion, like Gudrun's, has a masochistic as well as a sadistic dimension, and therefore, though he feels "a passion almost of cruelty" (72) with Minette and enjoys her slavelike defenselessness (69), she cannot hold him long. Far greater is his passion for his equal in cruelty, with whom he can exchange roles on the destructive seesaw of dominance.

Compared to Gerald's love affairs, the relationship between Birkin and Ursula appears cooler, more separated, and more equal. The presence of diabolically submissive women in the novel tends to refine the notion of what Ursula's apparent submission to Birkin means. Compared to Minette's infusing herself into Gerald's will, Ursula's acceptance of Birkin's way seems like the concurrence of a free agent, like a treaty ratified for the common good. As such, it parallels the "pledge" from lesser being to greater described in the original essays on American literature. It is a voluntary "yielding" in separation or singleness, rather than an enforced violation of the beings of either party.

Yet Ursula's yielding is a concurrence in Birkin's idea of how they should be together, even though, as we saw in the last chapter, his idea involves the relinquishing of her sexual desire. And her acceptance of his way does not proceed from an intellectual recognition that he is right, but rather from her discovery, in the tearoom scene, that he is a superior being, more than a man, "one of the sons of God such as were in the beginning of the world, not a man, something other, something more" (305).

She discovers Birkin's power in roughly the same part of the body that harbors Gerald's when he is drawing it from Minette's submission, and Ursula submits to Birkin because of it. Yet for several reasons, these relationships are not analogous. For one thing, Birkin already has the power in his body and does not need to draw it from Ursula. For another, the extreme dominance-submission of Gerald's relationships always leads to inflamed sex and merging, while Ursula's qualified submission signals her acceptance of single being and "stillness" rather than sex. Whereas in the sexual relationships Minette actually loses her being, fusing into Gerald, and Gerald seems always to desire being absorbed into Gudrun, like a child returning to the womb, Ursula recognizes Birkin in asexual separation from him. Finally, Ursula's recognition of Birkin's superiority does not mean that she will accept his leadership in Minette's slavelike fashion. Nor will she revolt as utterly from it as Gudrun does from Gerald's (while relishing his power)—Gerald's relationships again serving as complex foils for the "paradisal" way.

Women in Love, therefore, represents a subtle fictional argument on the question of who should dominate between the sexes and why, and it does seem to come to a conclusion: that woman should tacitly submit to the higher being of her husband but that she should retain her independence of mind and body and not relish her subjection. Rather than flinging herself about on the seesaw of power, she should accept the man's superior wisdom but remain distinct from him in her opposition, balanced and still (the sexual dimension of both possibilities for Lawrence being evident in his images).

Women in Love also argues the questions of whether men should pledge themselves to each other apart from women and whether lesser men should follow the lead of greater. Ursula is given equal time at the end of the novel, when she pronounces Birkin's desired blood brotherhood "an obstinacy, a theory, a perversity" (473). Here as elsewhere when Ursula opposes Birkin, Lawrence presents both views, presumably to let the fiction decide the issue without interference from his own predilection. In "Morality and the Novel," he describes such a practice as the only method of writing truly moral fiction and explains that, left alone, the novel will provide a truth superior to any idea the novelist has in his head (*Phoenix* 528).

Such was Lawrence's theory, but in practice the ideas he had while writing tend to be discernible in his novels—if only because, as he believed, the issues work themselves out in the novels. Both sides may be presented, but one side eventually has the edge. The essays from the same period reveal that Lawrence did have a predilection for "manly love." Birkin shares it; Ursula opposes him; and, though moment by moment *Women in Love* refuses to affirm either side of the quarrel, in its conclusions the emotional resources of the novel nudge us toward the idea that Birkin is right. At the same time, the terms of the argument over blood brotherhood in the novel suggest that the male union is ideally hierarchical, that one of the brothers may be wiser and therefore destined to lead the other (as is explicitly the case between Lilly and Aaron in *Aaron's Rod*).

The novel finally implies that not only Ursula but Gerald, too, is properly Birkin's pupil. Ursula accepts Birkin's ideas and her story has a happy ending, whereas Gerald does not even engage him in the quarrel as deeply as Ursula does, and his story is tragic. Birkin, at least, could teach Gerald what he needs to know to stay alive. Not only does he foresee the means of Gerald's death, he also says to Gerald early on, "You seem to have a lurking desire to have your gizzard slit" and "it takes two people to make a murder: a murderer and a murderee" (27). These perceptions, too, are supported by the novel. Gerald has known all along that Gudrun may be his spiritual killer: well before they are lovers he recognizes her as "his ultimate victor" (234), and he does not contradict her enigmatic assertion that she will strike the last blow (162). He has been warned, apparently, that she is lethal, and he pursues her in spite of it, or perhaps because of it, because he desires to be a murderee.

Gerald might have lived if he had listened to Birkin and taken what he said as a warning to be acted upon. The book also finally seems to be on Birkin's side when he cries with a tear-streaked face, "He should have loved me. . . . I offered him" and insists against Ursula that it would have made a difference. The difference it would have made is limited by Birkin to a "further life" Gerald might have had, after death, "with his friend" (471). But elsewhere the novel implies that pledging blood brotherhood with Birkin might have saved Gerald. Symbolically, Gerald dies of the process that is "imminent" in Birkin as well until he chooses "the paradisal entry into pure, single being" instead (245–47). It would follow logically that Gerald might also have been saved by committing himself as Birkin did to a "pure relationship" with a woman and leaving the conventional world.

But, surprisingly, the narrator tells us that, though "star

balance" is what Gerald needs, he cannot do it on his own. He needs Birkin's help. Birkin saved himself, but Gerald needs Birkin to save him:

> He was willing to be sealed thus in the underworld, like a soul damned but living for ever in damnation. But he would not make any pure relationship with any other soul. He could not. . . .
>
> The other way was to accept Rupert's offer of alliance, to enter into the bond of pure trust and love with the other man, and then subsequently with the woman. If he pledged himself with the man he would later be able to pledge himself with the woman: not merely in legal marriage, but in absolute, mystic marriage.
>
> Yet he could not accept the offer.
>
> (345)

These thoughts are not obviously in the mind of any character, except possibly in Gerald's; the passage ends with Gerald's feelings ("he was strangely elated at Rupert's offer. Yet he was still more glad to reject it, not to be committed" 346). The suggestion that Gerald must pledge with Birkin or be damned comes not from Birkin's ego but from either Gerald's own superior understanding or the central consciousness of the book.

This passage, therefore, combined with Birkin's meditations in "Moony," implies that Gerald's tragedy is the result of his inability to pledge with Birkin: that is the only way he can escape freezing (the northern version of the African damnation). Neither does the book encourage reader indifference concerning Gerald's fate. If Gerald is "God" of this book's dark satanic mills, he is also Promethean (as suggested earlier), and he is consistently presented as beautiful, with a great potential for life that needs only to be released. His resistance and death must surely register as tragic, with the effect of affirming any alternative that might have saved him.

Ursula's resistance to Birkin's idea of that alternative is not given comparable emotional weight. Whereas Birkin mourns Gerald with eloquence and dignity, Ursula reacts to his grief in a jealous and petty way, thereby making her opposition to blood brotherhood look childish. "Haven't you seen enough?"

she asks, instead of comforting him, and she asserts her claim on Birkin in competition with the dead man's: "You've got me. . . . Aren't I enough for you?" (472). It might even be fair to say that when Ursula is allowed to go on jealously fighting blood brotherhood over Gerald's corpse, it is not a case of equal time; she is being given enough rope to hang herself for her inferior understanding. And along with her, of course, hangs her side of the argument.

Ursula never acknowledges that Birkin's understanding is superior; she simply adopts many of his ideas as the book progresses while continuing to resist him on other points. Neither do any of the other characters recognize Birkin as a seer or leader. In fact, he is often the object of their ridicule. Yet, for some reason, all the major characters ask Birkin for answers on important questions; a remarkable amount of the book's dialogue begins with some other character, most often Gerald, at least ostensibly asking Birkin for enlightenment.

Gerald passively resists nearly everything Birkin says, yet he continues to ask questions and attends closely to the answers. He even repeatedly asks Birkin to divine his future and tell him how to live:

> "Now do you think I shall ever feel that for a woman?" he said anxiously.
> Birkin looked at him and shook his head.
> "I don't know," he said. "I could not say."
> Gerald had been on the *qui vive*, as awaiting his fate.
>
> (268)

He asks Birkin if he should marry Gudrun and presses him so hard for an answer that Birkin finally says, "Ask Gudrun, not me. You're not marrying me, are you?" (342–44). He always demurs when asked to tell Gerald how to live, but eventually, when sufficiently pursued, he will say what he thinks ("If I were you I would *not* marry" 344).

Birkin does not hesitate to answer most other sorts of questions, and he pronounces on a variety of subjects. "What *do* women want at the bottom?" Gerald asks, echoing Freud (though the desire's location is peculiarly Lawrentian) (418). Ursula asks Birkin why "there is no flowering, no dignity of human life now" (118). Even Gudrun, who is not close to Birkin, asks him if "the English will have to disappear," and she, too, thinks he can read her fate:

> It was strange, her pointed interest in his answer. It might have been her own fate she was inquiring after. Her dark, dilated eyes rested on Birkin, as if she could conjure the truth of the future out of him, as out of some instrument of divination.
>
> (386)

Gerald, Gudrun, Hermione, and Ursula discuss such general questions with each other, but they do not ask each other for the answers; only Birkin is given such invitations to pronounce.

The mocking opposition of the same characters who ask for his guidance does constitute a countering voice of sorts. Gerald and Gudrun laugh (literally behind Birkin's back as he drives a car) at Birkin's idea of "ultimate" marriage. "I know nothing about *ultimate* marriage, I assure you: or even penultimate," Gudrun sneers, and Gerald replies, "Only the ordinary unwarrantable brand! Just so—same here. I am no expert on marriage and degrees of ultimateness. It seems to be a bee that buzzes loudly in Rupert's bonnet" (281).

The sympathetic focus of the novel is on Birkin, however, and the harsh light cast on his critics (especially on the Pompadour Café crowd) gives Birkin rather the look of an embattled and self-doubting prophet. Gerald and Gudrun are allowed to jeer, but the novel implies that they would have done well to listen. The passage quoted earlier gives Gerald a clear choice between "damnation" and "absolute, mystic marriage" (345); and Gudrun gets Lawrence's stiffest condemnation in the end, for having chosen "the obscene religious mystery of ultimate reduction . . . of diabolic reducing down" (443), instead of the "paradisal" way (saying, "*Je m'en fiche* of your Paradise!*" 282). In the end, Gudrun seems to be turning into a clock:

> She was watching the fingers twitch across the eternal, mechanical, monotonous clock-face of time. She never really lived, she only watched. Indeed, she was like a little, twelve-

hour clock, vis-à-vis with the enormous clock of eternity. . . .
the thought of the sight of her own face, that was like a twelve-
hour clock dial, filled her with such deep terror, that she has-
tened to think of something else.

(457)

The final disposition of fates makes clear that Birkin was
right. But even early on, before Birkin's ideas have been
proven, the novel displays some bias for him. The scene in
the motor car, for instance, ends with sympathy for Birkin,
characterizing the mockery behind him as a threat that he can
rise above: "Birkin, as he drove, felt a creeping of the spine,
as if somebody were threatening his neck. But he shrugged
with indifference. It began to rain. Here was a change. He
stopped the car and got down to put up the hood" (283).

Lawrence himself declared *Women in Love* "a record of the
writer's own desires, aspirations, struggles; in a word, a record of the profoundest experiences in the self" ("Foreword,"
viii). Birkin's discernible identity as a fictional surrogate for
Lawrence helps to explain both some of the bias and the fre-
quency with which others ask his advice; Lawrence was a
well-known writer who was often urged to give his opinion
(certainly in print, and probably in person) on a variety of
subjects. But this identity also adds an important and disturb-
ing dimension to the leadership theme of this novel. Birkin is
sometimes wrong, sometimes unreasonable, and often self-
critical, but he is also described as "an utterly desirable man"
(122) who has "an uncanny force" that Gerald calls "almost
supernatural." He is even able to defeat the physically superior Gerald in skin-to-skin combat (262–64). This character,
who is eventually recognized to be "more than a man," who
is the superior being to whom Ursula learns to submit, who
can correctly read the fate of Northern humanity (symbolically represented by Gerald) and show it the way out of its
decline, is the self-portrait of messianic Lawrence, who
would declare in his own voice, a few years later in *Fantasia*,
that he would like the working man to give him "back the
responsibility for general affairs."

But, happily for *Women in Love*, this image of the self as

seer is humbled, even in the final scene, by fierce opposition from Ursula: "You can't have two kinds of love," she says at the end, "because it's false, impossible." Though Birkin gets the last word ("I don't believe that"), the impression a reader is likely to take away from this novel is of struggle and conflict, rather than assertion and resolution.

The political polemics that were to shape Lawrence's subsequent fictions were already in his mind, however, and one final comparison with the original essays on American literature should make clear how thoroughly a part of *Women in Love* such thinking is. Even without accurate methods for assigning dates of composition, internal evidence shows that these essays derive from the same stage of development in Lawrence's thinking as does *Women in Love*: for, alone among Lawrence's philosophical works, these essays, like that novel, link the bowels not only with sensuality and single being but also with the politics of dominance. The function soon to be usurped by the erect penis in Lawrence's political map of the body is in this stage of his thinking performed by the bowels. Not only are they associated with life-giving deathliness and homoeroticism, they are also the repository of an individual's power, and it is this creatively destructive power in the male that the female should revere.

Fantasia and other essays from the early twenties develop a life-centered theory of the cosmos and a model of human consciousness as a nonmental phenomenon primarily to explain child development. These essays argue for a harsher, less loving method of raising children, aimed at producing men who will march away from women to fulfill the impulse that is greater than sex, "the desire of the human male to build a world."[48] *Fantasia* explains consciousness as an interaction between "four great affective centres of the body." The "sympathetic," located in the front of the body, is attracted to others and desires to merge into oneness with the world; the "vol-

48. Lawrence, *Psychoanalysis/Fantasia*, 60.

untary," in the back, is repelled by others and desires to dominate them; the top half of the body is "spiritual," the site of awareness of others; the bottom is "sensual," a word that Lawrence as usual in this period associates with isolation and power rather than pleasure—this zone is the origin of the sense that "I am I." These four centers correspond to four nerve ganglia, one of which, the lumbar ganglion in the lower back, is the site of separate identity and masterhood. Sexual consciousness does not proceed from these four primary centers but from four subsidiary ones, lower and higher than the principal four.[49]

Hence, because Ursula discovers an electric power, a power presumably of the nerves, "at the back and base of the loins" in Birkin, some critics reason that she is discovering Birkin's lumbar ganglion. Because the source she discovers is "more satisfying . . . than the phallic source," it is not one of his sexual centers. Because it is "here she discovered him one of the sons of God . . . not a man, something other, something more," she seems to be finding unusual power in his lumbar ganglion, which would make him both naturally separate and a born leader of men (305–6). This reading, which partially removes Birkin and Ursula's breakthrough from association with the body's "dark river of dissolution," is sometimes offered as a solution to the dilemma we have been concerned with all along, the problem of the way out of degradation being apparently inseparable from the way down into it.

In *Women in Love*, however, as we have seen, the coincidence of imagery between the "African degradation" and Ursula's discovery in Birkin is quite exact. Although what Ursula discovers may have to do with Birkin's lumbar ganglion, it clearly has to do with his bowels as well. And in fact the early versions of the essays on American literature confirm that in 1917–18 Lawrence saw the lower centers as actually being seated in the bowels—not merely by association, or as the

49. Ibid., 38–39, 74–78, 85.

nerves governing the digestive process, as they are in *Fantasia*—but by logical necessity. In these essays (which, again, correspond in time with *Women in Love* while *Fantasia* does not), there are no separate centers for sexuality, but only the two, upper and lower, breast and bowels. In 1917–18, Lawrence believed that both sensuality and the desire for dominance were not a function of the nerves but actually intestinal urges, expressions of the desire to devour and digest:

> In the bowels lies the dark and unfathomable vortex of our sensual passion, sensual love . . . within the bowels lies the burning source of the sensual consciousness. Here the Self is positive and centripetal. . . . from this centre I draw all things into me, that they enter in passional communion into my self, become one with me, an increase and a magnificence in my self. This is the process of my sensual becoming, which culminates at last in the great dark glory of real almightiness, all things being added unto me for my power and perfection, wherein I am whole and infinite. . . .
>
> In the thrill and pulse within the bowels I gather the new creature into myself, into blood knowledge, I encompass the unknown within the dominion of myself.
>
> (*SM* 52–53, 56)

To desire is to eat is to own is to be powerful. Sensuality is actually imperialism of the self. Lawrence seems to see nothing incongruous in making "sensual passion" itself a part of this imperialism of the bowels.

Freudian theory also supports the idea of the bowels as the source of a sense of power, primarily because a child's production of feces is the psychological archetype for future creations. Lawrence's idea, however, concerns digestion rather than excretion. The identification of sensuality with digestive imperialism occurred to Lawrence because small children like to put things in their mouths:

> The process of this sensual fulfilment begins in the tiny infant, when instinctively it carries everything to its mouth, to absorb the mysterious mouth and abdominal knowledge of the unknown thing, carry this unknown in a communion of most intimate contact, into the self. . . . This is the beginning of the process of sensual fulfilment, which ends only in that strange,

supreme passion, when the "I" is singly consummate and almighty, in supreme possession of the All.

(*SM* 53)

What the child desires is to be sensually fulfilled in absorbing and mastering the thing.

This scheme makes sexuality seem indistinguishable from other forms of dominion and provides the justification for Lawrence's conflation of sexuality and politics in this period, his reciprocal appropriation of the imagery of each to describe the other. It may have the added advantage of implying that the drive for political dominance is a laudable substitute for sexual expression because both are manifestations of the same desire. Ursula certainly finds Birkin's "marvellous fountains" of power "more mysterious and potent than any she had imagined or known, more satisfying, ah, finally, mystically-physically satisfying. She had thought there was no source deeper than the phallic source." If "the darkest, deepest, strangest life-source of the human body, at the back and base of the loins," is more satisfying than the phallus (306), then power is more fulfilling than sex, and a natural hero gives more to a woman nonsexually than sexually. This glorification of the intestines also supplants woman's superior access to the divine and removes guilt about anal eroticism.

Lawrence wants to assert that men have a nonmental power greater than women's that justifies both a man's leadership of his wife and his marching away from her with other, similarly endowed male warriors to form a "sensual" hierarchy of distinct beings dedicated to improving the world. Birkin's power is not something that Ursula shares. But because women, like men, possess bowels, it is logical that Lawrence should subsequently attribute the source of power to the exclusively male organ, and that shift probably explains his return to genital sexuality in the late novels, despite contemporaneous declarations of loathing for sex.[50] And despite this logically necessary shift, traces of Lawrence's original as-

---

50. "And I, who loathe sexuality so deeply, am considered a lurid sexuality specialist," he wrote in 1926. Moore *Letters* 2, 954.

sociation of the bowels and power persist. In *Lady Chatterley's Lover*, Connie's regenerative submission to Mellors's lordly power is accomplished and celebrated in an act now widely understood to be anal intercourse. Here Connie can only be "a passive, consenting thing, like a slave, a physical slave."[51]

Lawrence's paintings also attest to his association of the bowels or buttocks with power relations and the leadership politics he thought would regenerate Western civilization. Most striking is the image he called *Renascence of Men* (see frontispiece). In this watercolor a naked, kneeling man prostrates himself in fealty to another naked man squatting just in front of him. The follower displays his buttocks prominently in the foreground of the lower left, and they are balanced by the curve of the leader's buttocks in the upper right.

The focus on buttocks is by no means limited to paintings with political import: at least half of Lawrence's known paintings, whether they are called *Rape of the Sabine Women* or *Throwing Back the Apple*, center on (usually male) buttocks. *Red Willow Trees*, for instance, is far more about buttocks than it is about trees. Most of the trees are in the background, while in the foreground three naked men display themselves from the rear, two squatting and one resting his rump in the cleft of a tree, where it is framed and presented to us. Even Lawrence's justly praised *Contadina*, his oil painting of a naked Italian peasant's torso, devotes its upper right quadrant to the naked buttocks of another figure.[52]

Such images have an obsessive quality; so do Lawrence's recurrent formulations of why this area of the body is significant in human relations. In the early essays on American literature, the bowels are the organ of both power and passion; in "The Reality of Peace," they are home to secret shameful desire, which must be accepted and made part of life; in *Women in Love*, they are the source of individual integrity as well as spiritual corruption, and the hero's superhuman

---

51. Lawrence, *Lady Chatterley's Lover*, 297.
52. *The Paintings of D. H. Lawrence*, privately printed for subscribers only (n.p.: The Mandrake Press, 1929).

power emanates from his buttocks. In *Fantasia,* Lawrence skirts the scatalogical and erotic by locating heroic power in the nerves under the buttocks. Finally he definitively limits the gender of heroes by associating power with the ithyphallus. He uses these images to assert that leadership politics have an innate physical origin, but their specific character and centrality to his political thought again suggest that his politics themselves were at least in part an attempt to rationalize an interest that he found unacceptable in himself.

Conclusion

Private Parts and Public Events

In their initial formulations, Lawrence's leadership politics seem designed to control female power and sexuality while allowing for an acceptable (that is, nonerotic) form of male bonding. Clearly, his emotional life affected his political thinking. Its importance is discernible even in his reactions to the public influences contributing to the rise of authoritarian thought in this period. The Great War and its effects are the obvious immediate cause of the urge to order in Lawrence and his contemporaries, and various heroic philosophies, already popular before the war, helped to determine the forms of its expression. But Lawrence's own account of his life during the war years makes clear that his private obsessions also shaped his response to that public disaster; and, although he admired Nietzsche in his youth, he embraced neither Nietzsche's political philosophy nor his views of women until the later period. In fact, no public influence or event, not even the success of feminist agitation in the 1920s, is sufficient to explain the timing of Lawrence's turn toward antifeminist authoritarian thought.

Lawrence's early work contains Nietzschean themes, such as the view that Western civilization is atrophied and in need of spiritual regeneration, which may be provided by violent conflict. He may even have taken the title of his most ambitious early work from Zarathustra's promise to show "the rainbow and all the steps to the overman" to his disciples.[1] But that novel is not about the steps to Nietzsche's idea of the

---

1. Friedrich Nietzsche, "Thus Spake Zarathustra," *The Portable Nietzsche*, trans. Walter Kaufmann (New York: Viking, 1954), 136.

superman. In his *Rainbow* period Lawrence felt that "the great serpent to destroy" was "the Will to Power,"[2] and his "Sons of God" were simply men and women who knew how to live free of economic and social constraint.

The "Heroic Vitalism" that Eric Bentley believes is shared by Lawrence, Carlyle, Nietzsche, and others is "a religion of Dionysian life and energy" that recognizes an unequal distribution of the divine force and therefore often underlies the politics of dominance. Lawrence began as a vitalist; his early works contain the idea that the functions of living organisms are due to a principle distinct from physical and chemical forces. Nothing in the early works, however, suggests that he would eventually preach heroic politics, as he began to do in the period when he wrote *Women in Love*. Furthermore, when his politics changed, so did the nature of his vitalism. It began as a sense of the inherent divinity of all life, but it became mysticism, a belief in supernatural power, including the power of death, which, because it is supernatural rather than organic, may express itself through some creatures and not others. Organic vitalism is potentially female-centric birth worship, but supernatural energy can be assigned to the male to counter the female's procreative power, something it seems Lawrence wanted to do.

Even Bentley sees Lawrence as having been not so much influenced by Carlyle and Nietzsche as having developed similar ideas because of similar personal experiences. Bentley finds parallels between their natal families and notes that all three were committed Christians who lost their faith, which left them with a need to create a new reunion of "religion and politics, the eternal and the temporal, the metaphysical and the historical." But experiences beyond those of his early years were required to make Lawrence's thinking truly compatible with Nietzsche's. Nietzsche rejected "the eternal feminine," setting up what Bentley called a "visionary hero" to be his "masculine viceregent" against her; he also preached

2. Cambridge *Letters 2*, 272.

comradeship and solitude for his "Higher Men."³ In his early period Lawrence favored intimacy with a woman over comradeship and solitude, and submission to the eternal feminine over her subjection to the masculine hero. Whereas Nietzsche's example argues that misogyny is an essential ingredient of hero worship, his influence is not sufficient to explain Lawrence's turn toward the belief that "a race falls when men begin to worship the Great Mother" (*SM* 101).

That Lawrence's very temperament seemed to change during the war years invites one to overemphasize the war itself as an influence on his thinking. Most critics agree with Bentley that the war shattered Lawrence's nerves, estranged him from England, made him an opponent of democracy, and "emptied the universe of all meaning for him."⁴ Lawrence himself argued that it was not the war but the mob spirit at home that killed England, made it "the corpse of a country to him."⁵ His feeling is understandable: negative public opinion contributed both to the banning of the novel nearest his heart and to his being hounded out of Cornwall as a German spy. But the existence of a private, unadmitted crisis simultaneous with these events is evident even in the novel that Lawrence based on his life in those years.

In "The Nightmare" chapter of *Kangaroo*, Lawrence as narrator rages against the English public for trying "to break the independent soul in any man who would not hunt with the criminal mob" (216). The protagonist, Somers, is poor, and Lawrence has the public trying "with their beastly industrial self-righteousness, to humiliate him as a separate, single man" (217). He condemns the violation of Somers's separate being by the army, but not because they might have ended his life by sending him to the trenches. Somers has "no conscientious objection to war" (216) and no fear of being killed

3. Eric Bentley, *A Century of Hero-Worship: A Study of the Idea of Heroism in Carlyle and Nietzsche, with Notes on Wagner, Spengler, Stefan George and D. H. Lawrence*, 2nd ed. (Boston: Beacon Press, 1957), 218, 110, 128.
4. Ibid., 219.
5. D. H. Lawrence, *Kangaroo* (1923; rpt. New York: Viking, 1960), 216, 221, 264. Hereafter this work will be cited in the text.

in it, because "it is not death that matters, but the loss of the integral soul" (219). In these passages, integrity of the self is synonymous with manhood and requires separation from others. Therefore 1916–19, the period of the mob's "reign of terror" (215), were the "years when the world lost its real manhood" and "practically every man lost his . . . own manly isolation in his own integrity, which alone keeps life real" (216–17). Because of this loss, Somers develops the "dread, almost the horror, of democratic society" (264).

Given their use in the rest of his work, the terms of this description suggest another analysis of why these years "changed his life for ever" (226). It is true that the Lawrences were subjected to harassment because of war hysteria and that they lived in extreme poverty, surviving largely on the charity of friends. But these events did not create his hatred of the mob and the capitalist system; he had hated both already, before he felt the mob's power directly, in the period that even he recognized as belonging to the good old world ("It was in 1915 the old world ended," 220). While he was writing *The Rainbow*, his chief reason for wanting a revolution was to guarantee a living wage to everyone, so "no man amongst us, and no woman, shall have any fear of the wolf at the door, for all wolves are dead."[6] And though he called himself a "democrat," he felt sure that "the mob" would oppose his idea of heaven on earth: "the mob shall not crush us nor starve us nor cry us to death. We will deal cunningly with the mob, the greedy soul, we will gradually bring it to subjection." This subjection, as suggested earlier, must be principally an economic matter or a means of self-defense, since it is in this very letter that Lawrence says, "the great serpent to destroy, is the Will to Power."[7] In early 1915, he would already like to "wring the neck of humanity" for the war, "the spear through the side of all sorrows and hopes." And even before the banning of *The Rainbow* he wonders, "What is the use of giving books to the swinish public in its present state."[8]

6. Cambridge *Letters* 2, 282.
7. Ibid., 272–73.
8. Ibid., 268, 276–77.

While writing *The Rainbow*, he objects to the war, the mob, and industrial capitalism, but not on the grounds that they violate his manhood and singleness. He hopes to see humanity regenerated through the abolition of property and law, the fulfillment of all strong desire, and the mingling of each married couple "in entire nakedness of body and spirit."[9] Singleness, isolation, and manhood become his desiderata only when "the merging, the clutching, the mingling of love was become madly abhorrent to him," as he says of Birkin in *Women in Love* (191). Although Lawrence labels the isolation he then favors as "manly" and even "phallic," it seems to consist of separation from women but not from other men. Lawrence's isolated, manly heroes all desire to be pledged to a "unison" with other men: Somers is passionately attached to a young farmer, Birkin wants to "break into a oneness" with Gerald, and Lawrence enjoins men to "look round for the man your heart will point out to you. And follow—and never look back."[10]

Lawrence's emotional investment in these ideas and his association of them with the lower digestive tract are surely the only explanations for an odd moment in *Kangaroo*, when he narrates the nadir of Somers's wartime experience. The doctors examining him for the draft inspect his anus, and Lawrence seems to drop the mask of fiction to curse them: "because they had handled his private parts, and looked into them, their eyes should burst and their hands should wither and their hearts should rot" (261). Lawrence seems to feel that Somers's reaction is one that anyone would have, but the violence of it is only understandable when we remember Lawrence's association of the anus with male power, shameful (probably homoerotic) desire, and integrity of the self, which can be affirmed through the anal caress and violated in sex with powerful women.

The erotic elements of his political thought make clear, too, that his turn against women was not simply a response to the

9. Ibid., 191.
10. D. H. Lawrence, *Psychoanalysis and the Unconscious/Fantasia of the Unconscious* (New York: Viking, 1960), 218.

success of the feminist movement, as does the timing of this change. Hilary Simpson, in *D. H. Lawrence and Feminism*, usefully summarizes various stages of Lawrence's thinking about women's independence and argues that he was sympathetic to feminist goals so long as they were not achieved; Simpson sees his antifeminism of the 1920s as a reaction to the public changes in women's status and behavior.[11] His reaction, however, clearly preceded the achievement of feminist goals. It seems to have begun in 1915, during the wartime quiescence of feminist agitation, and soon after his visit to Cambridge, when the Lawrences separated for a short time; and it deepened in the most difficult years of their marriage, which also preceded the end of the war, when they lived alone on the Cornish coast and Lawrence apparently flirted with homosexual love while his wife had affairs with other men. Frieda Lawrence asserted her personal and sexual independence all through the war years, as did no doubt other individual women, probably contributing at least as much thereby to the antifeminist reaction as did the more public manifestations of New Womanhood.

In Lawrence the antifeminist reaction appeared simultaneously with his earliest authoritarian thought; the question remains whether he is to be considered an isolated case or in some sense paradigmatic. The relationship between antifeminism and authoritarianism in modernist literature is an issue I hope to investigate in another study.

11. Hilary Simpson, *D. H. Lawrence and Feminism* (De Kalb: Northern Illinois University Press, 1982).

Index

Aaron's Rod, 102, 137, 144, 182, 186, 191
Accident in a Mine, 145
African sensuality, 44, 47, 51–52, 81–86 passim, 153–54, 211, 224
Anal eroticism, 44–49 passim, 123–27, 136, 153–54, 223–28 passim, 233. *See also* Bowels; Buttock fetishization; Sodomy
Animal life, 58–65, 71, 89, 98, 108, 109
Antifeminine views: authoritarian, 5–9, 105, 234; Lawrence's, 15, 48, 128–32, 145–46, 161, 170, 196–205, 230–31, 234
Anti-Semitism, 184
Aphrodite, 157
Apocalypse, 91–92
Apocalyptic mode, 20, 49–50
Arches, 73–74
Arnold, Armin, 186
Asquith, Lady Cynthia, 13
Authoritarianism, 114, 183–85, 229; antifeminism with, 5–9, 105, 234; and phallic worship, 154; and Rananim, 176

Beetles, 11, 44, 45, 83, 84, 150–51, 153
Bell, Quentin, 14
Benda, Julien, 7
Bentley, Eric, 8, 230, 231
Biblical references, 49, 50, 54, 57–58, 91–92, 99–100
Birrell, Frankie, 11
Birth, 98–101, 106, 109, 115–16, 154, 201

Blood brotherhood, 136, 164, 208–9, 214, 217–20
Blood knowledge, 32, 196
Book of Enoch, 91–92
Bowels, 45, 125, 136, 151–54, 206, 223–28 passim
Brown, Norman O., 126
Burnet, John, 148–49
Buttock fetishization, 44, 45, 123, 124, 181, 227–28

Captain's Doll, 111
Carlyle, Thomas, 8, 230
Cavitch, David, 153, 162
Chamberlain, Houston, 185n
Child rearing, 100–106, 223
Christian era, 2, 3, 147
Clarke, Colin, 46, 50–51, 52, 56–57, 209
Consciousness, 58–65, 110, 111, 223–24
Contadina, 227
Cooper, James Fenimore, 184, 187, 196–97
Corruption, 37, 54, 149, 150–51; heterosexual, 33–34, 46, 51–52, 83–84, 113, 151; and homoeroticism, 11, 14–15; in procreation, 115. *See also* Dissolution
Crews, Frederick, 203
"Crown," 17, 85, 136–52 passim, 188, 206; and destruction/decadence/corruption/death, 2–3, 39–41, 115–16, 146–47, 149, 189; on heterosexuality, 41, 81, 114, 138, 142, 146; and homoeroticism, 14,

235

142–46 passim, 161–65 passim, 190

Darkness, 62–65, 68, 79, 82, 83
Death, 2, 3, 50, 82, 83, 147; and heterosexuality, 13, 33–49 passim, 72–73, 77–80, 146; homicidal, 12–13, 38, 41–43; and homoeroticism, 15, 146, 188, 189; self, 30–31, 38–39, 120. See also Dissolution
Decadence, 36, 44–45, 49, 50–51, 146. See also Corruption; Dissolution; Reduction
Delany, Paul, 10, 13, 153, 165
Delavenay, Emile, 184–85n
Democracy, 6, 7, 176–77, 187–88, 204
Destruction, 2–3, 20–25 passim, 33, 36–37; sex as, 15, 27, 34, 38, 41–46 passim, 55–56, 79, 100, 120–23 passim, 128; in procreation, 100, 115–16. See also Death; Decadence
Dissolution, 24, 36–37, 50–51, 62, 83, 120–21, 149; male power and, 45, 61; through sensationalism, 39–40. See also Destruction; Separation
Divinity, 58, 71, 146–47, 160
Dostoyevsky, Fyodor, 58
Drieu La Rochelle, Pierre, 6, 7–8, 9

Edge, John, 191
"Education of the People," 188–89, 199, 200
Egypt, 43, 44–46, 83–84
Eliot, T. S., 7
Englishmen, 1, 13, 155, 156, 157–58
English Review, 155, 184, 186
Equality, sexual, 4, 92–93, 112, 174, 178–81
Eternities, 3, 146–47, 150

Fantasia of the Unconscious, 17; antifeminine views in, 167–68, 186; body's power centers in, 125, 223–24, 225, 228; child development in, 223; creation in, 201; decay in, 36; horses in, 91, 93; so-

cial visions in, 172, 173, 182, 186, 191, 222
Fascism, 5–6, 8–9, 183–85
Female sexuality, 129–30, 200, 205; in The Rainbow, 116–18, 136; in Women in Love, 48, 114, 116, 118–19, 129–30, 136, 168, 170, 171, 200. See also Passivity, female; Procreation
Female submission, 166, 181, 208, 213, 215–16, 217; political, 4, 201; in sex, 48, 128–29, 130–31, 194–95, 205, 215–16, 227
Feminism, 179, 234. See also Antifeminine views; Independence, female
Fiedler, Leslie, 203
Ford, George, 54, 153
Forster, E. M., 13, 66, 82, 141, 142, 160, 192
Fox, 111
"Fragment of Stained Glass," 42
Freeman, Mary, 49
Freud, Sigmund, 1–2, 3, 126, 129, 165, 225

Garnett, David, 11, 14, 163
Garnett, Edward, 11, 163
Genesis, Book of, 54, 91, 92
Gide, André, 8, 141
Goats and Compasses, 145
Goodheart, Eugene, 172
Grant, Duncan, 10–11
Gray, Cecil, 145

Hall, Radclyffe, 141
"Hardy." See "Study of Thomas Hardy"
Hardy, Barbara, 107–8
Hawthorne, Nathaniel, 166, 203
Heraclitus, 3, 148–50, 151, 152, 185
Hitler, Adolf, 6
Hocking, William Henry, 165
Homicide, 12–13, 38, 41–43
Homoeroticism, 4, 9–15 passim, 46, 139–46, 152–53, 160–69 passim, 190–94. See also Blood brotherhood
Horses, 88–98 passim, 106–12 passim, 180, 213

Hough, Graham, 46
Howe, Graham, 46
Howe, Marguerite Beede, 47–48,
    73n, 96, 122, 123, 135–36, 162
Huxley, Aldous, 7–8

Ibsen, Henrik, 157–58, 159
Independence, female, 214–15, 217,
    234
Intestines. See Bowels
Italians, 155–56, 157, 158–59, 160–
    61
Ithyphallus, 204–6, 228

Kangaroo, 144, 164, 182, 184, 190–91,
    231–32, 233
Keats, John, 50
Kermode, Frank, 46, 49
Keynes, John Maynard, 10–11, 14
Kinkead-Weekes, Mark, 51n, 78
Knight, G. Wilson, 48–49, 51, 128,
    150, 152

"Ladybird," 44
Lady Chatterley's Lover, 17, 18, 209;
    pregnancy in, 102; sexuality in,
    48, 128, 154, 164–65, 200, 204,
    205, 227
Lawrence, Frieda, 102–3, 159–68
    passim, 234
Leavis, F. R., 46, 47
Lewis, Wyndham, 6
Look! We Have Come Through!, 164
Lost Girl, 102
Love, 32, 118

Male bonding. See Homoeroticism;
    Blood brotherhood
Male power, 4, 111–12, 182, 192n,
    194, 201, 205–6; anus/bowels/
    buttocks as source of, 45, 181,
    206, 223, 225, 226–28, 233; and
    dissolution/ corruption, 45, 61,
    113
Male submission, 117, 134, 182
"Manifesto," 126–27
Mansfield, Katherine, 165, 168
Man Who Died, 102, 154
Marriage, 32, 47, 171, 188, 221
Masochism, 40

Mechanization, 24, 36–37, 38, 44
Meyers, Jeffrey, 46, 153
Miko, Stephen J., 51n, 146, 172
Miller, James E., Jr., 7
Millett, Kate, 128, 205
Milton, John, 29
Miscarriage, 93–107 passim
Misogyny, 8, 9, 145, 230–31. See also
    Antifeminine views
Montherlant, Henry de, 5–6, 7
Moore, H. T. , 46, 167
"Morality and the Novel," 217
Moral relativism, 3, 51
Morrell, Ottoline, 10, 14, 174
Motherhood, 165, 166, 198–99; fas-
    cism and, 6; in The Rainbow, 96–
    97, 106, 109, 117; in Women in
    Love, 31–32, 118
Movements in European History, 183
Moynahan, Julian, 46
Murry, John Middleton, 14, 46–47,
    55, 164, 165, 168
Mussolini, Benito, 7, 184

Nathan, Peter, 8, 9
Nazis, 6
Nietzsche, Friedrich, 8, 184, 185,
    229–31

Ontology, 20–22, 35–38, 98–100, 201
Orgasm, 129–30, 205
Orwell, George, 8

Paintings, Lawrence's, 144–45, 227
Parenthood. See Child rearing;
    Motherhood
Passivity, female, 129, 194–95, 215,
    227. See also Female submission
Patai, Daphne, 8
Phallus: vs. anal eroticism/bowels,
    44–45, 206, 223, 226; and power,
    204–6, 223, 226, 228; worship of,
    154, 155, 158, 160
Plumed Serpent, 17, 48, 162, 167, 182,
    191, 205, 206
Poe, Edgar Allan, 195
Politics, 3–9, 66–68, 170–206 pas-
    sim, 210–11, 222–34 passim. See
    also Authoritarianism; Utopian
    visions

Pound, Ezra, 7, 17, 184
Power, 61, 181, 201, 204. *See also* Authoritarianism; Feminism; Male power; Submission
Pregnancy, 93–109 passim, 115
Procreation, 31–32, 108–9, 113, 114. *See also* Birth; Child rearing; Motherhood; Pregnancy
"Prologue" to *Women in Love*, 14, 132, 138, 139–40, 141, 143, 145
"Prussian Officer," 42–43
Psychoanalysis and the Unconscious, 182

Rainbow, 10, 19–39, 46–113 passim, 130–36 passim, 144, 162, 207, 211; banning of, 10, 207; birth in, 98–101, 106, 109, 154; and corruption/destruction/dissolution/death, 13, 30–31, 33–34, 46, 51–56 passim, 72–84 passim, 100, 146; and Lawrence's marriage, 163–64, 181–82; and male power, 192n; politics in, 3–4, 5, 66–68, 171–77 passim, 230, 232–33; revisions to, 13, 16, 52, 55–56, 72–80 passim, 146, 171–81 passim, 206; self-realization in, 4–5, 13, 32, 65–81 passim, 96–108 passim, 113, 147, 178, 179–82, 196; sexual fulfillment in, 4–5, 13, 32, 46, 63–64, 71–81 passim, 110, 113, 116–18, 130–31, 135, 146, 148, 173, 179, 181
Rananim, 66–67, 69, 92–93, 174, 176, 177
"Reality of Peace," 3, 136–37, 150, 152, 189, 190, 227
Reduction, 3, 39–41, 57, 149; through sex, 40–41, 61, 81, 114, 138, 142, 146
Red Willow Trees, 227
Reflections on the Death of a Porcupine, 17n, 39, 142
Renascence of Men, ii, 227
Revelation, Book of, 49, 50
Revisions, 18; to "The Crown," 17n, 39, 142, 146; to *The Rainbow*, 13, 16, 52, 55–56, 73–80 passim, 146, 171–81 passim, 206; to *Sons and Lovers*, 103; to *Twilight in Italy*, 154–61 passim; to *Women in Love*, 3, 19–20, 141, 146, 150, 180, 186, 191, 206
Romanticism, 50
Ross, Charles, 77–78
Russell, Bertrand, 4, 39, 144, 175, 185, 192; Lawrence's blood-brotherly love for, 14, 164; Lawrence's Cambridge visit with, 10

Sadism, 40
Sagar, Keith, 73–74, 97–98
Sanders, Scott, 153, 172
Satanic associations, 35
Schwarz, Egon, 9
Self-realization, 65–71, 113–14, 147, 178–82 passim, 196; in deathliness/destruction, 5, 13, 38–39, 46, 73–81 passim; and procreation, 32, 93–114 passim; through sex, 4–5, 13, 32, 38–43 passim, 63–64, 71–87 passim, 99, 100, 110, 113–14, 123, 160, 181, 196
Sensationalism, 3, 39–40, 85, 113
Separation, 7, 32, 119–20, 195–96, 216, 233; through anal caress, 123, 125–27; through reduction/dissolution, 3, 36. *See also* Singleness; "Star balance"
Sex, 4–5, 10, 127–69, 179, 181–82, 196; destruction/dissolution/death with, 13, 15, 27, 33–50 passim, 55–56, 72–84 passim, 100, 113–14, 120–23 passim, 128, 146; and politics, 4–5, 114, 146, 154, 173, 186–94, 200–205, 226; self-realization through, 4–5, 13, 32, 38–43 passim, 63–64, 71–87 passim, 99, 100, 110, 113–14, 123, 160, 181, 196. *See also* Anal eroticism; Female sexuality; Homoeroticism; Phallus; Sodomy
Shaw, George Bernard, 25
Shelley, Percy Bysshe, 12, 50
Signature, 39
Simpson, Hilary, 131–32, 234
Singing of Swans, 145
Singleness, 195–96, 216, 233

"Sisters," 19, 20, 103, 132–35, 137, 178
Socialism, 4, 193
Sodom, 153–54
Sodomy: heterosexual, 13, 48–49, 127, 128, 129, 152; homoerotic, 144, 192–93
Sons and Lovers, 17, 102, 133, 162; children in, 103; homoeroticism in, 144; self in, 67; sex in, 63, 84, 131
Sons of God, 43, 91–93, 178
Soucy, Robert, 9
Spring, 144–45
"Star balance," 32, 46, 123–27 passim, 195, 212, 213
Studies in Classic American Literature, 186, 188, 203–4
"Study of Thomas Hardy," 2, 65, 68–69, 91, 111, 146, 162; Aphrodite in, 157; and procreation, 100–101, 108; self-realization in, 40–41, 43, 66, 74, 75, 77, 80, 81, 85, 93, 98–100, 180–81; sex in, 40–41, 43, 74, 77, 81, 85, 86, 99, 110, 118, 119–20, 180–81, 189–90, 199; and the unknown, 37–38, 80, 82, 85, 93
Submission: male, 117, 134, 182. *See also* Female submission
Swift, Jonathan, 126
Symbolic Meaning, 186

Taoism, 113, 150, 152
Trespasser, 102, 131
Tuberculosis, 10, 167
Twilight in Italy, 14, 154–56, 158, 160–61

Unknown, the, 37–38, 80–86 passim, 93, 98, 113
Utopian visions, 4, 146, 170–80, 185; Rananim, 66–67, 69, 92–93, 174, 176, 177; socialist, 4, 193

Vitalism, 90, 230

War, 3, 10, 11–12, 39–40, 78–79, 229, 231–32, 234
"Wedding Ring," 19
White Peacock, 102, 131–32, 144, 192n
Whitman, Walt, 188, 190, 191
"Why the Novel Matters," 16
"Witch à la Mode," 131
Women in Love, 3, 4–5, 12–62 passim, 73, 81–84, 113–53 passim, 205–33 passim; and female sexuality, 48, 114, 116, 118–19, 129–30, 136, 168, 170, 171, 200; homoeroticism in, 14, 139–42, 143, 145–46, 152–53, 161, 162–63, 168, 171, 191; male power in, 111, 112, 113, 181, 223, 226, 227–28; and politics, 5, 114, 146, 170, 171–72, 186, 193–94, 223; procreation in, 31–32, 102, 103, 114–15, 116, 118, 136; revisions to, 3, 19–20, 141, 146, 150, 180, 186, 191, 206; singleness/separation/ "star balance" in, 32, 46, 119–27 passim, 195–96, 212, 213, 216, 233
Wordsworth, William, 50
Work, 179–80
Working man, 191–92

Yeats, W. B., 6, 171

Compositor: Wilsted & Taylor
Printer/Binder: Braun-Brumfield, Inc.
Text: 10/12 Palatino
Display: Palatino